Facebook® Advertising
FOR
DUMMIES®

by Paul Dunay, Richard Krueger, and Joel Elad

WILEY

Wiley Publishing, Inc.

WILEY

About the Authors

Paul Dunay is an award-winning B2B marketing expert with more than 20 years' success in generating demand and creating buzz for leading technology, consumer products, financial services, and professional services organizations.

Paul is Global Managing Director of Services and Social Marketing for Avaya, a global leader in enterprise communications, and author of *Facebook Marketing For Dummies* (Wiley). His unique approach to integrated marketing has led to recognition as a BtoB Magazine Top 25 B2B Marketer of the Year for 2009 and winner of the DemandGen Award for Utilizing Marketing Automation to Fuel Corporate Growth in 2008. He is also a five-time finalist in the Marketing Excellence Awards competition of the Information Technology Services Marketing Association (ITSMA) and a 2005 gold award winner.

Richard Krueger is co-founder and CEO of AboutFace Digital, a social media marketing agency focused on Facebook as a network for acquiring customers, building brand, and driving sales. Recognized as a serial entrepreneur with extensive business development, branding, public relations, technical product development, and business management experience, Richard has a successful track record in leading the business strategies on behalf of social media and interactive entertainment companies. He has served as founder, CMO, and part of the original management teams of companies that brought true innovation in the areas of broadband infrastructure, content syndication, social media, mobile entertainment, online gaming, and local search.

Joel Elad has written six books about various online topics, including *LinkedIn For Dummies*, *Starting an Online Business All-in-One Desk Reference For Dummies*, and *Web Stores Do-It-Yourself For Dummies*. He is the head of Real Method Consulting, a company dedicated to educating people through training seminars, DVDs, books, and other media. He holds a Master's Degree in Business from UC Irvine, and a Bachelors Degree in Computer Science and Engineering from UCLA. He has contributed to *Entrepreneur* magazine and Smartbiz.com, and has taught at institutions like the University of California, Irvine.

Dedication

We dedicate this book to advertisers everywhere who are in the middle of the biggest sea change in marketing history. We believe there has never been a better time to be a marketer, and that tools like Facebook are rewriting the rules. In fact, we believe that Facebook will become the preferred platform for marketers and advertisers to acquire new customers, interact with existing customers, and sell products and services. We hope that by providing you with straightforward, step-by-step advice, as well as sharing our real-world experiences in marketing companies via Facebook, you'll become better at your craft and thereby take us all to levels in marketing we've yet to explore.

Authors' Acknowledgments

This project could not have succeeded without the support of many people who truly helped make this book a success.

First, we would like to acknowledge all of our families for allowing us to pursue our passion for Facebook Advertising. We appreciate all your understanding and support, throughout the time we took away from you to write this book.

We would like to thank the superb team at Wiley: Amy Fandrei, who reached out to us because of our blogs and supported us through the entire process. Christopher Morris, our project editor, who kept us on track every step of the way and helped us conform the book to *For Dummies* standards. And all the other Wiley folks behind the scenes who made the book possible.

Thanks to scores of bloggers, too many to list, who kept us informed about changes Facebook was making in their Facebook Advertising platform and what they meant to users. Most of all, we'd like to thank Facebook founder Mark Zuckerberg, and his team of young entrepreneurs and software developers, for their vision in realizing the most popular online social network on the planet.

Publisher's Acknowledgments

We're proud of this book; please send us your comments at http://dummies.custhelp.com. For other comments, please contact our Customer Care Department within the U.S. at 877-762-2974, outside the U.S. at 317-572-3993, or fax 317-572-4002.

Some of the people who helped bring this book to market include the following:

Acquisitions, Editorial

Sr. Project Editor: Christopher Morris

Acquisitions Editor: Amy Fandrei

Sr. Copy Editor: Teresa Artman

Technical Editor: Michelle Oxman

Editorial Manager: Kevin Kirschner

Editorial Assistant: Amanda Graham

Sr. Editorial Assistant: Cherie Case

Cartoons: Rich Tennant (www.the5thwave.com)

Composition Services

Project Coordinator: Patrick Redmond

Layout and Graphics: Joyce Haughey, Laura Westhuis

Proofreaders: ConText Editorial Services, Inc., Lauren Mandelbaum

Indexer: Cheryl Duksta

Publishing and Editorial for Technology Dummies

    Richard Swadley, Vice President and Executive Group Publisher

    Andy Cummings, Vice President and Publisher

    Mary Bednarek, Executive Acquisitions Director

    Mary C. Corder, Editorial Director

Publishing for Consumer Dummies

    Diane Graves Steele, Vice President and Publisher

Composition Services

    Debbie Stailey, Director of Composition Services

Contents at a Glance

Introduction 1

Part I: Getting Started with Facebook Advertising 7
Chapter 1: Profiting from the Facebook Revolution 9
Chapter 2: Setting Up Your Facebook Account 23

Part II: Launching Your Facebook Advertising Campaign 41
Chapter 3: Matching Your Ads to Your Marketing Strategy 43
Chapter 4: Buying Strategies 63
Chapter 5: Understanding the Types of Ad Campaigns 81
Chapter 6: Getting Set to Implement and Measure Results 95

Part III: Managing Your Facebook Advertising Campaigns 117
Chapter 7: Creating Pages for Your Campaign 119
Chapter 8: Testing and Optimizing Your Ad Campaign 137
Chapter 9: Tracking Conversions to Sales 159

Part IV: Minding Your Metrics 179
Chapter 10: Checking Out the Data 181
Chapter 11: Creating Reports 199
Chapter 12: Extending the Facebook Experience 231

Part V: The Part of Tens 249
Chapter 13: Ten Facebook Page Promotion Techniques (Besides Ads) 251
Chapter 14: Ten (or So) Facebook Ads Beginner Mistakes 263
Chapter 15: Ten Nontraditional Facebook Ad Campaigns 275
Chapter 16: Ten Resources for Facebook Advertisers 289

Index 305

Table of Contents

Introduction 1

About This Book 2
How This Book Is Organized 2
    Part I: Getting Started with Facebook Advertising 2
    Part II: Launching Your Facebook Advertising Campaign 3
    Part III: Managing Your Facebook Advertising Campaigns.............3
    Part IV: Minding Your Metrics......................................3
    Part V: The Part of Tens 3
Foolish Assumptions 4
Conventions Used in This Book 4
Icons Used in This Book 5
Where to Go from Here 5

Part 1: Getting Started with Facebook Advertising 7

Chapter 1: Profiting from the Facebook Revolution 9

Introducing Facebook Advertising 10
Finding Your Way around Facebook Advertising....................12
Seeing the Familiar Aspects of Facebook Advertising.............14
    Design your own advertisements 14
    Manage your own ad budget 14
Understanding Unique Aspects of Facebook Advertising....................16
    Targeting profile attributes 16
    Using clickable ads that don't leave the original Web page...........18
    Gathering responder information with Facebook Insights.............19
Direct and Relationship Marketing Aspects of Facebook Ads................19
    How direct marketing techniques affects your advertisements....20
    Understanding relationship marketing as part of your sales cycle....22

Chapter 2: Setting Up Your Facebook Account 23

Creating a New Facebook Business Page 23
Creating Your First Ad Campaign 27
Elements of a Great Ad Campaign 33
    Titling your ad..33
    Writing body text 34
    Choosing an image..36
    Choosing your destination URL 37
Preparing your Facebook Business Page for Your Ad Campaigns..........38
    Adding or updating the necessary elements on
        your business Page..38
    Selecting elements for ad campaign landing pages or targets 39

Part II: Launching Your Facebook Advertising Campaign... 41

Chapter 3: Matching Your Ads to Your Marketing Strategy 43

Picking a Target Group from the Facebook Audience 44
Establishing the Scope of Your Ad Campaign...47
    Local campaigns 47
    Regional campaigns...48
    National and international campaigns 50
Align Your Ad Campaign with Your Marketing Objectives 52
    Building your brand..53
    Driving sales 55
    Forming a community (alternate title — building your Fan base).....57
    Listening (and responding) to feedback...61

Chapter 4: Buying Strategies 63

Choosing a Payment Model..64
    Cost per impression 65
    Cost per click..65
    Determining cost per click...67
Basing Bids on Recommended Range...70
Tracking Your Campaign Budget...71
    Running a budget report in Ads Reports 72
    Understanding report results...76
Adjusting as You Go Along 78
Pausing or Stopping a Campaign...79

Chapter 5: Understanding the Types of Ad Campaigns 81

Differentiating between Ad Types 81
Using Ads with Social Attributes 86
Understanding the Importance of Images 89
Multiple Concurrent Campaigns..92
    Reaching internal and external Web sites 92
    Scheduling your Ad 93

Chapter 6: Getting Set to Implement and Measure Results 95

Allocating Resources to Create and Monitor the Campaign...................96
Integrating Your Off-Line Campaigns 97
Testing Your Ads 99
    Creating test campaigns...99
    Determining ad success 101
Placing Ads through a Facebook Rep 102
    Getting in touch with a Facebook rep 102
    Taking over a home page 103
Developing Performance Objectives..105
    Defining conversions 107
    Analyzing results...107

Exploring Alternative Facebook Advertising Options 108
  Advertising within applications (FarmVille, Mafia Wars)............. 108
  Advertising by creating an application 110
Cross-Promoting via External Networks... 112
  Cross-promoting with blogs 112
  Cross-promoting with e-mail blasts.. 114

Part III: Managing Your Facebook Advertising Campaigns 117

Chapter 7: Creating Pages for Your Campaign 119

Choosing a Landing Page.. 119
  Opting for an internal Facebook landing page 122
  Opting for an external Web site landing page 124
Creating a Separate Tab for Your Campaign..................................... 127
  Using FBML to create a custom tab... 127
  Installing FBML on your Page.. 129
  Building a custom FBML tab on your Facebook Page.................. 132
Capturing Customer Data with Forms 134

Chapter 8: Testing and Optimizing Your Ad Campaign 137

Using Facebook Reporting Data.. 137
  The Advertising Performance report 138
  The Responder Demographics report 140
Optimizing Your Campaign 143
  Refining bid range pricing on your ads 143
  Gaining audience perceptions... 146
  Maximizing results.. 147
Measuring Insights with Facebook Insights 150
  Users who Like your Page.. 150
  User demographics... 153
  User Page Views 154
  Media consumption 155
  Story and discussion feedback 156
  Page Activity (Mentions, Reviews, Discussions, Videos, Photos).... 157

Chapter 9: Tracking Conversions to Sales........................ 159

Setting Up a Process to Convert a Lead to a Sale............................. 159
  Defining a conversion... 160
  Understanding the types of conversions 162
  Converting a lead 165
Following Up with Your Leads 167
  Verifying a lead.. 168
  Calling on a lead.. 169
  Tracking leads in a CRM system 169

Converting a lead to a sale 172
Tracking the ROI 173
Tracking Your Conversions 175
Metrics to track 176
Optimizing conversions 177

Part IV: Minding Your Metrics 179

Chapter 10: Checking Out the Data 181

Getting to Know Ads Manager 181
Understanding campaign notifications 184
Analyzing Lifetime Statistics 187
Viewing graphs 189
Reviewing multiple campaigns 192
Reviewing weekly stats on your ad campaigns 193
Adjusting Account Settings 195

Chapter 11: Creating Reports 199

Introduction to Facebook Reports 200
Generating Reports 201
Creating an Advertising Performance report 205
Creating a Responder Demographics report 210
Creating a Responder Profiles report 213
Gaining Insights from Facebook Insights 214
Tracking interactions 216
Measuring User engagement 222
Breaking out demographics 225
Exporting data 225
Piecing Together a Dashboard 226
Identifying what's important 227
Exploring third-party tools 227

Chapter 12: Extending the Facebook Experience 231

Introducing Social Plugins 232
Benefiting from Facebook Plug-ins 234
Fostering community 234
Building engagement 235
Adding Social Plugins to Your Web Site 236
Choosing Social Plugins for Your Business 237
Like button 238
Recommendations 239
Login (with Faces) 240
Comments 241
Activity Feed 243
Like box 244
Friendpile 245
Live Stream 246

Part V: The Part of Tens *249*

**Chapter 13: Ten Facebook Page Promotion
Techniques (Besides Ads)** **251**

Promote Your Page Offsite 252
Put Compelling or Unique Content on Your Page 253
Have a Clear Focus on Your Page's Purpose 253
Make Your Content Easy to Share 254
Get Your Users to Collaborate 255
Provide Something Exclusive to Your Facebook Page 256
Build a Facebook App 258
Create and Interact with Facebook Groups 259
Post a Facebook Marketplace Listing 260
Market Yourself, Not Just Your Page 262

Chapter 14: Ten (or So) Facebook Ads Beginner Mistakes **263**

Not Using a Picture or Graphic in Your Ad 263
Not Refreshing the Ad Often 265
Not Split-Testing Your Ad at Least Once 266
Not Targeting Your Audience 266
Targeting Your Audience Too Tightly 267
Testing Your Ads for Too Short or Long of a Time 268
Focusing on CPC or Membership, Not Profit per Click or Engagement 269
Writing a Simple or Boring Headline 270
Not Including a Strong Call to Action 270
Not Connecting with Your Audience on a Relationship Basis 271
Not Following Facebook Advertising Guidelines 272

Chapter 15: Ten Nontraditional Facebook Ad Campaigns **275**

Paging a Party of One 276
Showing Off Contest Entries' Creativity 277
I Want to Work for You! 279
Can You Solve the Riddle? 280
Bring the Community to the Mountain 281
Wanted: A Few Young Minds 282
Are You a Tough Mudder? 282
Build a Better Book Group with Facebook 284
No Purchase Is Too Large 285
Be Your Own Brand 286

Chapter 16: Ten Resources for Facebook Advertisers **289**

All Facebook Is All about Facebook 289
Get Inside Facebook with Inside Facebook 291
Do an About Face with AboutFaceDigital 293
Hear the Buzz — Marketing for Technology 294

It's the Age of Advertising: Ad Age, That Is.................................295
Stay Up to Date with Social Media Today.................................296
Get the Picture with iStockphoto...297
Get the Scoop Directly from Facebook......................................300
Access the Libraries Created by the Facebook Developer Team.........301
Like Facebook Ads? Why Not Like the Facebook Ads Page?.................302

Index.. *305*

Introduction

*1*n 2004, Harvard student Mark Zuckerberg created a Web site that would take the world by storm. As of mid-2010, Facebook had more than 500 million users, 70 percent of whom resided outside the United States. Even more amazing, 50 percent of all users checked their Facebook account at least once per day. Billions of photographs, status updates, Web links, and notes are shared among Facebook users every month. With all that activity, it shouldn't be a surprise that businesses started to show up, wondering how to reach out and talk to this vibrant global community.

Facebook responded by offering different solutions for companies, public figures, and brands to interact with Facebook users on both a professional and personal nature. An initial effort called "Fan pages" gave way to "business Pages," by which users can follow the activities of a business through their own News Feed on Facebook. When Microsoft made an equity investment in Facebook in 2007, Facebook allowed Microsoft to sell banner advertising on their site. Over the next few years, Facebook has changed their strategy and created different types of advertisement opportunities that companies of any size can use.

Of course, in true Facebook style, their advertisements were slightly different from the typical online ad model. On Facebook, advertisements can have "social" elements, which allow advertisers to show a potential user which of their friends have already interacted with that advertiser. These ads also have an "engagement" factor that allows users to interact with advertisements directly, allowing them to, say, click an option to Like a Business Page, or RSVP to a Facebook Event, without having to leave their current Web page.

Despite these differences, several elements about Facebook advertising are quite familiar. Like other Web sites, Facebook allows businesses or people to design their own advertisements, set their own daily budgets, and track the progress of their ad campaigns. Facebook allows advertisers to provide some targeting information to focus the audience that will see the advertisement. In fact, this feature contains one of the greatest strengths of Facebook advertising — a series of targeting filters that allow you to set extremely specific guidelines and take advantage of the copious amounts of information each Facebook user has already provided about him- or herself. If you want to target 35–44-year-old females in Midwestern states who like Brad Pitt flicks or Danielle Steel novels, you can make sure your Facebook Ads display to only those Facebook users who match these criteria.

We wrote this book to help you with the aspects of designing, testing, running, and maintaining advertisement campaigns on Facebook. Because advertisements can be seen as an "intrusion" on people's interactions with each other, it's important to look at how your advertisements, and overall Facebook presence, can simply extend the conversation instead of intrude on it so that you can gain acceptance and users — and, hopefully, conversions to paying customers or loyal users. A lot of power is available to any eager person willing to reach hundreds of millions of active users, and this book is designed to help you reach that audience as successfully as possible.

About This Book

This book covers all aspects of creating, launching, and maintaining your Facebook Ad campaigns: From establishing a presence and an account on Facebook, to designing your first ad campaign, implementing strategies, understanding your options, testing your concepts, updating your ad messages, targeting specific users, understanding your ad results, and thinking about the future of your ad campaigns and Facebook business presence, and everything in between. There's a lot of advice and concepts but also some step-by-step instructions to get things done, and it's all right here in this book.

How This Book Is Organized

We divide this book into five handy parts. This book is organized as a guide; you can read each chapter in order, or use specific chapters to supplement your own efforts. Throughout the process of building your Facebook Ads, you can think of this book as a reference, where you turn to the chapter you need that applies to your situation, find the knowledge you need to consider, and then continue in your process. We do a little amount of cross-referencing, too, so if you need to look elsewhere in the book for more information, you can easily find it.

Part 1: Getting Started with Facebook Advertising

Part I starts with the basics, as we talk about the world of Facebook, how to establish yourself and your business on Facebook, and be ready to start running advertisements.

Part II: Launching Your Facebook Advertising Campaign

Part II goes into the ad launch process, where you devise strategies for which markets you wish to target, which pricing models you want to consider for your ads, how to make your budget go the farthest, which types of ads you want to run on the site, how to test your ad concepts, and what other advertising options exist on the site.

Part III: Managing Your Facebook Advertising Campaigns

Part III is designed to help you maintain your existing Facebook Ad campaigns, as we discuss how to build targeted landing pages that your users will see after clicking an ad. We also discuss how to explicitly target your advertisements for the highest results, and how to track the results of your ad campaign, even as far as those new users' activity on your own Web site.

Part IV: Minding Your Metrics

Part IV takes a keen focus on understanding and interpreting the results of your ad campaigns. We discuss the Ads Manager utility within Facebook, where you can monitor the ongoing statistics of your different ad campaigns, and begin to identify trends, successes, and failures. We then go into how you can pull specific reports on your ad campaigns, showing you results of those campaigns down to the last click. We finish this part by looking to the future and how you can integrate other parts of Facebook into your own Web site so that you can continue the conversation with your Facebook users on your own domain.

Part V: The Part of Tens

Part V is the traditional *For Dummies* Part of Tens — lists that detail a number of Facebook Ad resources to consider and some lists of best practices of what works, as well as the biggest mistakes and things to look for to limit how much you need to fix.

Foolish Assumptions

We assume that you know how to use your computer, at least for the basic operations, like checking e-mail, typing up a document, or surfing the great big World Wide Web out there. If you're worried that you will need a Ph.D. in Marketing to write your own Facebook Ads, relax. If you can bring up Facebook in your Internet browser, you can write your own Facebook Ad. Hopefully, you've done some form of advertising in the past so that you have an idea of what kinds of ads you may want, as well as how to write a headline and advertising message.

We use the word "page" to talk about any regular Web page, but we use the word "Page" to talk about a specific kind of Facebook page where a business or brand has its own presence on the social networking site.

This book assumes that you have a computer that can access the Internet; any PC or Apple Macintosh line of computer will be fine, as well as Linux or any other operating system with a Web browser. Please note, though, that we don't get into the core specifics of how to write marketing copy or find the necessary keywords for your specific Facebook Ad. In some parts of the book, we talk about specific applications (like Microsoft Excel, so we presume that if you have Microsoft Excel, you know how to use it for the purposes of building a spreadsheet and entering data).

This book doesn't describe the basic operations of a computer, accessing the Internet, or using an Internet Web browser such as Safari, Internet Explorer, or Firefox. We try to keep the information here specific to Facebook, and the pages within Facebook that support the ad creation and management process. Beyond that, if you need more information about connecting to the Internet or using a Web browser, any standard Internet reference works fine.

Conventions Used in This Book

To make sure instructions are clear and easy, we follow these conventions:

- When you need to take a specific action in a step list, they are printed in **bold**.
- When you see something printed this way — `http://facebook.com` — you're looking at a Web address (URL) or perhaps (and rarely) a snippet of markup language.

Icons Used in This Book

The Tip icon notifies you about something cool, handy, or nifty or something that we highly recommend. For example, "Just because there's a dancing clown out front doesn't mean that it's the best restaurant on the block."

Don't forget! When you see this icon, you can be sure that it points out something you should remember — maybe even something we said earlier that we're repeating because it's very important and you'll likely forget it anyway. For example, "Always check your fly before you walk out on stage."

Danger! Ah-*oogah*! Ah-*oogah*! When you see the Warning icon, pay careful attention to the text. This icon flags something that's bad or that could cause trouble. For example, "No matter how pressing the urge, no matter how well you know these things, *do not* ask that rather large woman next to you when she is 'due.'"

This icon alerts you to something technical, an aside or some trivial tidbit that I just cannot suppress the urge to share. For example, "FBML is known as FaceBook Markup Language, which is similar to HTML, or HyperText Markup Language." (By the way, FBML may be going away, so consult *Facebook Application Development For Dummies* by Jesse Stay for the replacement method of iFrames.)" Feel free to skip over this book's technical information as you please.

Where to Go from Here

You can start reading this book anywhere. Open the table of contents and pick a spot that amuses you or concerns you or has piqued your curiosity. Everything is explained in the text, and stuff is carefully cross-referenced so that you don't waste your time reading repeated information.

Part I

Getting Started with Facebook Advertising

The 5th Wave   By Rich Tennant

VP Sales

"It's web-based, on-demand, and customizable. Still, I think I'm going to miss our old sales incentive methods."

In this part . . .

If you've ever had to move to a new town, you understand the need to explore your new area and get comfortable with your new surroundings so you can adapt to your new environment. Believe it or not, that same analogy can be extended to the world of Facebook. If you want to set up shop as an advertiser, your best chance of success is to become comfortable with the overall environment before you start advertising.

In this first part, we cover the Facebook site in general and discuss how and where you can place advertisements on the site. We also discuss how your business can have a free presence on the site by building your own Facebook Page (yes, that's with a capital P) where your business can have "Fans" or people that follow your business' status on Facebook. Your ad campaigns will be more authentic and successful if you are a member of the community where you advertise.

Chapter 1

Profiting from the Facebook Revolution

In This Chapter

▶ Discovering what Facebook advertising offers

▶ Seeing the similarities between Facebook and other advertising

▶ Identifying the unique functions of Facebook advertising

▶ Understanding the direct and relationship marketing aspects of Facebook Ads

The old adage in real estate is that the three most important qualities of a property are "Location, location, location." Many say the same thing about advertising as we watch ads pop up (and under) all over the place. You can't watch a NASCAR race, drive along the road, read a magazine, or listen to the radio without hearing, seeing, or experiencing a message from an advertiser. Naturally, advertisers want to be where people are, and incorporate their products and messages into everyday life, from the bus stop bench to the clock on your doctor's office wall. As the World Wide Web has evolved, and more and more people incorporate the Internet into their daily lives, advertising naturally followed them online. And the Web has never been the same.

Online advertising has experienced a phenomenal growth, from the early days of text-only ads to the online streaming videos and media-rich ads that we can see today. In that time, advertising has taken on different forms (banner ads, pop-up ads, pop-under ads, everything but the Pop-Tarts ad) and different ways of charging the advertiser. One of the main functions of advertising, though, has been that ads allowed popular content to stay free of charge for users on the Internet. People got to host their own Web sites, have free e-mail accounts, and carry on all sorts of discussion with ad-supported Web sites and companies. In fact, the most popular Web sites today are the search engines, like Google and Yahoo!, that help direct people to what they are seeking on the Internet and receive a lot of revenue from the ads displayed alongside the search engine results.

Today, the hottest category of Internet usage for most people is the social networking space, where people use social Web sites to stay connected and communicate with their friends and colleagues. The current leader in personal social networking is Facebook, with more than 500 million members as of this writing. Members can talk to their friends, share photos and stories, comment on each other's status, and join groups and discussions on their favorite topics. Facebook also has third-party applications that run on its site, allowing people to take and share quizzes, play online games, and support their favorite causes. Alongside all this activity and discussion, quietly and unobtrusively placed, are advertisements that anybody can purchase, create, and launch by using Facebook advertising.

Facebook is in a unique position: It has a wealth of information about its users, with more content being generated daily, and Facebook has figured out how to allow advertisers access to that information without affecting the privacy of any particular user's sensitive data.

In this chapter, we talk about the basics of Facebook advertising, from what an ad looks like to its basic structure and placement, and the different types of ads and pricing models that Facebook offers. We cover some of the basic principles Facebook Ads uses that are similar to other online advertising sites, as well as highlight some of the unique aspects that Facebook offers to their advertisers. We end the chapter by discussing the two types of marketing an advertiser should keep in mind when using Facebook Ads: direct marketing and relationship marketing. By showing you all of these concepts, we will demonstrate that Facebook Advertising gives you the power to advertise your exact message to your exact audience in a hip and non-threatening environment, which should be any marketer's dream.

Introducing Facebook Advertising

When you use Facebook, whether you're on your home page, reading comments on your Friends' Walls, or playing your favorite online Facebook game, you'll probably notice at least one advertisement, usually on the right side of the page. These are Facebook Ads, and they are available to anyone with an advertising budget, from $1 to $1 billion. (That last option is probably just for Dr. Evil from *Austin Powers*.) Large advertisers, such as Pepsi, Proctor & Gamble, and Walmart, run ads on Facebook, but it also offers a great opportunity for many small businesses. A quick look at the Facebook for Business Page (see Figure 1-1) shows ads from companies like Nike to a company selling eBay auction templates.

Every advertisement on Facebook has the same four core elements:

- A **title** (25 characters or fewer)
- An **image** (optional but we strongly recommend having one; 110 x 80 pixels)
- The **ad copy or message** (135 characters or fewer)
- A **link** to a Facebook or other Web page (when someone clicks the ad)

Figure 1-1:
Facebook
Ads appear
along the
right side of
the page.

Facebook also adds a link entitled Like to do one of two things. If the advertiser is promoting a Facebook business Page, then clicking Like will add that user to the Facebook Page as a Fan. Otherwise, this link let users vote whether they like the advertisement. This is one way how Facebook enables its community to help police the types of ads that get displayed on the site. It also adds an interactive nature to the ads because when someone clicks the Like link for an ad, their friends find out that the person liked the ad, which may prompt some friends to view the ad as well.

If you're a Facebook member, you've likely seen ads displayed on the right side of most Facebook Pages. These ads include a headline, an image, and body copy (text). As we mention earlier, Facebook also includes a Like link with which members can either join a Facebook Page or express their thumbs-up approval for the ad. Like most traditional display ads, the user is then redirected to another page within Facebook or an external Web site.

Increasingly, Facebook Ads also include an option to engage in a social action, such as "Like," or "RSVP to this Event," like in Figure 1-2. Ads that include a social action are referred to as *social ads* or *engagement ads.* Social ads can even include a video (instead of a still image) that allows the user to view the video from directly within the ad unit.

A Sponsored social ad inviting visitors to "click the bucket"

Figure 1-2:
A social
ad offers
visitors
the ability
to engage
in a social
action.

On your Facebook home page, only one ad appears as the Sponsored ad, as shown in Figure 1-2. For most other Facebook Pages — also called *Rest-of-Site* pages — you should see at least three ads along the right side of the page, named the *Ad Space*.

Finding Your Way around Facebook Advertising

When you're ready to use Facebook Ads, start by going to its home page (www.facebook.com/ads), as shown in Figure 1-3.

Your Facebook Ad account will be tied to either your personal Facebook account or your Facebook Pages account, which is tied to your business. We walk you through how to create your own Pages account in Chapter 2. After these accounts are set up, Facebook walks you through the four-step process of building your own Facebook Ad:

Figure 1-3:
Start at the
Facebook
Advertising
home page.

1. Design your ad.

   a. *Write your title and ad message (or* body text, *as Facebook calls it).*

   b. *Attach an image to be included in the ad.*

   c. *Designate an internal Facebook Page or external Web page.*

2. Target your ad.

   Use Facebook's different target filters to assign the specific audience that you want to view your ad.

3. Price your ad.

   You designate a campaign name for your ad, set a budget for that ad, and decide whether to use a CPC or CPM pricing model when the ad is displayed. (Read more about CPC and CMP pricing in later chapters.)

4. Review your ad.

   You go over all the information you entered in Steps 1–3, and make sure the ad is to your liking. After you review everything and make sure that it's correct, you submit the ad to Facebook for approval.

You can read about all these steps in more detail in Chapter 2.

Seeing the Familiar Aspects of Facebook Advertising

Certain elements of Facebook advertising are very similar to other ad solutions out there, like Google AdWords. Some of these elements — such as writing your own advertising messages (a catchy title, some enticing call to action) and managing your own advertising budget (setting ad bid prices, doing daily or total ad budgets) — are proven winners that simply make sense for an online advertiser and create a better experience and return on investment (ROI).Because of these similarities, anyone with some experience in online advertising can use the Facebook Ad platform with no sharp learning curve. Later, we discuss some of the unique aspects of Facebook Advertising to further demonstrate the power and reach of this platform.

Design your own advertisements

When running an ad on Facebook, it's time to channel your inner Don Draper (from the AMC TV show *Mad Men*) and come up with your own design. After all, it's up to you to write your own ad. And this is a good thing because you're the one writing an ad that speaks directly to the customer you're trying to attract instead of having to pick from templates or stale prescripted messages. You're free to design targeted advertisements that match your goals, product catalog, or intended cause.

Facebook guidelines, however, do govern what you can and cannot put in an ad. Most of these guidelines have to do with protecting other people's copyrighted or trademarked information; or preventing anything obscene, offensive, or illegal from being displayed. Failure to abide by these guidelines can result not only in your ad not running but even removal of your Facebook account. You can find out more at the Facebook Ad Guidelines page at `www.facebook.com/ad_guidelines.php`.

Manage your own ad budget

With Facebook Ads, like other ad systems, you can set your own daily, weekly, monthly, or yearly budget, so you have virtual control over how much you spend. This allows you to plan your ad campaigns so you know your ads will be on Facebook during specific periods of time. Too, you keep yourself from spending your entire yearly ad budget in one or two days.

By managing your own ad budget, you can also decide when to spend more or less based on how effective your ads are performing. We discuss this strategy in Chapter 4 when we talk about how to calculate the effectiveness and ROI of your ads.

Of course, the value of being able to manage your own advertising budget occurs only when you take the time to decide when and how much to spend on your advertisements. Before you start running any major campaign, ask yourself a few questions:

- ✔ How much money do I have, total, to spend on Facebook advertisements? What percentage of my overall ad budget will I dedicate to Facebook Ads?

- ✔ How long do I want this ad campaign to be visible on Facebook?

- ✔ For what specific dates or timeframes will I need extra visibility or spending?

After you've thought about total spending, decide your per-ad spending. Many online advertising systems, including Facebook, have a *bidding system* for determining an ad's price. A *bidding system* is a method in which the advertiser defines the ad they wish to run and then create and enter their own bid price, which they are willing to pay the ad system for running this ad on that ad system. The bidding system will also look at any competing advertisements in their system inventory and suggest a bidding price or bidding range for this new ad request that the ad system would likely accept.

Facebook bases its ad pricing on a *closed bidding system*. This means that you can't see what others are bidding for ads, nor can they see your bids. Facebook provides a recommended bidding range, although you can choose to under or overbid their suggested range. However, if your cost is too low, the ad will not appear. Sometimes a penny too low on a bid can mean the difference between an ad being seen and one that isn't.

Similar to other systems, you have two different methods you can use to bid for your ads:

- ✔ **CPC (cost per click):** This is the method most often used, preferred by advertisers who closely track the performance of their ad. In the CPC method, the advertiser doesn't pay until a potential customer clicks the ad and is taken to the intended target page of that ad. This way, the advertiser doesn't pay every time an ad is merely displayed, and each click can be tracked to see whether that potential customer performed any action after clicking the ad.

- ✔ **CPM (cost per [thousand] impresssions):** This method was how online ads were originally paid for by advertisers. Whenever Facebook displays your ad, that counts as an *impression* against your ad budget. You can bid on the rate charged per 1,000 impressions.

   Some advertisers still opt for this method, especially in cases where they are looking for visibility instead of getting the customer to perform a specific action. The cost is much less with CPM because the advertiser is not paying for performance.

For those of you wondering why cost per *thousand* is abbreviated as CP*M* instead of CP*T*, the M refers to the Roman numeral system, in which M stands for 1,000.

We discuss more about CPC and CPM, as well as specific bidding strategies for both models, in Chapter 4.

Understanding Unique Aspects of Facebook Advertising

The most recent Interactive Advertising Bureau (IAB) Revenue Report (done by PricewaterhouseCoopers) estimated that $22.7 billion was spent on Internet advertising in 2009. Ten years ago, the estimates on Internet ad spending ranged from $1–2 billion. Part of this phenomenal growth is attributable to Internet companies figuring out bigger and better ways of serving the advertiser more — and, in most cases, better — information that advertisers can use in their efforts. As Internet technology has improved, Web sites have been able to incorporate images, then audio, video, and Flash technology into their ads to make them more attention-grabbing and user-friendly. Search engines were able to relay keywords typed in as a user's intent and geared ads targeted for those keywords.

Facebook Ads, unlike other ad systems (such as Google AdWords) can provide some great features for their advertisers mainly because of one thing: information. Facebook sits on a mountain of information about each of its users, from user profile information to the discussions, groups, and other ads that each user clicks or fills out while using Facebook. New information is generated daily, and Facebook has figured out how to harness that information in a way that shields the privacy of each particular user's sensitive data while providing a richer experience for the advertiser.

Targeting profile attributes

If you're designing an ad for a search engine like Google or Yahoo!, the most you know about your viewer is typically the keyword(s) that user types when using the search engine. Therefore, your ad has to be attractive to those visitors using those keywords as you try to figure out whether your product or service matches what they're searching for.

With Facebook, however, you can know a lot more about each person who will potentially view one of your ads. The typical Facebook user completes an extensive profile that tells the world (or just their Friends) everything from their Interests, Likes, and Dislikes to their Age, Gender, and Marital Status. Because this information is stored in each Facebook user's profile, Facebook can offer its advertisers the ability to target specific profile attributes so that you, the advertiser, can set very specific audiences for your ad.

Say, for example, that you're trying to advertise a shop that sells wedding dresses in Los Angeles. With other ad systems you might run search engine ads targeting phrases like *wedding dress* or *getting married,* but with Facebook you can actually tell Facebook to display your ad only to those 35,620 Facebook users (see Figure 1-4) who are Women, 25 to 44 years old, whose Marital Status is Engaged, and whose location is Los Angeles or a surrounding area.

Facebook has 11 profile attributes that you can set for each ad, including location, age, sex, education, and so on. For more on this, see Chapter 2.

Targeting your audience is as important as the message itself. Develop personas to represent your target audience. Learn what they're interested in — their educational background, relationship status, and where they live. Reach only the audience you desire by leveraging Facebook's targeting to meet your ideal customer profile.

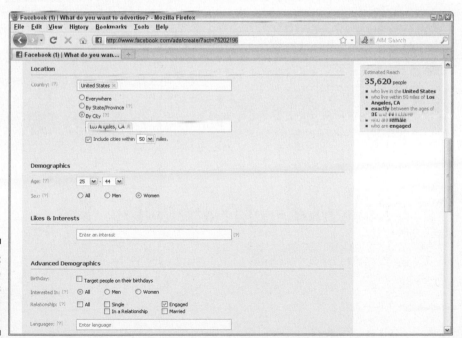

Figure 1-4:
Target the exact users who will see your ad.

Using clickable ads that don't leave the original Web page

The design of most online advertisements is to redirect the viewer to a specific Web page, or pop open a new tab or window to get to a message that the advertiser wants the viewer to see and then hopefully perform some sort of action. This is why we discuss landing pages at various places throughout this book, primarily in Chapter 7. However, some Facebook Ads offer a feature not possible with other systems: namely, the ability for the viewer to click the ad, perform the *call to action* (what you want the viewer to do), and never be taken off the original Web page where the ad was displayed.

With Facebook Ads for Pages and Events, the ad actually includes another element not found in other ads. That extra element is a button or link that the user clicks to perform the necessary action on Facebook's server. This button or link then changes to a confirmation message when the action is complete — and, most importantly, never updates, redirects, or changes the Web page that the user was on when the ad was clicked.

For example, take the ad for AllPosters.com in the left side of Figure 1-5. If you click the Like link, the ad subtly changes, replacing the link with a confirmation message (You like AllPosters.com, as shown on the right side of Figure 1-5), but the rest of the page stays the same, allowing the customer to go about their Facebook experience as usual.

Figure 1-5:
You can interact with Facebook Ads without leaving the page!

This feature is significant because it enhances the relationship marketing aspect of Facebook Ads. You, the advertiser, can interact with new customers without interrupting their daily activity. You become part of their overall experience as they are added to your Fan page or event RSVP list without losing track of their everyday Facebook interactions. The immediate confirmation of the action without the jarring effect of the visitor being moved to a new Web page often means that user is more likely to stay with that advertisers' brand in the future.

Gathering responder information with Facebook Insights

If you're going to advertise on Facebook, we highly recommend having a Page on Facebook as well. (We talk about how you can build a Facebook Page for your business in Chapter 2.) Not only will having a Page include you in an ongoing conversation with your customers and visitors by using Facebook, but it also gives you more information that you can use to update and refine your ads.

Facebook keeps track of visitor information for your business Pages through an interface called Facebook Insights. You can see user exposure, actions taken, and behavior related to either your social ads or your business Page, which allows you to monitor trends so that you can better gauge the effects of your ads beyond the common metrics of click-through rate and CPC.

We discuss the ins and outs of Facebook Insights, and how to use the data to update your ad campaigns, in Chapter 8.

Direct and Relationship Marketing Aspects of Facebook Ads

As you begin to use Facebook Ads to create and run your ad campaigns, you should understand two of the basic marketing disciplines that are coming into play in your efforts to reach the consumer:

✔ Direct marketing
✔ Relationship marketing

Your individual ads and ad campaigns are very much a direct marketing effort. You have specific goals, messages, and offers in mind, and you can measure the cost, ROI, and effectiveness of each ad that you run. Here, you are thinking about how each ad is acted upon and how it directly affects your business.

However, your presence in general is more of a relationship marketing effort. You're not simply running ads to get a one-time sales bump and then fade away. Your goal with these ads is to increase overall usage in your company's products, brand image, or even your Facebook presence.

Therefore, keep both disciplines in mind while you devise and implement your advertising strategy. The best success stories come from businesses that play to both these discipline's strengths while understanding the benefits their ad campaigns can bring in dollars as well as good will and brand presence.

How direct marketing techniques affects your advertisements

Facebook is an ideal direct marketing channel, offering direct marketers a cost-effective buy and easy-to-deploy testing environment from which to hone in on their target audience and refine the message. Direct marketing is a science in which measurement of response is an essential component. Facebook provides a platform from which to experiment and measure the results almost instantly.

It's no wonder that direct marketers are flocking to Facebook. When measuring results, a one percent difference in outcome could easily translate into hundreds or thousands of additional sales, depending upon the scale. That's why Facebook is a direct marketer's dream. The site allows you to run very focused and incremental tests, optimizing what works, and expanding your scope to reach up to tens of millions of consumers. For example, the Bradford Exchange uses Facebook Ads to market their Star Trek Electric Train (see Figure 1-6), where interested parties click the ad to buy the train from their Web site. (See Figure 1-7.)

Figure 1-6:
You can directly market your products on Facebook...

To have an effective ad campaign, here are some basic rules to consider when creating a direct marketing campaign via Facebook:

✔ Always test your message on a small percentage of your target group before you launch a full-out campaign.

✔ Test only one element at a time in a series of experiments so that you can **access** what effect each change caused.

✔ Focus initial testing on the target audience; then refine the offer.

✔ Test pricing based on CPC and CPM (even though CPC will typically outperform).

✔ It's better to send a bad offer to the right audience as opposed to a good offer served to the wrong audience.

When it comes to direct marketing, the important thing to remember when using Facebook Ads, is that you should try to test ads, compare results, and update your efforts as you go along. We cover these concepts in more detail throughout the book. Just know that you should achieve better success if you take the time to employ some of these direct marketing techniques with your Facebook Ad campaigns.

Figure 1-7:
. . . to sell something on your own Web site.

Understanding relationship marketing as part of your sales cycle

Throughout this chapter, we talk about the immediate nature of this ad system, and how you can measure, test, and retest your different ad campaigns. However, with Facebook (as opposed to a search engine), you might need to engage in some relationship marketing to complement your direct marketing. Think of your advertising presence as an ongoing part of your business, not just a one-time sales promotion.

In many cases, don't expect that your first ad to a new consumer will lead to a direct sale. Instead, you should view your clicks and interactions with viewers as steps in a relationship as you use Facebook Ads to build a relationship with each customer. Some examples of your goals and measurable results for relationship marketing would be

- ✔ The number of new people on your mailing list for a given month
- ✔ The number of Fans on your business Facebook Page
- ✔ The number of comments or Like votes to your Facebook posts

After you make an initial connection, make sure to do a steady amount of follow-up to move that customer along the right path from curious bystander to repeat paying customer.

Here, you have to consider how each ad affects that relationship, and whether you are running too many, too few, or just the right amount of ad campaigns to create that balance. You need to think like your prospects and ask yourself whether each campaign helps your customers find what they need or want — and most importantly, whether each campaign moves each visitor in the right direction, from stranger to loyal follower of your business.

Chapter 2

Setting Up Your Facebook Account

In This Chapter

▶ Creating a new Facebook business (Fan) Page

▶ Creating your first Facebook Ad campaign

▶ Deciding on the elements for a great ad campaign

▶ Preparing your Page sections for potential ad campaigns

*W*hen in Rome, do as the Romans do. When you're planning to use Facebook Ads to advertise something, be a part of the Facebook community. The best way to maximize the Facebook advertising system is to be a part of that system, which means having a presence there — a constant, active, thriving presence that's always being updated. We're not saying that you have to be a Facebook star, but your ads will have a better chance of success if you "mingle with the locals" (as it were) and have a solid, respectable presence that you can point to with your ads or build off your marketing success.

In this chapter, we walk you through the various steps needed to activate a business Page (yes, that's *Page* with a capital *P*. A business Page is different from a regular Facebook user profile, which is spelled with a small *p*) and your Facebook Ad account. Because an ad "account" is standard for anyone who advertises, we guide you through building your first ad campaign on Facebook. After that's done, then we talk about important elements you should consider in your ads and on your business Page.

Creating a New Facebook Business Page

Even though Facebook is designed as a true "social" network, where a majority of people use the site for personal connections and communication, Facebook recognizes that businesses, brands, and public figures want to use the site for nonpersonal goals as well. Facebook has developed a slightly different kind of account and page for members of the nonpersonal persuasion. Initially, these accounts were called *Fan Pages,* as in "Become a fan of Coca-Cola" or "Become a fan of Rihanna," but Facebook now refers to these accounts as Pages, which Facebook users can Like to indicate their membership to that Page. Unlike the personal Facebook profiles, where a person could have a maximum of 5,000 friends, a business Page could have unlimited interested users. Whereas personal profiles can "friend" and "message" each other, business Pages can only change their status, which gets broadcasted to any interested users or "fans" of that business.

The good news is that on a business Page, you can do many of the things that any Facebook user can do, including the following:

- ✔ Upload pictures and videos.
- ✔ Create and maintain discussion threads.
- ✔ Install applications on your Page.
- ✔ Create new Wall posts for which your Fans can comment or create their own posts.
- ✔ Join relevant Facebook groups.

As of this writing, Facebook is moving away from *Fan Page* and using *business Page* to refer to the pages for an artist, a brand, or a business. Instead of "becoming a Fan," Facebook users can simply "like" a business Page to follow that business and become Fans.

When you're ready to set up an official Facebook Page for your business, just follow these steps. If you don't have an existing Facebook account, that's okay. Just follow these steps, and you'll eventually create one.

1. **Go to www.facebook.com, the Facebook home page.**

   If you're already logged in to your personal account, click Account and then Logout from the top-right menu. You should be taken to the general home page shown in Figure 2-1.

2. **Click the Create a Page for a Celebrity, Band, or Business link to start the registration process.**

3. **On the Create a Page screen that opens, under the Official Page header, choose from three options (see Figure 2-2):**

   - Local Business
   - Brand, Product, or Organization
   - Artist, Band, or Public Figure

   If you select Local Business or Brand, Product, or Organization, you'll be asked to choose from a drop-down list the best category that matches your business or product. Some choices include: Consumer Product, Food and Beverage, Game, Online Store, Professional Service, Retail, and many more.

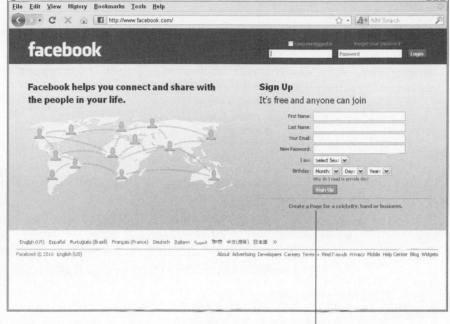

Figure 2-1:
Start by
creating
a new
Facebook
account
for your
business.

Create a Page for a celebrity, band, or business link

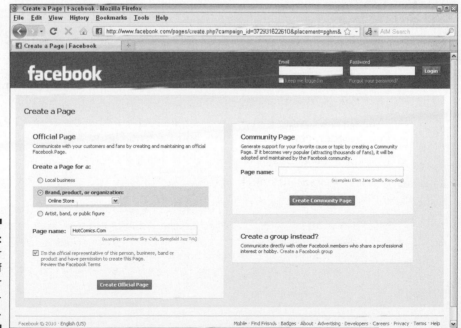

Figure 2-2:
Select your
type of
business or
organiza-
tion.

4. **Create a name for your Page and certify that you are the official representative**.

   a. *In the Page Name text box, write the name of your Page.* **Note:** *You don't need to include words like Fans in the Page name. Just stick to the name of your business.*

   b. *Mark the check box to certify to Facebook that you are the authorized representative to create this account, as shown in Figure 2-2.*

5. **Click the Create Official Page button**.

   On the resulting Create a Facebook Account screen that opens, you'll be asked whether you have an existing Facebook account.

   • *If you have your own Facebook account:* Provide your login information here.

   • *If you've never created a Facebook account:* Select the I Do Not Have a Facebook Account option (see Figure 2-3), enter the required information in the text boxes, and click the Sign Up Now button.

6. **Check your e-mail program for a confirmation e-mail from Facebook.**

   From that e-mail, click the link to be taken back to Facebook to see your newly created business Page; see Figure 2-4.

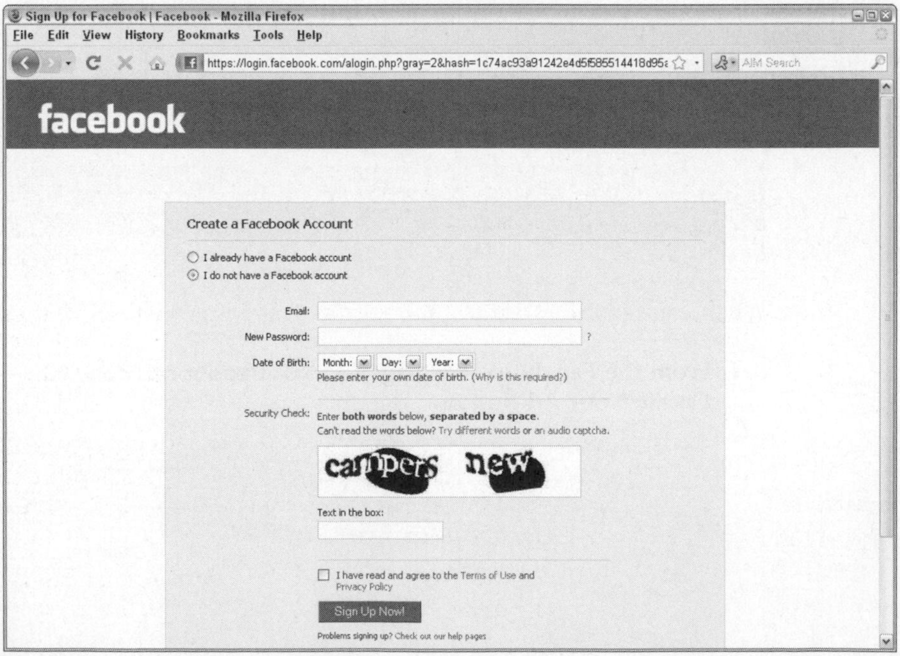

Figure 2-3:
You can
create
a new
account
here.

Make sure that the link in the confirmation e-mail you click starts with `www.facebook.com/`. Position your cursor over the link so you can see the actual Web link at the bottom of your Web browser, or copy and paste the link printed in the e-mail to your Web browser just to be safe. Recently some Web sites are pretending to be sites like Facebook and aim to steal your user information for illegal purposes.

Figure 2-4:
See your new Facebook business Page, ready to be filled in!

Creating Your First Ad Campaign

When you sign up for Facebook, whether you're using a personal or business account, you actually already have a Facebook Ad account. All you have to do is create your first ad to get started. After you create your first ad, Facebook will ask you to create a funding source (either a credit card or PayPal) for your ads to be eligible to be displayed.

When you're ready to start your first ad campaign, just follow these steps:

1. **From the Facebook Ads page — `www.facebook.com/ads` — click the Create Your Ad button.**

   You'll be taken to your first step, Design Your Ad (see Figure 2-5), where you first decide specifically what your Facebook Ad is promoting by setting the location where the advertisement will forward interested parties. You can pick one of the following options:

   • An external destination (a Web site page not on Facebook). Here, you would simply fill in the Destination URL field, like in Figure 2-5.

   • An internal Facebook Page, Group, Application, or Event that you want to advertise in your ad. Here, you would click the I Want to Advertise Something I Have on Facebook link. After that, you would see a drop-down list of any events, groups, applications, or Pages of which you are the Administrator, and you can then choose the internal Facebook content to be linked to your ad.

2. **Write the title and ad message for your message, and we strongly recommend that you add an image to enhance your ad.**

   a. *Provide a title (25 characters or fewer) and your ad message (135 characters or fewer) into the appropriate text boxes.*

   b. *If you have an image that you can put with your ad, click Browse to navigate to the image on your computer and then insert it into the ad.* Understand that your image file cannot be larger than 5 megabytes, and should be sized as no longer than 110 pixels wide by 80 pixels tall. The aspect ratio on your image should be either 4:3 or 16:9.

   You can a variety of different images to your ad, such as your company logo, a picture of the product, or even a smiling person who might use the product. By default, if you are advertising a Facebook Page, you will see the profile picture of that Page being used as your image, which you can change.

   c. *Click the Continue button.*

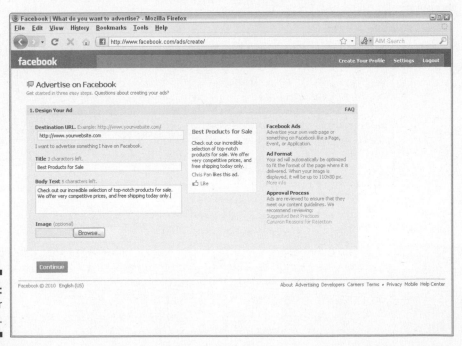

Figure 2-5:
Design your ad here.

3. **From the second step page (Targeting), use the Facebook filters to pick the exact audience you want to see your ad.**

As shown in Figure 2-6, you can pick the location of your target audience (the country — or in some cases, the state and/or city), age, gender, languages spoken, or specific keywords that indicate their likes or interests.

Facebook has 11 profile attributes that you can set for each ad, including the following.

- *Location:* You can target as many as 25 countries with each ad. For some countries, Facebook allows you to further target specific geographic regions or cities. For those of you running a local business, this option can ensure that you show ads only to those people who can physically walk into your business.

- *Keywords:* Besides Location, this is probably the most used targeting filter. Based on keywords that individuals put in their profile (under Interests, Favorites, and so on), you can show ads to only those people who have that keyword in their profile. So, if you're trying to reach people who enjoy the TV show *Desperate Housewives,* you can set that filter by entering the name of the show in the Keywords target field. Understand that as you add keywords, Facebook may suggest additional keywords you can add based on people's Likes and Interests.

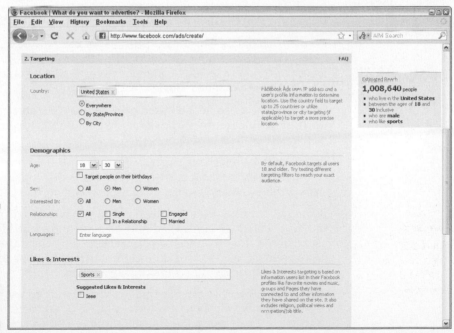

Figure 2-6:
Pick the exact target audience you want to view your ad.

When using multiple keywords, you need to separate them with the word "or." So, for example, if you are trying to reach people who enjoy either Desperate Housewives *or* Gossip Girl, you would write: "Desperate Housewives" OR "Gossip Girl."

- *Age:* Based on the birth date that the user provides, Facebook can determine a user's age, which allows you to target specific age range demographics to display your ads. After all, if you're targeting college freshmen, your ad needs to speak to that generation. Likewise, if your desired audience comprises senior citizens, the ad needs to appeal to their particular tastes and sensibilities. Perhaps your product is geared for women between the ages of 35 and 45? No problem.

- *Sex:* Perhaps your ad is intended to reach a specific gender. With Facebook Ads, you can set which gender (or both) can see your ad.

- *Education:* Based on the profile data each user enters into Facebook, you can target your audience to reach people with a specific education level, whether high school graduate, college graduate, or even someone still in college.

If you're trying to target people in college, Facebook offers you the option to enter a specific college or university name, as well as the name of a major and graduation year as additional targeting filters.

- *Workplace:* If you're trying to reach workers at a specific company (say, IBM or Coca-Cola) you want to reach specific job types (Project Managers), you can use the Workplace filter to target your ad.

- *Relationship Status:* This target is primarily used for advertisers trying to target a product or service tied to weddings or related to marriage. If you're trying to advertise a singles site, you can target people who are listed as single.

When you target someone based on relationship status, your ad won't be visible to users who did not complete the Relationship Status part of their profile.

- *Relationship Interests:* This target is primarily used for advertisers of products or services that have to do with someone's intended relationship partner, whether it's about dating or something more "private."

- *Birthday:* This filter is especially handy if you want to display an ad with a special offer that's valid only on someone's birthday. The user will see this ad only if he uses Facebook on the day noted as his birthday. (Specific birthdate information of each user is always protected, based on the user's privacy settings.)

- *Connections:* You can run ads that are visible only to users who are already Fans of your Business Page, who RSVP'ed to your events, or who are a member of one of your groups. You can also target Friends of your Connections, especially when you're interested in growing the number of Fans or members that you have.

• *Languages:* If you're running different ads to target different cultures or countries, you can use the Languages filter to make sure the appropriate ad is displayed for the language for which you wrote the ad.

For this example, we target 18–30-year-old men in the United States who like sports. Facebook estimates more than one million potential Facebook members who fit this target. (Don't worry; we will cover targeting in more depth in Chapter 3.)

The more targeting filters you use, the lower your estimated reach will be, meaning a smaller audience will be exposed to your ad, and therefore, you may not see a large amount of responses to your ad.

4. **After you pick your target audience, scroll down and click Continue.**

5. **In the third step, Campaigns and Pricing (see Figure 2-7), create a name for your campaign.**

6. **Create a daily budget for your campaign.**

Pick the account currency you want to use, and then decide how much you want to spend on a daily basis to run this ad on Facebook, as shown in Figure 2-7. You can choose to run your ad every day or pick specific days to display your ad. We cover ad-buying strategies in more depth in Chapter 4.

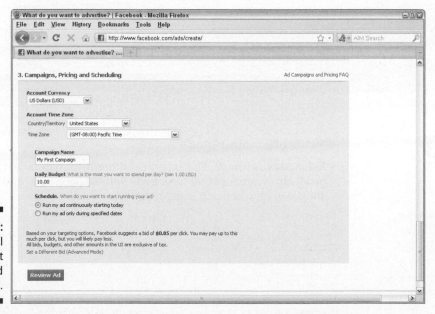

Figure 2-7:
Set an initial daily budget for your ad campaign.

7. **Click the Review Ad button to review your ad for accuracy.**

    On the Review Ad page that opens, look over the sample ad (as in Figure 2-8) to make sure it looks exactly how you want it shown to your target audience. One quick note: Even when you insert an image, for some reason, the image will not show up in the Ad Preview on this screen. If you inserted an image, don't worry; it will run with your ad. You can give this ad a unique name so you can refer to it later if you want to change or reuse this ad. (As a default, the ad will use your title as its initial name.)

8. **Provide Facebook with the billing information so it can charge you for running your ad.**

    You also need to provide Facebook with a form of payment so it can bill you when your ad is run. Either fill in the boxes as shown to provide a major credit card, or click the I Have a Coupon to Redeem link to give the promotional code for Facebook Ad credit.

9. **Click the Submit button to submit your ad to Facebook**.

As of this writing, Facebook reviews every ad campaign submitted to make sure that each advertiser follows Facebook policies. You should hear back from Facebook within one to two business days, on average, whether your ad was approved, and if so, when it will start running.

That's it! You created your first ad campaign, and your Facebook Ad account is active and ready.

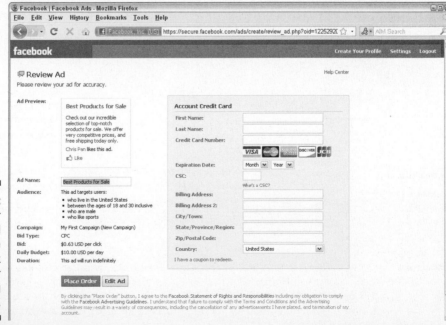

Figure 2-8:
Look over your ad and provide Facebook with your billing information.

If you ever need to pause or delete any ad that you've created, you can do so from the Ads Manager. We discuss the steps necessary in Chapter 3.

Elements of a Great Ad Campaign

You don't just want to create a regular, run-of-the-mill ad campaign. You want to create a *great* ad campaign. Here, we take a closer look at some of the immediate aspects of your ad, and then use the next few chapters to discuss some of the larger aspects of your entire ad campaign, from harnessing the powerful targeting features to spending your ad budget in a wiser fashion.

Start with the ad itself, which comprises the title, ad message, and optional image used in your ad, plus the targeted destination link of your ad. Although there is no perfect "right way" to build your ad, our experience with ad campaigns has given us some recommendations, tips, thoughts to keep in mind.

Titling your ad

A headline can be a very powerful tool for bringing attention to any advertisement. After all, most people just read the headlines when they skim at a newspaper. With the limit of only 25 characters for the headline — *title* — of your Facebook Ad, you literally have to choose your words very carefully.

In some cases, like when you advertise a Facebook Event, your title may be "locked" so you cannot alter it at all.

First and foremost, be aware that Facebook has some specific rules regarding the title of your ad:

- ✔ You must use actual words in a grammatically correct manner. That is, you can't substitute ¢utesy $ymbols for letters; or use excessive repetition (like *Sale, Sale, Sale*), emoticons (like J), unnecessary symbols (such as 4or *), and so on.

- ✔ Use keywords that specifically relate to your ad message. For example, don't use *Free iPhones* in your title if you're selling discount sporting goods.

- ✔ Limit your use of punctuation. You can't use exclamation points; and don't end your title with an ellipsis (. . .), dash, or other excessive punctuation.

Basically, your ad title needs to be readable, clear, and precise, not like something a teenager would send via text message. Beyond the basics of the rules, however, you want your title to be eye-catching and relevant — something that will make a Facebook user stop what they are doing, and read your ad to consider clicking it to take advantage of your offer or promotion.

Writing body text

After you craft your headline, it's time to write your ad's message. You have 135 characters to play with to communicate a call to action and do some form of initial setup or explanation as to what you offer. For those of you who enjoy tweeting on Twitter, coming up with a message using only 135 characters isn't that tough, but for the rest of us, it means choosing each word very carefully.

Just like for the title, Facebook has some rules for how your ad message body text should appear. The main thing is to use complete sentences with proper spelling, grammar, and punctuation. The other important element is that whatever you promise or advertise in your ad message *must* be present in the landing page or destination of the ad link. You cannot advertise one thing and then redirect people to something unrelated.

Now that we've discussed what you have to write, think about what you *should* write. You can find entire books that address the art of copywriting, advertising, or online marketing, but here are some basic tips to keep in mind:

- ✔ **Relate to your audience.** Because you get to target your ad to a very precise audience, don't forget to make your ad message targeted as well. Instead of trying to be as broad as possible, use keywords, terms, and language that your target audience will recognize and respond to. You'll have a better response from your intended targets if they recognize the vocabulary used in your ad.

- ✔ **Have a clear call to action.** It's not enough that your advertisement shows off your company or brand. Your ad should ask viewers to do something — buy something on sale, join a group or newsletter, receive a free tip sheet — that they can get only by clicking your ad. The concept in sales is of "asking for the sale": You don't just put the offer out there, but rather you ask the question, "Will you buy the item I am selling?" Your ad will hopefully compel people to click that ad to take advantage of your call to action.

- ✔ **Be clear with your offer.** Leave the mystery writing to folks like John Grisham. Your goal is not to tease the audience so they click your ad in hopes that your Web site will convert them. Your goal is to have an ad that is clear so your audience knows exactly what you are offering them before they click over. This way, every click you get is someone's genuine interest in acting on your offer. Otherwise, you can blow your budget very quickly and have very little to show for it.

- ✔ **Learn from others.** If you're stuck on what to write for your ad copy, look at other Facebook Ads. Go to your Facebook home page, your Friends' pages, or any Group pages where you are a member. Read the ad copy in each ad and see whether any ideas come to you. This will also give you exposure to what your competition is running, so you can try to make your ad distinct. See what ads catch your attention, and then ask yourself, what about their ad text made your eyes stop?

For example, if you're trying to recruit people to Like your Facebook Page, your ad may initially look like the first image in Figure 2-9, where you add the simple message "Visit our Page and become a Fan! Click here." Remember, though, this ad has to catch the user's attention and compel them to stop what they're doing, consider your message, and act on it by clicking a link. Give people more information as to what they can expect to find on your Page (like The Body Shop does in their ad, as shown in the second image in Figure 2-9) or be specific that you're only offering special content on your Facebook Page, like Quikbook.com does in its ad (in the last image in Figure 2-9).

Figure 2-9:
Turn an
okay ad
into an eye-
catching
one through
your
message.

Visit our Page and become a Fan. Click here !

The Body Shop USA   x
Become a fan of The Body Shop for access to exclusive deals, giveaways & more!
👍 Like

Quikbook.com   x
Save big on your next hotel stay! Like Us for access to exclusive Facebook-only sales & specials; deals you won't find anywhere else.
👍 Like

You can look at a number of ads by looking at your Ad Board (either click More Ads at the bottom of your Ad Space on your home page or go directly to `www.facebook.com/ads/adboard`), which looks like Figure 2-10. Here, you can view several ads and get some ideas.

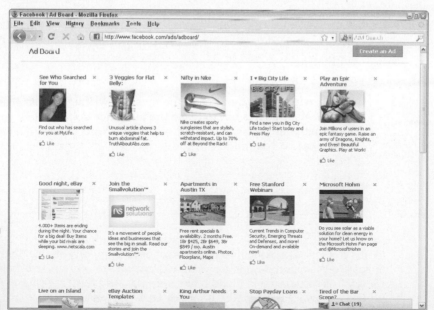

Figure 2-10:
Compare
Facebook
Ads.

Choosing an image

One of the unique advantages of Facebook Ads versus other platforms is the ability to include an image with your ad to help reinforce your offer and attract viewer's attention. When choosing an image, though, keep the following in mind:

✔ **Keep it simple.** Your image displays at a size of 110 x 80 pixels, so using a complicated or "busy" image probably won't work well in a Facebook Ad. The best images are those that display one object, person, or logo. For example, the image of the Constitutional Convention used in the Route Out ad (see Figure 2-11) is so compacted that only the "We the People" emblem is noticeable. By contrast, the simple bead necklace photo in the Bead Lovers Korner ad stands out better.

✔ **Your image needs to "match" your ad.** This advice might seem self-explanatory, but it bears mentioning. When you choose an image to augment your ad, the image has to have something to do with the advertisement. If you're running a photo of a laptop, the ad should be laptop-related, for example.

✔ **Your image must conform to Facebook guidelines for ad images**. According to Facebook, the file size for your image should not be larger than 5 megabytes. Facebook does not support the use of animated or Flash images for your ad. The aspect ratio for your image should be either 4:3 or 16:9, and the size of your image should not be greater than 110 by 80 pixels. If your image size differs from this size, Facebook will automatically resize your image to 110 by 80 pixels.

✔ **Be careful when using trademarked or copyrighted photos.** If your image includes a copyrighted or trademarked image, you might not be able to use it in your Facebook Ad. Facebook has rules in place that don't allow you to use certain images. So, if you're thinking of using a picture of an iPhone, perhaps a visual drawing of something that looks like an iPhone would be a better choice.

Figure 2-11:
Keep your
images as
simple as
possible.

Many Web sites provide free or stock photos that you can use if you have no access to the right graphic for your ad. Just do an Internet search for "free photos" or "stock photos" and make sure that the terms of whatever Web site you pick allow you to use the photo in an advertisement.

If all else fails, use your company logo or an image from your Web site. That way, your graphics will be consistent between your ad and Web site.

Choosing your destination URL

You caught the attention of a Facebook user who likes your ad and clicks it. Now you are going to send that user to another Web page or Facebook Page. So, the choice becomes what destination your ad should have. You get to choose the destination link for your ad, so choose wisely.

As you're coming up with options for what to use as your destination URL, here are some points to keep in mind:

- ✔ **Your link should be trackable.** Even if you want your ads to just send people to your Web site's home page, you should include something to make sure you can track the results or indicate to the incoming page that this viewer came from a Facebook Ad. Some people do this by embedding a tracking number or field in their link. (For example, www. yourwebsitename.com?source=facebook.) Others create a special landing page accessible only by using the precise link from the Facebook Ad. For example, you could create a special directory and Web page on your site, such as www.yourwebsitename.com/fb/facebook.html, that's not referenced or linked from your home page or anywhere else, and the only way someone can get to that Web page is to click the link from your ad. (We discuss more about landing pages in Chapter 7.) Pick a method that's easy for you, and when you want to track your results, you can use tools like Google Analytics (www.google.com/analytics) or GoStats (www.gostats.com).

- ✔ **Don't squeeze the visitor when they arrive.** With other ad systems, the destination URL or landing page goes into a long sales letter or tries to capture a lot of information and make an immediate sale. As we mention earlier, because your ads are building a relationship, your destination URL shouldn't ask for a bunch of information up front or rush a sale. Don't overwhelm your visitor with too much sales copy or extra actions, like pop-up ads.

    Asking for Personally Identifiable Information (such as name, date of birth, phone number, or Social Security number) on the Web page of your destination URL goes against Facebook's current rules — unless you're advertising an e-commerce transaction and a product is clearly being sold from your ad.

- ✔ **Create one page for each ad.** This is especially true if you are running multiple ads at any one given time. Many advertisers create a unique landing or destination page for each ad that they create. This way, the destination URL can refer exactly to the offer mentioned in the ad instead of sending the viewer to an existing Web page that could have a lot of text, images, and offers on it. You want to keep the destination simple and present your ad offer only on the destination page. This way, when you track your results, you have a better idea of whether that specific offer was good enough to entice a response. We talk more about tracking your results in Chapters 10 and 11.

Preparing your Facebook Business Page for Your Ad Campaigns

Step back for a moment and look at your Facebook business Page again. Although you might be using your Facebook Ads to point new customers to your own Web site, you will hopefully be interacting with these customers on Facebook through your business Page as well. Therefore, you want to make sure your business Page is fully set up for any new visitors. Just like you'd put the finishing touches on a brick-and-mortar store before a Grand Opening, you should take a look at your Facebook business Page before you start running your ad campaigns so that your presence helps you and makes you look more professional and approachable.

Adding or updating the necessary elements on your business Page

If you're sending people to your Facebook Page for your business, make sure that your business Page has enough of the right elements to ensure that new visitors get the full picture about your business. Remember that your business's Facebook presence needs to be seen as an ongoing, full-fledged effort independent of any individual ad campaign.

Therefore, if you just recently created your Facebook business Page, or just inherited or took over the business Page from someone else, see whether these elements have been added to your page:

- ✔ Basic info on the company (contact information, store address, hours, phone, and so on)
- ✔ Detailed info on the company (company overview/mission statement, a list of main products, and the official company Web site URL)
- ✔ Links to relevant Web sites
- ✔ Wall posts that reference the company being mentioned in any online articles, interviews, or Webcasts
- ✔ Event listings of any company activities open or available to the public (online events; not necessarily live, in-person events)

You should make sure that all the elements on your Facebook business Page are consistent with your own Web site or business logo. This not only includes your logo, but any color choices you use for your business, any slogans or business messages, and anything related to your business brand.

One great example is the retailer Best Buy, which incorporates some custom pages along with basic information about the company. (See Figure 2-12.) Not only did Best Buy establish its Business Page but Best Buy also consistently provides updates and interactions with its Fans through Wall posts and messages.

Other companies then add things like Facebook-only specials and announcements to their business Page. For example, the Comic Bug, a Los Angeles–based comic book shop, decided to host a special raffle only available to its Facebook Fans who RSVP'ed for an upcoming event at the store. (See Figure 2-13.)

Selecting elements for ad campaign landing pages or targets

As you build your Facebook business Page and think about ad campaigns for your business, plan ahead to make sure that elements of your Facebook business presence are ready to go when you run a relevant ad campaign. Consider creating or augmenting some of these items, which could be your landing pages or ad targets in the future:

- ✔ **Facebook Event:** Having a Grand Opening sale? Anniversary sale? New product launch? If you have a specific event in your business, create a Facebook Event that gives people the details of that event, whether the event is in person, online only, or both. After you create the event, invite your Fans, ask your Fans to promote it to their friends, and post updates to the event as it approaches.

- ✔ **Photos tab:** If you're thinking of promoting a new line of products, or perhaps adding a new location to your brick-and-mortar business, you can prepare a set of photos showing off your expansion and let your ad campaign direct people to your Photo albums or Photo tab. Don't be afraid to show "action" shots of your business or customer photos, or have your Facebook Fans submit their own photos of your business to include on your business Page. The right photos can tell a better story than any writer could with words.

- ✔ **Product reviews:** It never hurts to have employees, customers, or casual Fans provide reviews of products you have available for sale. By encouraging reviews on an ongoing basis, you will always be ready for an upcoming promotion by pointing people to existing reviews of that product or category.

Figure 2-12:
Best Buy
uses its
Facebook
Page to
reach out to
customers.

Figure 2-13:
The Comic
Bug offers a
Facebook-
only raffle to
their
customers.

Part II

Launching Your Facebook Advertising Campaign

In this part . . .

After you join the Facebook community and built up a presence, it's time to start planning your Facebook ad campaign. Of course, the best campaigns will be those that execute a great strategy . . . or set of strategies.

In this part, we go over a number of the strategies and tactics you need to execute when planning your ad campaign. We look at the different targeting strategies you can take using Facebook's filtering options, and ways to stretch your budget by using the different payment models for your ads. We then discuss the different types of advertisements that you can run on Facebook. Finally, we end this part with a look at how to test your initial concepts, improve your expected results, and explore some external promotion methods.

Chapter 3

Matching Your Ads to Your Marketing Strategy

In This Chapter

▶ Picking a target advertising group

▶ Setting the geographic range for your ad campaign

▶ Deciding the scope of each ad campaign

▶ Fulfilling your marketing objectives through Facebook Ads

There are several forms of advertising for which you can't really segment or define your audience. For example, when you rent an outdoor billboard, you're basically advertising to the group "anyone who drives by." When you post a flyer, you're advertising to the group "anyone who walks by." Some mass market–advertising methods, such as TV or radio ads, run surveys on their audiences to give the advertiser an idea of the demographics behind their audience. However, those numbers are just averages and can vary daily. For some businesses, their audience target is based on quantity, not quality.

Facebook advertising, on the other hand, allows you and your business to create and run advertisements that are highly targeted when it comes to the viewing audience — and you should take advantage of that capability.

In this chapter, we focus on the targeting capabilities of Facebook, explaining how to target everything from a local to an international audience. We then look at aligning your ads with whatever marketing strategy you're employing, whether your goal is to build your business brand, increase sales, or augment your customer service outreach.

Picking a Target Group from the Facebook Audience

When you're determining your target group, you're basically answering the question, "Who do I want to reach with my ad?" In other words, if you could pick any Facebook user to view your ad (and hopefully click it), what would that user look like? We're not talking hair color or wardrobe, but what demographic you're trying to reach. Are you looking to target your video game company toward young single males ages 13–30? Perhaps you're trying to sell golf equipment to working professionals in their 30s and 40s who live on the West Coast? Or maybe you're just trying to announce your new donut shop to anyone within a 5–10 mile radius of your town. In any case, you need to define your target group.

Start by writing a profile of your target user. You can specify several factors, including

- **Age:** Do you want to specify a range of ages, such as 18–25? Or do you want a specific age, such as 21-year-olds who are eager to start enjoying their adult privileges?

- **Education:** Does your audience share a specific educational level, such as high school or college students? Are you trying to reach people enrolled in school, or graduates of a certain level? Perhaps your target audience is affiliated with a specific college, university, or institute of higher learning, or for example, college grads who may want to get an MBA from a school like UC San Diego (as in Figure 3-1).

- **Gender:** Is your product or business better suited to one gender? *Note:* Even if your product is something that one gender can't use, ask yourself whether your customer set includes members of the opposite gender who are going to buy this item for their partner or spouse. In other words, even if the product is "for guys," perhaps you want women to see your ad because maybe a woman would buy that product for a man, especially if it's a product best suited as a gift.

- **Language:** Are you trying to reach an audience that speaks a certain language, such as Spanish-speaking people who live in the United States? Are you trying to reach a certain cultural target group? If so, targeting the language spoken by the viewer is a great way to reach out to specific communities.

- **Location:** Is the location of your viewer important enough to specify it in your target group? For example, maybe you have a local business you're trying to advertise, or a large portion of your current customer base lives in a certain locale. (Perhaps you're advertising a geographic site like SanDiego.com to San Diego residents, like in Figure 3-2.) Does the nature of your business product lend itself to a certain geographic area? (You don't need to advertise ice scrapers in southern California, for example.)

✔ **Likes and Interests:** In Facebook, likes and interests are known as keywords, which basically specify any particular favorite item or interest that your target user would have written in their Facebook profile. Perhaps you're trying to reach fans of a particular entertainment franchise, like *Twilight* or *Star Wars*. You might want to target people who enjoy a specific outdoor sport or activity, or who play musical instruments. Maybe you have a new product line of branded merchandise, and you want to announce this to established fans of that brand. You have a lot of freedom here because you can pick popular or niche areas. For example, a seller of branded cell phone cases could market UCLA Bruin cases to UCLA fans (see the first image in Figure 3-3), while someone else can market Simpsons Google skins to Simpsons fans (see the second image in Figure 3-3).

When you specify a particular keyword for a Like/Interest, though, you exclude any users who don't spell that word exactly the same as you did, or who haven't entered that word into their profile.

Figure 3-1:
Target your
ad to people
who share
an educa-
tional goal.

Figure 3-2:
You can
promote
local busi-
nesses
or geo-
graphically
targeted
businesses.

Figures 3-3:
You can create ads that target specific Likes and Interests.

As you determine your target user, you also need to decide whether you want to widen your target base or stay close to certain specific demographics. You can always make this decision after you run some ad campaigns and study the effectiveness of previous campaigns, or you can build in some leeway into your initial targets. For example, if you are targeting 18–25-year-olds, you can add some leeway by lowering the minimum age to 16 or 17 and raising the maximum age to 27 or 28.

Don't forget that you might have some existing demographic information at your fingertips to help you determine an appropriate target group for your ads:

✔ **Your customer database:** If you've been in business for any given length of time, you've likely built up a customer database. Your database might not have detailed demographic information on every customer, but see what information is available. Perhaps you can determine that 88 percent of your customers are between the age of 25 and 34. You might find out that 75 percent of your newest customers live in either California or Florida. Go through any customer records you have to identify patterns, commonalities, or trends that could influence your advertisements.

Your e-mail provider may be able to help with your Facebook ad campaign. For example, Blue Sky Factory is an e-mail provider that can tell you how many of your e-mail addresses in your customer database are registered with Facebook (or other social networking sites like Twitter, LinkedIn, and so on). Tools like Blue Sky Factory make it easier to reach your existing customers who are already on Facebook but may not be connected to your Facebook Page.

✔ **Your product target demographics:** If you have a business selling a given product, look at that product. Who is that product designed for? Chances are that a manufacturer, distributor, or trade association has a wealth of desired demographic information that you could find as a retailer of that item. For example, the biggest target market of video games is males age 13–30. Do some research on the Internet or talk to your suppliers and look for groups of people more inclined to buy your product. After all, even if your product could be bought by anybody, the goal of a targeted ad is to reach the *most likely* purchaser, which should increase the chance of conversion (from viewer to customer) and increase the success of your business.

✔ **Your Web site usage log:** If you have a Web site for your business, you most likely have access to a report that shows you how people found your Web site. If a viewer typed in a string of keywords into a search engine, saw a results page, and clicked a link from that results page, you will be able to see that string of keywords in your report. (It's part of the incoming link the viewer used before they arrived on your Web site.) If you see a keyword (or set of keywords) being used over and over by Web searchers who end up checking out your Web site, consider using that keyword (or set) as part of your target group when building your Facebook Ad target group. There are a number of Web analytics programs that can help you analyze your usage logs and other Web site information, which we provide in Table 3-1.

Table 3-1	Web Analytic Tools
Name of Analytic Tool	*URL of Tool*
Google Analytics	www.google.com/analytics
WebTrends	www.webtrends.com
CoreMetrics	www.coremetrics.com
Omniture SiteCatalyst	www.omniture.com

Establishing the Scope of Your Ad Campaign

After you come up with a target group (or range), it's time to define your targeting filters when building your ad campaign. You enter your ad target information in Step 2 of the ad-creation process, appropriately labeled Targeting. From this information, you filter out Facebook users who don't match your targets, so only potential targets within your desired group are presented with your ad.

If you're building multiple campaigns — say, to test different ad messages or offers — use the same target filters for each campaign. That way, you can compare apples to apples wherein the only difference is the ad message or specific offer. Then you decide which message or ad is more effective instead of wondering whether a different target group has a different response rate.

Local campaigns

The easiest scope to implement on Facebook is a local campaign. When trying to reach a local audience with your Facebook Ad, you simply define a city within a given state, and then specify a certain mile radius around that city as your target audience.

1. **From the Facebook Ads page — `www.facebook.com/ads` — click the Create Your Ad button.**

2. **In the first step of the process, write the title and ad message for your message, and we strongly recommend that you add an image to enhance your ad.**

   Here, you need to design your ad by coming up with the advertisement itself and the destination the user sees when they click the link, which is an external URL to Facebook, or an internal Facebook Page, Event, Application, or Group.

3. **Scroll down the page to the second step of the process, Targeting.**

4. **Choose the base country by typing it into the text field provided, if it is not automatically filled in already.**

5. **In the Location section, select the By City radio button and then enter the name of the city you want to target into the City field.**

   Facebook prompts you while you type to suggest the name of a city in its database that matches what you're typing. After you pick the correct city, that listing shows up in the City field, as shown in Figure 3-4.

   If you type in the name of a city and Facebook squawks `No matches found`, nobody has yet defined a location to be that city, so you need to try another city name close by or the name of the larger metropolitan area that has defined Facebook users in that city.

To expand your reach a little, select the Include Cities Within check box (next to the City field) and then pick a miles value — 10, 25, or 50 — to expand the radius of possible targeted cities beyond the city you selected.

You can also expand your search by including several nearby cities, as shown in Figure 3-5, with a number of suburbs and cities within the greater San Diego, CA area.

Regional campaigns

When you want to expand your campaign to focus on an entire region instead of a city-by-city level, you probably want to start by specifying the states in the region you want to target. When you get to the Targeting screen (refer to the preceding section), follow these instructions:

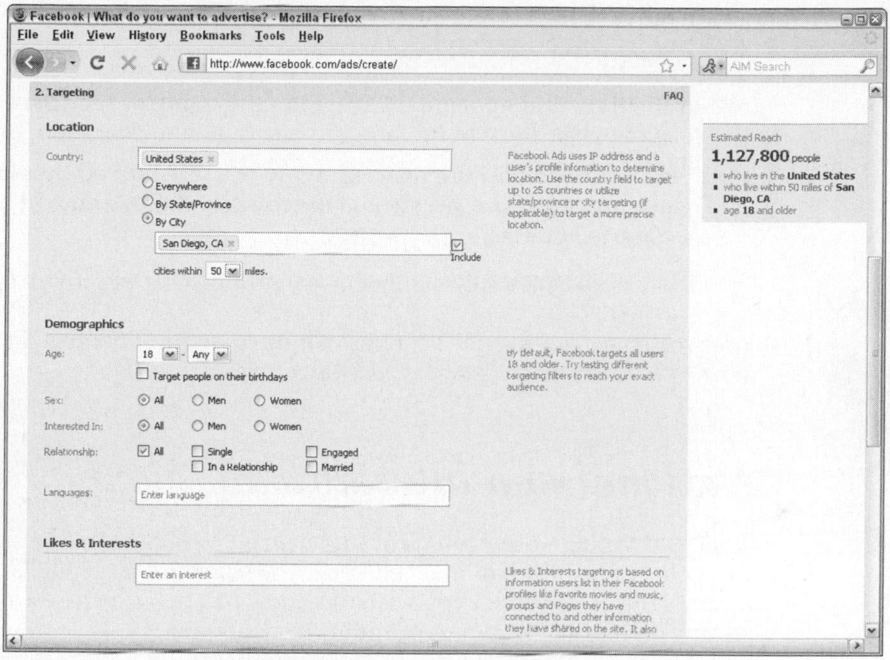

Figure 3-4:
Target your campaign to a single city.

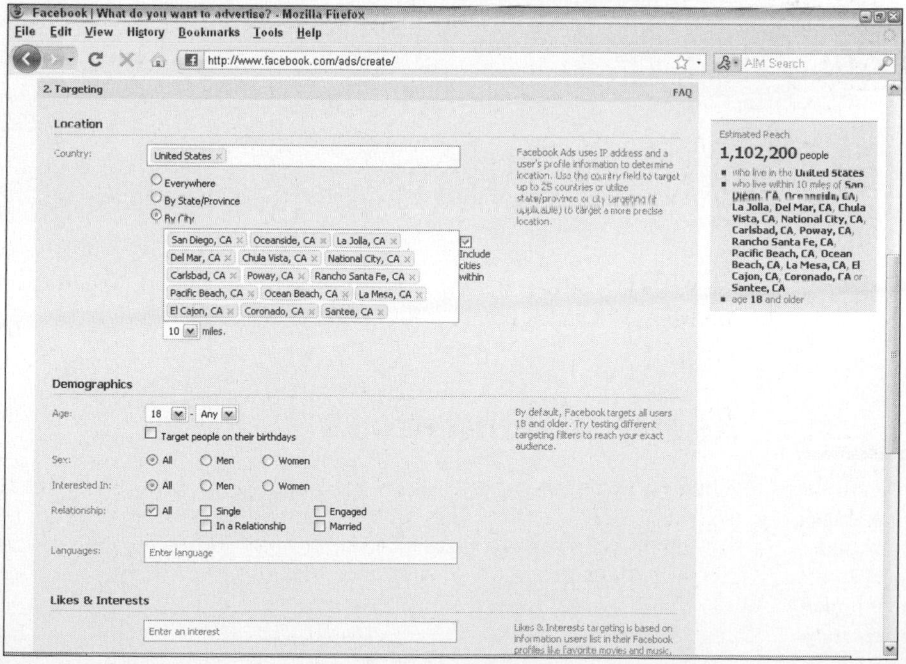

Figure 3-5:
You can target multiple cities in the same area.

1. **Make sure the correct country you want is selected in the Country field.**

2. **Select the By State/Province radio button.**

3. **In the field that appears, start typing the name of the first state or province you want to include in your regional campaign, as shown in Figure 3-6.**

4. **(Optional) Repeat Step 3 if you have more than one state in your region that you want to specify.**

   There is no limit to the number of states or provinces you can specify here.

Your region cannot include sections of more than one country. And if you pick more than one country, state or city targeting is unavailable.

National and international campaigns

As of this writing, when you want to run an ad campaign that reaches out to a national or an international audience, your location targeting is simply the name of the country(ies) you wish to target. You don't have to worry about picking certain states, cities, or radius measurements.

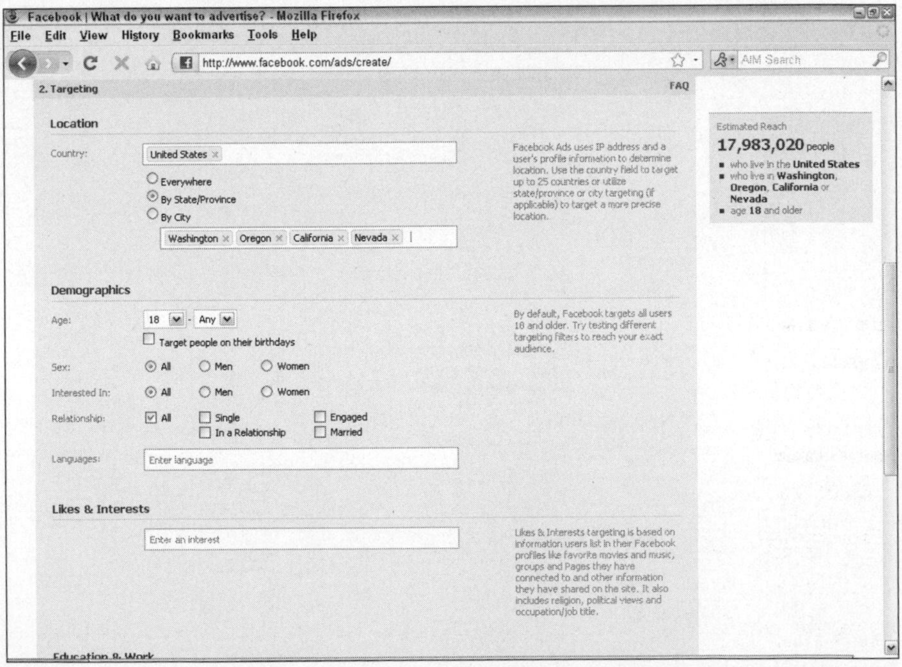

Figure 3-6:
Enter one or more states to create your region.

When you want to target a specific country, simply type that name into the Country field on the Targeting page. As default, Facebook automatically fills in your home country in the box. For example, for us, it shows the United States when we start an ad campaign, as shown in Figure 3-7.

If you want to run a campaign in more than one country, simply type the name of another country into the Country field until the correct country option appears. Say that you want to target European countries with your newest ad campaign. You can type in all the European countries until they appear as shown in Figure 3-8. You can list as many as 25 countries as targets for your campaign.

You still retain all your other targeting filters, such as age, interests, education, gender, and languages.

If you want to run language-specific campaigns in different countries, Facebook recommends you create a different campaign with each language you want to use. For example, use one campaign for all your Spanish speakers, a second campaign for French speakers, and so on. This way, each language campaign can be optimized so the message resonates with the native speakers of each language.

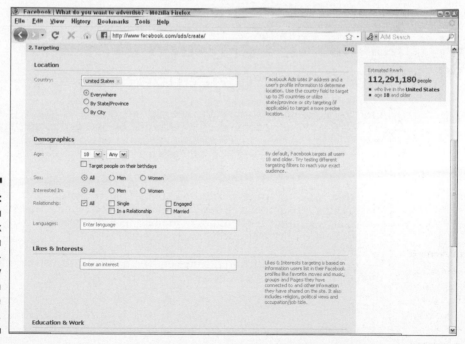

Figure 3-7:
With Facebook Ads, you automatically start with your home country.

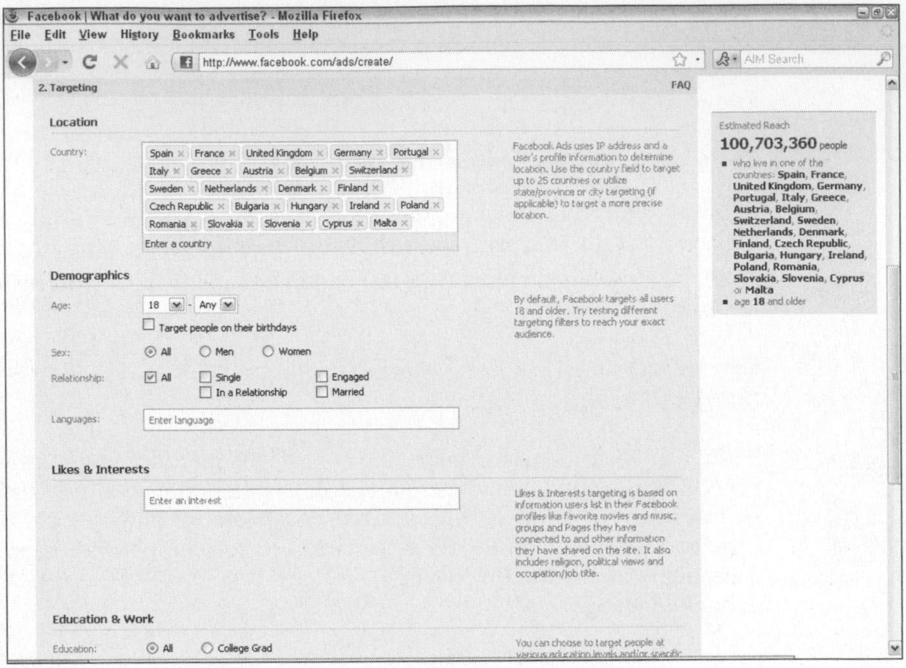

Figure 3-8:
Add coun-
tries as
targets for
your
campaign.

Align Your Ad Campaign with Your Marketing Objectives

After you decide who you want to see your ad, decide what you want your ad to say. Present your customers with a clear, concise, and focused message. As we mention earlier, your Facebook Ad is just one part of a larger marketing strategy, so make sure that your ads are consistent and in sync with the rest of your marketing strategy.

Of course, for your strategy to be effective, it has to match your intended goal for your ad campaign. There are many ways to reach your goals, but employing a strategy without a goal in mind is like preparing to dig a ditch without knowing where or why you're digging.

The goals we see mentioned most often by small business owners and people interested in advertising usually include these four:

- Building your brand
- Driving sales
- Forming a community
- Listening (and responding) to feedback

The following sections discuss how you can align your ad campaign strategy better with each of these objectives.

Building your brand

What do you think of when you think of your company's brand? More importantly, what do your *customers* think of when they see, hear, or think about your company? Building a company brand is not only one of the most important things that any company can focus on but it's also one of the hardest to truly measure. Yes, surveys can test for brand recognition and gauge public opinion, but it can be hard to quantify how a single ad campaign can affect a company's brand perception in the marketplace.

The key with building your brand is to ensure that your ad messages communicate the intended "brand message" of your company, rather than only promote or push a sales strategy on a given product. You can't just tell people what they should think of your company's brand, but communicate through actions, images, and the desire to build a relationship with a new customer and maintain that relationship over time.

As a real-world example, take a look at the video game company, Rockstar Games, running Facebook Ads to promote its Facebook business Page. (See Figure 3-9.) Its ads don't ask people to run out and buy its most recent game. Instead, Rockstar Games wants the viewer to become a fan and get automatic updates, access to game trailers, and the ability to download and use applications that reinforce its different brands. The image that Rockstar uses is directly from one of its video games, which reinforces that brand.

When building your brand, here are some things to keep in mind when designing your Facebook Ads:

- ✔ **Focus on your message.** Ultimately, what message do you want your company's brand to say to people? If you're trying to be the most dignified, trusted authority in something, don't use a silly, goofy, "hip" ad in hopes to cater to "the young people." Your ads are an extension of your brand, so whatever message you want your brand to represent is the *exact* message your ad should be saying. Take a look at the two ads in Figures 3-10. NuSpark Marketing conveys the serious message of a one-stop marketing shop that can handle a variety of important marketing jobs, while BikerOrNot.com conveys the fun, social hangout that their community offers.

- ✔ **Use the most up-to-date images, slogans, and messages.** If you're about to unveil a new logo, slogan, or imagery in your company's ads, make sure that the Facebook Ads use the same imagery at the same time you roll out everything else. When your Facebook Ads use last year's graphics, it makes you, your company, and your ad look old, dated, and tired.

✔ **Consider using CPM instead of CPC.** Because it's harder to measure the effect of an ad that pushes your brand, you might want to consider paying for each impression of the ad, through CPM, rather than paying a specific price when someone clicks the ad with CPC. This is a financial decision as well as a strategy decision, and we discuss bidding strategies in Chapter 4.

✔ **Use a soft call to action.** Your goal is for your ad viewer to become a fan, not a customer. For the marketer at heart, this goal might be the toughest one to implement. Rather than issuing an impassioned call to action with a ticking-clock deadline, your ad might simply ask for someone to Like your business Page, or RSVP for an upcoming event. Your initial goal might be to simply get your brand on the viewer's radar, which you can convert to a paying customer down the road. This soft approach — getting your foot in the door, as it were — allows you to introduce your company slowly, with numerous wall posts, announcements, photos, and information so that you become part of your viewer's Facebook activities, and hopefully make the transition to become part of their buying activity as well.

Figure 3-9:
Your ads can rein-force your brand without direct sales efforts.

Figures 3-10:
Your ad
message
should be
appropriate
to your
business.

Driving sales

If you're thinking to yourself, "Yes, brand is important, but what I really want to do is generate some sales and move some product," we are here to say that nothing is wrong with that! As long as you understand that your goal is to drive sales of a product, make sure your ad campaign is working as hard as you are with that singular focus. Just remember that you don't want to make over-exaggerated promises to your potential customers in your quest to break sales records or overrun your sales force with leads.

Facebook Ads lend themselves very well to the practice of driving sales through ad campaigns, and not just for products — you can promote sales of your service as well. Take a look at the ad in Figure 3-11, which promotes three laser hair-removal sessions for a fixed price of $250. This ad hits all the correct marks because it

- ✔ Portrays a clear offer
- ✔ Has a call to action with a deadline to motivate that action
- ✔ Is specific with the offer

Although the ad includes an image that might not be directly related to the service, it's hard to capture the actual service in this ad. In this case, a suitable alternative was used to reinforce the message of removing unwanted hair.

When you're planning a Facebook Ad campaign to drive sales, here are some tips to keep in mind:

- ✔ **Use the most important keywords in your ad.** This might seem like an obvious tip, but it's one worth mentioning. Because you're limited in the number of characters in your title (25) and ad message (135), every character counts. Your ad is not a mystery that you hope people click (unless, perhaps, you're promoting a new mystery game or contest), so focus your ad to speak directly to your target audience. To accomplish that, you need to use the right keywords to make someone stop, read your ad, and consider clicking it.

  When Threadless was running a t-shirt sale and used Facebook Ads to promote this (see Figure 3-12), the ad title used three important keywords:

Keyword Topic	Keyword Used
Company Name	Threadless
Product	T-Shirt
Sale	Sale

The ad message reinforces the t-shirt sale with the enticing price point *Starting at only $5* and the implied time limit of Sale Ends Soon to motivate action.

✔ **Have a specific call to action in the message.** Although you hope that any new customers from this ad campaign will continue to buy your products, you're hoping for more than awareness here: You want them to click the ad this time and take an action. Therefore, you need to communicate something to motivate them to click your ad and take that action. As we mention earlier, having a time limit or deadline *(Act Now)* can be a great motivator. Avoid using broad phrases like *Find Out More* and *Check Us Out.* Be specific as to what customer will get if they respond. For example, *T-Shirts Starting at $5* or *Download Wallpapers, Ring Tones, and Free Games* are more specific and use a better call to action.

✔ **Segment your ad to find the best performers.** The value of testing your ad really comes into play when you're driving sales because you can compute the actual value of each customer you receive by measuring the new sales generated. Therefore, as you test and measure the effectiveness of your ads, don't be afraid to create multiple ads — even at multiple price points — to maximize your return on investment (ROI).

As you try different campaigns and identify your best-performing ads, don't be afraid to devote more of your budget to that ad. You might even want to segment your ads based on the audience. Say you mainly have two groups of buyers — college kids and high school kids — and you know that college kids spend more. You might have two different ad campaigns, wherein you spend more to target college kids, but you still reach out to the high school kids at the appropriate level of ad spending. You can see from our mock examples below in Figures 3-13 that a travel agency could have two different ads for two different markets, like college and high school kids.

Figure 3-11:
Use ads to
drive sales
of a product
or service.

Figure 3-12: Make sure your ad has important keywords in its title.

Figures 3-13: Create multiple ads to reach different target groups.

Forming a community (alternate title — building your Fan base)

Nowadays, many customers don't just buy products from Company X: They are *users* of Company X, and even part of Company X and the company brand. People identify themselves from the brands they choose to include in their lives, and social media like Facebook allows companies big and small to be a part of their users' lives and interact on a continual basis. In other words, many companies have a community of users and customers who interact with the company and brand on a daily basis.

Your Facebook Ad campaigns can help your company form that community with your current and potential customers. Whether you're a consumer products company, a local service provider, or even a nonprofit organization, you and your company can benefit from a community, now and in the future.

Here are some tips to keep in mind:

> ✔ **Use your current Fans to get new Fans.** Facebook Ads has a targeting option where you can choose to run your ad to "Target users whose friends are connected to . . ." and pick your business Page. This way, when your ad gets displayed, it shows only to Friends of your Fans, so each ad will have an automated message (see Figure 3-14), like *Joe Serrano likes Social Ads Tool* underneath your ad. This acts like a Friend

referral, which is one of the most powerful and trusted sources when people act on an online offer.

✔ **Encourage customers to get involved.** Your message can be as simple as *Hey, Take a Picture and Send It In, Leave a Comment,* or *Mention Our Company in Your Next Status Update,* but the point is to have your customers become part of the community so that they feel some ownership and connection to this new community. This connection should motivate them to continue being involved in the future. Contests and promotions are a great way to spur that initial involvement, but be sure to engage your customers often and steer them only lightly toward actual product sales.

✔ **Use updates to keep your customers involved.** When the Team Terrapin Facebook Page went up, they not only used advertisements to get new members for their yachting group but they also posted a number of vibrant updates to keep new and current Fans engaged and interested in their progress, whether it was preparation for a regatta or text message status updates from the blue ocean when a signal was available.

✔ **Get your employees involved.** To have an authentic, vibrant Facebook community, your employees (or some of your employees) need to get involved and engage the members of the community, whether to maintain and generate discussions, share news of new accomplishments, or answer questions and concerns. It's best to engage your employees before you roll out these campaigns because their feedback might lead to creating a better community.

✔ **Consider developing or advertising with a third-party application.** If you've used Facebook, you'll likely agree that many Facebook users are addicted to the applications offered on the site. One of the quickest ways to gain community acceptance and get the word out about your company (beyond an ad campaign) is to partner with a developer or hire someone to write your own company-branded application, which you can promote with an ad campaign.

TripAdvisor, for example, created the Cities I've Visited application, which Facebook users can use to show off where they've traveled. (See Figure 3-15.) With more than 5 million users, TripAdvisor gets free exposure every time people download or use that application on their own Facebook Page.

✔ **Augment your Facebook business Page.** As we mention earlier, your viewers and potential customers might judge you based upon the level of Facebook activity that you and your company generate, so make sure that your Facebook Page is not only up to date but that it also has some functions or activities to keep community members busy, occupied, and happy. GameLoft, for example, has tabs within its Facebook Page not only for new games like Iron Man 2 or Splinter Cell (see Figure 3-16); GameLoft also maintains a YouTube page, Photos page, Discussions, Events, Links, and Videos.

✔ **Post updates to your business Page regardless of sales impact.** When your company announces a new initiative, sales effort, or other press-worthy mention, you should post an update to your page. You can also post other items to connect with your audience, though, to give more value to your community.

One example is Reynolds Wrap, which maintains a Facebook business Page that, among other things, offers recipes and comments. (See Figure 3-17.) There's no exact formula for how many posts can be purely business related versus how many should be community-building posts. The one rule is that you should never just put 100 percent of your posts as pure business updates.

Figure 3-14:
Show your users which of their friends already Like you.

Figure 3-15:
Get the word out with an application as well as ad campaigns!

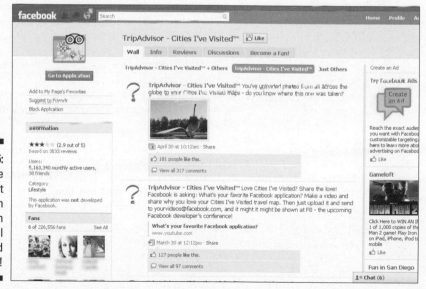

Figure 3-16:
Have lots
of options
for your
community
on your
Facebook
Page.

Figure 3-17:
Offer some
value to
your com-
munity
members.

Listening (and responding) to feedback

One of the benefits of having a presence on Facebook and engaging in two-way communication with your customers and Fans is that they have the ability to talk back, and you can respond directly to their comments. Some companies have a clear goal of using their social media accounts (like Facebook) mainly to listen and respond to feedback from their customers. This means being accessible and ready to answer questions and offer solutions, advice, or a friendly "virtual ear" in hopes of diffusing a difficult situation or reinforcing a positive brand.

When you want to go beyond the ad campaign and reach out directly to your users, here are some things to keep in mind:

✔ **Become part of the conversation.** Go beyond the ads to comment on people's pages when your brand or company is mentioned. When someone comments on your Facebook business Page, and a response is appropriate, be sure to provide that comment or resolution. Create a discussions page that is relevant to your business, like the ArcLight Cinemas (a small movie theater chain in California) hosting discussions about movies on its Facebook business Page, as shown in Figure 3-18.

✔ **Follow up quickly and regularly.** Nothing is worse than a string of comments from formerly interested users with zero feedback, comments, or new posts from the company. Like an abandoned blog or outdated Web site, an unresponsive Facebook business Page makes your company or brand look terrible in the eyes of the user community. We're not saying you need to respond within five minutes of a post, but make sure that someone has it in his schedule or responsibility list to read and maintain your Facebook Page.

✔ **Provide some employee training or rules on your responses.** When you assign someone the responsibility of maintaining a Facebook Page, make sure that she has some sort of training or experience with how to publicly respond to comments. For some people, it's intuitive, but others could quickly embarrass you and the company. The larger your company, the more it might be necessary to adopt certain rules or best practices as to how questions get answered, what kind of information gets publicly mentioned, and how problems or disputes get solved.

✔ **Put most frequently asked questions on your Facebook Page.** Don't be afraid to make your Facebook Page into a resource center for your users or customers. Put some valuable information, like the most frequently asked questions, on your Facebook business Page.

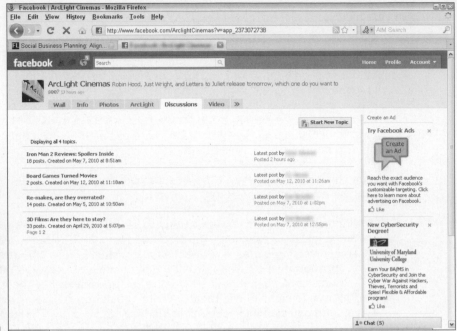

Figure 3-18:
Host discussions and get involved with what your customers are saying!

Chapter 4

Buying Strategies

In This Chapter

▶ Deciding which ad payment method to use

▶ Figuring out the amount to spend per advertisement

▶ Keeping track of your ad campaign spending

▶ When and how to make changes to your campaign

▶ Stopping an ad campaign temporarily or permanently

*W*ouldn't you love to win the lottery, then walk into your favorite department store with a personal bodyguard (who carries your money for you), pick out everything on the racks that appealed to you, then head to the clerk with your piles and piles of stuff, and say, "Ring me up"? Unfortunately, we don't have unlimited budgets for whatever we want, so keeping track of your spending is an important aspect of most business dealings, and online advertising is no different. Thankfully, you can track your ad spending down to the penny (and yes, we literally mean *to the penny*), so you can make every ad dollar spent really count.

Of course, keeping track of your spending is only part of the battle. Other decisions to keep in mind are how much you spend per unit, whether you're spending too little or too much per unit, and how to time when to change your limits. And there are a number of strategies to keep in mind. The most important aspect to an online ad campaign is this: Your decision making is *not* over when the campaign launches, but rather an ongoing matter that needs to be studied and adjusted when necessary.

In this chapter, we review some of the buying strategies you need to consider when creating, running, and maintaining your Facebook Ad campaigns. We start by studying the different payment models available to you as a Facebook advertiser. Then we go into the actual bidding process when you place your ad in Facebook's Ad inventory, and review what to look for after your ad campaign is underway, from reporting to adjusting and even the ever-possible pausing of a campaign.

Choosing a Payment Model

For many advertising mediums, there is only one payment model to consider: namely, the cost set by the printer or publisher. Magazines, newspapers, and other print media use *rate cards* that tell you exactly how much any given size advertisement will cost. (Figure 4-1 shows an example of a major newspaper's national rate card.) And sure, discounts and considerations are given to advertisers depending on contributions, length of campaigns, and so on. However, when you tell the advertising medium, "I want to run an ad like so," you get a simple answer of what it will cost.

In the world of online advertising, though, different payment models have evolved. As we discuss in Chapter 1, in the early days of the Internet advertisers had simple fixed models based on the number of times a banner ad was displayed. As technology evolved and advertisers saw the ability for true one-to-one marketing with detailed tracking and statistical models, new payment models came into play. Today, still newer, more sophisticated options are being considered by some online publishers, but the two models to consider when advertising on Facebook are

- Cost per impression (CPI or CPM)
- Cost per click (CPC)

Figure 4-1: Major media has rate cards stating their general ad prices.

2010 Advertising Rates & Information: National Rates

National Non-Contract Rates

Ad Size	General	WSJ 10% Comb
Full Page	$35,221	$31,699
Full Page Spread	70,442	63,398
Junior Page	29,938	26,644
Junior Page Spread	59,876	53,888
1/2 Page	18,534	16,681
1/2 Page Spread	37,068	33,361
1/4 Page	9,270	8,343
1/8 Page	4,637	4,173
1/16 Page	2,318	2,086

Contract Volume Rates

Pages	Discount
4	4%
7	8
10	10
13	12
17	14
22	16
26	18
39	20
52	22
78	24
104	26
130	28
156	30

Contract Frequency Rates

Issues	Discount
6 consecutive weeks	2.5%
13 per year	2.5
26 per year	5.0
52 per year	8.0

Category Rate: Automotive, Education, Financial Advisory Services/Publications, National Retail Products, New Issue and Financial Announcement, and Travel advertisers are eligible for a special 30% discount. National Retail includes price-point advertisements from retailers and manufacturers.

The Category Rate is only available nationally. Also, Category Rates do not qualify for an additional 10% ██████████████combination discount.

Color: The rate for color advertising is 35% added to the national advertising rate. Full-page spread-bleed, full-page spread, and full-page advertisements are accepted for color; junior-page, half-page vertical and half-page horizontal, and quarter-page horizontal advertisements are accepted for color as available per issue. Only available nationally.

Guaranteed Positions: Selected guaranteed pages or positions in ████████, when available, are 15% additional and are only available nationally. Top of advertising column and next to or under reading matter are 15% extra, when available

As far as which method is the best choice for you, that depends on your goals as an advertiser as well as your strategic needs for the ad campaign. The following sections compare and contrast these methods.

Cost per impression

When we talk about cost per impression (often abbreviated as either CPI or a specific model, CPM, for cost per thousand impressions), we refer to a concept often used in online advertising when it comes to Internet Web traffic. *Cost per impression* refers to measuring the worth and cost of a specific ad being displayed in an ad campaign. This pricing model is used with banner ads, text links, and even e-mail advertisements.

An *online ad impression* is a single appearance of an advertisement on a Web page or e-mail. Each time an ad loads onto the user's screen, the Web site's server can count that display as one impression. The ad displays can also be tracked by studying the server log entries or placing an identifying tracker within the Web page hosting the ad. Typically, if a user reloads the same page, or if an internal user action might cause some images to reload, those actions (and any other nonqualifying actions mutually agreed upon by the advertiser and the Web site running the ad) are not counted as impressions against the advertiser.

The important thing to understand about CPM is that you, the advertiser, will pay every single time your ad is sent to a user's screen and displayed, regardless of whether that user clicks the ad or takes action because of the ad.

Benefits to pursuing cost per impression advertising are the following:

- Your CPM is typically much lower than the CPC, so your ad budget should be more consistent.
- If your goal is to promote your company brand or announce something (rather than offer a call to action), you simply want visibility, which comes with CPM.

Cost per click

When we talk about *cost per click* (*CPC*), sometimes known as *pay per click* (*PPC*), we're referring to an advertising payment model wherein the advertiser pays for running an advertisement only when that ad is clicked by the viewer. Typically, on platforms such as search engines, advertisers associate their ad with a keyword phrase relevant to their target market, and the search engine allows each advertiser to place a bid for the cost per click, rather than pay a fixed price. When that keyword phrase is typed in by a viewer, the ads with the highest placed bids for a click would be posted at the top of the page, organized by descending bids for a click. These ads may be labeled as *sponsored links* or *sponsored ads* (see an example in Figure 4-2) to clue the viewer that the placement is dependent upon the advertisers paying to run an ad — not because the search engine automatically recommended that link as a search result.

On other platforms, such as content sites, a fixed CPC is charged to the advertiser instead of a bid system. When the content site displays relevant content to the ad message, the content site runs those ads on the same page. The placement of each ad on those pages is up to the content site. Some sites give featured placement to longer-term advertisers. Other sites offer top spots on a first-come, first-served basis. And some content sites limit the amount of ads per page, so placement is not an issue.

In either case, the actual CPC is the amount of money that an advertiser pays search engines and other Internet publishers for a single click on its advertisement that brings one visitor to the target link from that ad, usually the advertiser's Web site. The three most popular providers of CPC advertising are the top three search engines: Google AdWords, Yahoo! Search Marketing, and Microsoft Bing. All three operate under a bid-based model. The actual cost per click of any ad on their sites varies, depending on the search engine and the level of competition for a particular keyword.

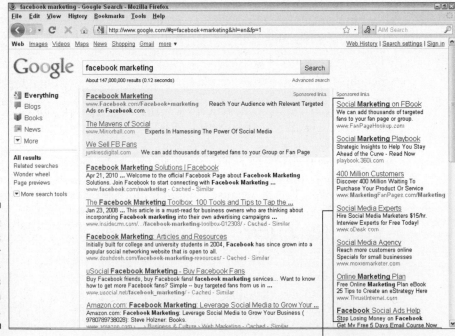

Figure 4-2:
CPC ads can appear as sponsored ads on search engines.

Sponsored ads

Dial M for 1,000

CPM is frequently used in advertising to represent *cost per thousand* because *M* is the Roman numeral for 1,000. When used in advertising, CPM relates to the cost per thousand page impressions. When someone says something like, "Our CPM is $5," this means that the cost of displaying your ad 1,000 times is $5, so your cost per ad impression is $0.005.

The CPC advertising model is open to abuse through click fraud. This type of Internet crime that occurs when a person, automated script, or computer program imitates a legitimate user of a Web browser, clicking an ad for the purpose of generating a CPC without having actual interest in the target of the ad's link. Such practice is the subject of some controversy and increasing litigation because of the advertising networks being a key beneficiary of the fraud. Google and other sites have implemented automated systems to guard against abusive clicks by competitors or corrupt Web developers. Facebook is naturally less susceptible, since you can only Like a page once, for instance.

Determining cost per click

The two primary models for determining CPC are flat-rate and bid-based. As of this writing, Facebook Ads are solely bid-based. In either case, you — the advertiser — must determine what you think is the potential value of a click coming from any given source. In other words, what is it worth to you if someone clicks your ad and comes to your Web site? Usually, you should base this value on the type of individual you're expecting to receive as a visitor to your Web site, as well as what you hope to gain from that visit (usually revenue), both short-term and long-term. Some factors that advertisers consider to determine a value are the following:

✔ **How targeted is the viewer who is seeing the ad?**

The more targeted the viewer, the more likely that viewer will act on your offer. This is because your ad is more relevant to that viewer — in advertising, this is usually accepted thinking. If you've implemented a number of targeting filters (see Chapter 3 for more information on targeting) then you should be willing to spend more on this lead over a lead from a search engine, for example.

✔ **Is the viewer intending on making a purchase?**

Was the user browsing when viewing the ad or looking for a place to buy? The search engine advertising equivalent of this question is like this: If someone is typing in one word, like *shoes*, they are probably in the beginning stages of looking. But if they type in *San Diego Coach Women's Shoes*, that person is probably more likely to be ready to make a purchase. On Facebook, people are on the site to talk to friends and socialize, so there is less of an intention to purchase in general.

✔ **What is the location of the user?**

Some ad systems, including Facebook, offer geo-targeting so you display an ad to only those folks who are or live close to your business. Being able to advertise to your local audience only is a big plus for Facebook advertising.

✔ **What is the day and time the viewer clicked the ad?**

Some dates/times can be more lucrative than others.

Flat-rate PPC

In the flat-rate model, the advertiser and publisher agree upon a fixed amount paid for each click. As we mention earlier, in many cases, the publisher has a rate card that lists the CPC within specific places on that Web site or network. These varying amounts are often related to the content on pages, with content that generally attracts more-valuable visitors having a higher cost than content that attracts less-valuable visitors. In this case, *valuable* refers to the value of the advertising that would be displayed on these pages. For example, publishers charge more for content pages that could attract a click worth $100 (such as, for example, content that might attract a new home buyer to fill out a mortgage application) than content that would attract a $0.50 click for someone to buy a new pair of jeans.

Often, advertisers can negotiate lower rates, especially when committing to a long-term or high-value contract. Be sure to discuss this possibility before signing any contract to see what can be negotiated. There is no steadfast or ballpark number on what is long-term or high value, as it depends on the Web site. For a big, global Web site like Facebook, high value is usually $10,000 per month or greater, as of this writing, for example.

The flat-rate model is particularly common to comparison shopping engines, which typically publish rate cards. Although the comparison engines' rates are sometimes minimal, advertisers can pay more for greater visibility. Comparison shopping sites are usually neatly compartmentalized into product or service categories, allowing a high degree of targeting by advertisers. In many cases, the entire core content of these sites is paid ads. For example, if we look at Google's Product database (see Figure 4-3), we can see that targeted ads for camcorders go right on the Camcorders page of the Web site.

Bid-based PPC

In the bid-based model, or *blind bidding*, the advertiser signs a contract that allows it to compete against other advertisers in a private auction hosted by a publisher or, more commonly, an advertising network. Each advertiser informs the host of the maximum amount that he is willing to pay for a given ad spot (often based on a keyword), typically using online tools to do so. The auction plays out in an automated fashion every time a visitor triggers the ad spot. The resulting price any advertiser ends up paying is not known, so the advertiser is, essentially, placing a blind bid with a specific maximum price.

For example, when the ad spot is part of a search engine results page (SERP), the automated auction takes place whenever a search for the keyword that is being bid upon occurs. All bids for the keyword that target the searcher's geo-location, the day and time of the search, and so on are then compared, and the winner is determined. In situations where there are multiple ad spots (a common occurrence on SERPs), there can be multiple winners whose positions on the page are influenced by the amount each has bid. The ad with the highest bid generally shows up first, although additional factors (such as ad quality and relevance, as determined by the search engine or publisher running the ad) can sometimes come into play.

Advertisers pay for each click they receive, with the actual amount paid based on the amount bid. It is common practice among auction hosts to charge a winning bidder just slightly more (for example, one penny) than the next highest bidder or the actual amount bid, whichever is lower. This avoids situations where bidders are constantly adjusting their bids by very small amounts to see whether they can still win the auction while paying just a little bit less per click.

Figure 4-3:
Comparison shopping engines offer targeted ad buys.

Basing Bids on Recommended Range

Facebook Ads don't rely on a keyword phrase, necessarily, but rather the targeting filters that you assign when you create an ad. (Read about filters in Chapter 3.) Therefore, every time a Facebook user brings up his home page or another page within Facebook, the ad system has to decide which ad(s) to display on those pages, based on which ads qualify to be shown to that user, and how much each advertiser bid to have their ad displayed.

Therefore, when running an ad on Facebook, you see a recommended bid range based on the targeting filters that you assign. When you first build your ad, Facebook wants to know whether you plan on running your ad continuously or on certain days, and will recommend one fixed price bid per ad. (See Figure 4-4.) Facebook determine this initial price based on the targeting filters you have set and the ads already in Facebook's ad inventory.

Click the Set a Different Bid link to see the option to pick Cost per Impression or Cost per Click, and be given a suggested bid range instead of a fixed price. (*Note:* The fixed price is the exact middle of the suggested bid range.) The bid range appears next to the Max Bid field, as shown in Figure 4-5. Based on the sample ad we were building, Facebook recommends that the bid range be set between 75 cents and 98 cents for one click.

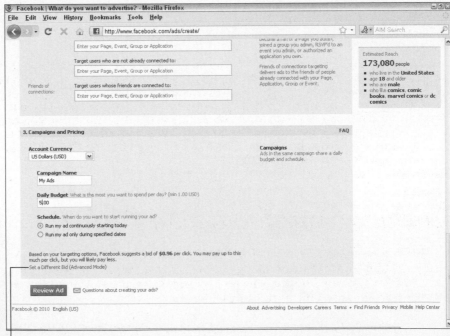

Figure 4-4: Facebook recommends a bid price for your ad.

Set a Different Bid link

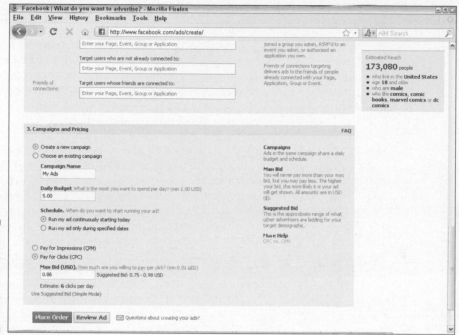

Figure 4-5:
Facebook
also recom-
mends a bid
range for
your ad.

If we change our pricing model to CPM, the suggested bid range in this example goes down to a range of 36 to 47 cents for 1,000 impressions. You do have
some flexibility in the price you pick for your ad.

One technique that several people use is to price their ad below the suggested
bid range, as much as 50 percent off the suggested bid range. Although this
strategy might not garner you as many clicks as Facebook projects you will
get, Facebook won't automatically deny your ad campaign because your bid
price is too low. You will see fewer impressions, but at least you are paying
less than expected — and your budget can go further. We have seen better
results if you choose the middle of the low end of the CPC bid range as your
check point when bidding.

Tracking Your Campaign Budget

After your ad is created and the impressions or clicks start coming in, don't
think that the heavy lifting is done and you just sit back and collect the glory
(and sales). The ongoing tracking and observance of your budget is essential
for a successful ad campaign.

You do have several options within Facebook for keeping track of your ad
campaign, though:

✔ **Ads Manager** provides you with all the basic information you need to manage your campaigns.

✔ **Ads Reports** allows you to download detailed statistics and get more data to work with regarding your ad performance. You can also find out about your audience through Ads Reports, which show you detailed demographic information and provide insights into the likes and interests of users who click on your ads.

In the following sections, we show you how to use Ads Manager and run Ads Reports and explain the differences between the report types so you can choose to pull the reports that are most relevant to your needs. We also review a few basic tips to help you apply the reporting data to optimize and grow your campaigns. We discuss Ads Manager and Ads Reports in more depth in Part IV of this book.

Running a budget report in Ads Reports

To run your first report, visit Ads Manager. You have two options for accessing the Ads Manager:

✔ Click Ads and Pages from your Facebook home page left navigation bar.

✔ Go directly to the Ads Manager page at `www.facebook.com/ads/manage`.

At the Ads Manager screen (see Figure 4-6), you can access Ads Reports by clicking the Reports link from the left-hand navigation bar. When the screen first loads, you see options for customizing your report: Report Type, Summarize By, Filter By, Time Summary, Date Range, and Format.

When you want to pull a report, just follow these steps:

1. **Pick the report type you want to run.**

   Five types of reports are available; see Figure 4-7:

   • Advertising Performance

   • Responder Demographics

   • Responder Profiles

   • Conversions by Conversion Time

   • Conversions by Impression Time

2. **Choose your Summarize By criteria.**

   This option determines how the statistics in your report will be broken down. Here, you can choose from

- *Account:* Shows the statistics for the entire account level

- *Campaign:* Breaks down the stats to the campaign level

- *Ad:* Breaks down stats to the individual ad level

3. Choose your Filter By criteria.

This option determines which of your ad campaigns will be included in your report. You can pick a specific ad, campaign, or all the campaigns within your account as the Filter for everything else in this report.

4. Define your Time Summary.

Choose what unit of time the report will organize the stats by. In this section, you see several different options, depending on how long your ads have been running and what type of report you chose in the first section. These options might include monthly, weekly, or daily. If, for example, you choose to run a monthly report, all the statistics are computed for the entire month. Comparatively, a daily report shows you statistics for each day of the campaign.

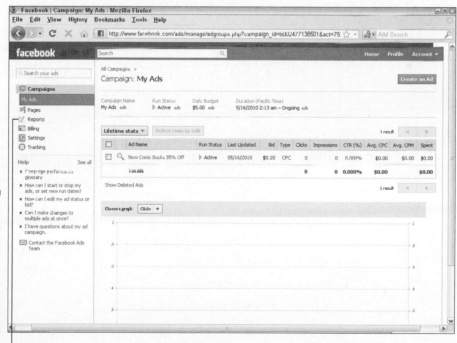

Figure 4-6:
Facebook
Ads
Manager
helps you
manage
your
campaigns.

Reports link

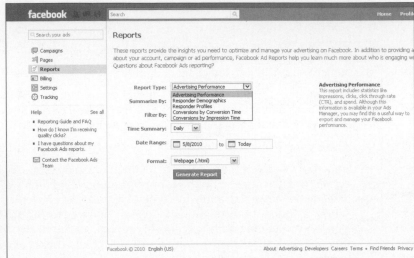

Figure 4-7:
Choose a
Facebook
Ads Report.

5. **Pick your Date Range.**

   In the Date Range fields, specify the time period for which you would like to see data. Select the start and end dates from the calendar that pops open when you click in each respective date field. The default date range that Facebook provides is the previous seven days, but you can pick any date range within the life of your campaign.

6. **Lock in your Format for seeing the report.**

   You can

   • View your report as a Web page written in HTML.

   • Export the report as a comma-separated values file (.csv). You can then import this file into all sorts of data-mining software, from Microsoft Excel to reporting programs like Crystal Reports. (Facebook labels this format as Excel .csv.)

   The information contained within the report will remain the same regardless of format.

7. **Click the Generate Report button.**

   Facebook uses the information you provided to calculate the necessary data and then either displays your report onscreen (like in Figure 4-8) or allows you to download the .csv file to your computer for further review (like in Figure 4-9).

Depending on what your goals are or what type of information you need, you might find it useful to run more than one of these reports. There's no limit to the number of reports you can run, so try running one of each to learn more about what statistics are available to you.

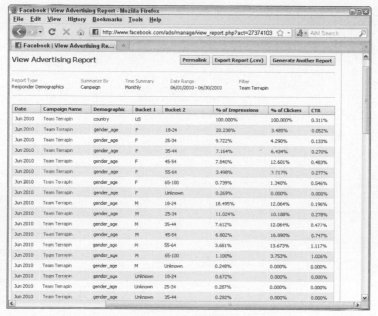

Figure 4-8:
View your
reports
onscreen
in HTML
format.

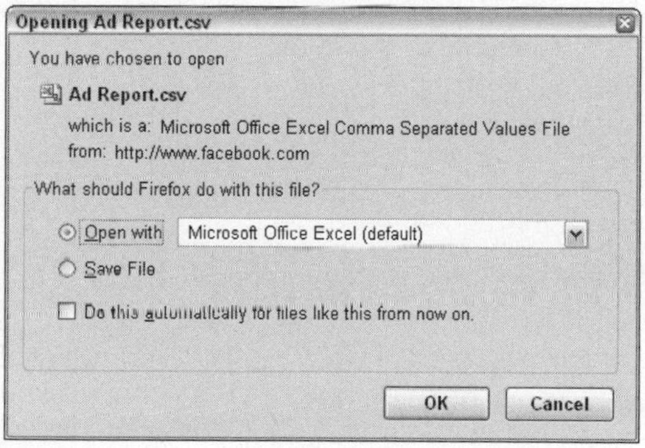

Figure 4-9:
Download
reports into
a program
like Excel
for further
analysis.

The Advertising Performance report (as shown in Figure 4-10) is the most basic report type, best used for campaigns with pure performance objectives. This type of report includes statistics such as Impressions, Clicks, Click Through Rate, Actions, and Conversions, not to mention Unique Impressions, Unique Clicks, and Unique Click Rate — and all in real-time. Keep in mind if that you're running ads for Pages or Events, the Clicks statistic is encompassing any clicks plus any Actions taken on the ad (such as Like and RSVP).

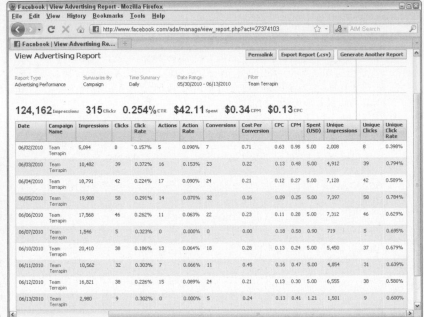

Figure 4-10:
The
Facebook
Advertising
Performance
report
shows
lots of
statistics.

Although this information is available to you elsewhere (such as your Ads Manager screens or graphs), you might find the Advertising Performance report a useful way to view all your statistics in one place over a longer period of time.

Understanding report results

Okay, you're looking at all this data, but what does it really mean? Unfortunately, these reports do not contain big red arrows and flashing lights with a bottom-line revenue estimate of how much money you made because of an ad campaign. However, the data within these reports can be very useful in identifying ads that work versus ads that are falling short of expectations. The key is to know what to look for in the numbers.

Start by defining some of the different fields of data in the Advertising Performance report:

✔ **Unique Impressions:** The number of different individuals who viewed the ad, campaign, or account for each given day, week, or month in your Advertising Performance report. This statistic differs from your regular impressions because each user is counted only a single time. In other words, even if a user sees your ad multiple times, she is counted only once for Unique Impressions.

✔ **Unique Clicks:** The number of unique users who click your ads. Like Unique Impressions, if a single user clicked your ad multiple times for some reason, she is counted only a single time here.

✔ **Unique CTR:** Calculated as the number of unique clicks divided by the number of unique impressions. So, for example, if your ad had 100 unique impressions and you had four unique clicks, your unique CTR would be 0.04, or 4%.

✔ **Actions:** Counted when users Like or become a Fan of your advertised Page, or RSVP "yes" or "maybe" to an Event through your ad. These positive engagement actions are also counted as clicks on your ad.

As you look through these reports, you want to know the answers to these questions:

✔ **Am I making money?** Let's get to the heart of the matter, shall we? In certain cases, such as generating more direct sales, you should be able to figure out whether your ad campaign was profitable to your business. Here's an example, and what you can find out along the way:

• Say that you paid for 100 clicks to your Web site, at $1 per click. *You spent $100 on this campaign.*

• You go to your Web site, and find out that out of those 100 new visitors, 3 people placed orders for products on your Web site. *Your conversion rate is 3%.*

• Next, you want to figure out the profit from those orders. You can either add up those orders to figure out gross profit, or if you have an average gross profit per order based on past sales, use that figure. Say that you make $40 per order on average. *Your total profit was 3 × $40, or $120.*

• So, you spent $100 in advertising to generate $120 in profit. Based on these numbers, *the campaign was a success.* You also know that *you can afford to pay $1.20 per click if necessary to break even.*

✔ **Who's clicking my ads?** You probably used targeting filters to limit your ad to a specific demographic (see Chapter 3), but even so, perhaps the people who are interested in your ad belong to an unexpected or narrowly defined demographic. You can run the Responder Demographics report to get a breakdown of the demographics of the viewers who clicked your ad. For example, say you were targeting 18–30-year-olds, and the Responder Demographics report (see Figure 4-11) shows almost all your clicks are coming from 13–17-year-old males. You might also see a common demographic trait that you didn't expect. For example, maybe you ran ads for both genders, and a high percentage of responders are female.

✔ **Are there common interests among people clicking my ad?** The Responder Profiles report shows you the likes and interests of viewers who clicked your ad. Just like with the Responder Demographics report, you might come to understand something new about the people who are most interested in your Facebook Ad. This can come in handy as you adjust your campaign to match this new insight. (See the next section.)

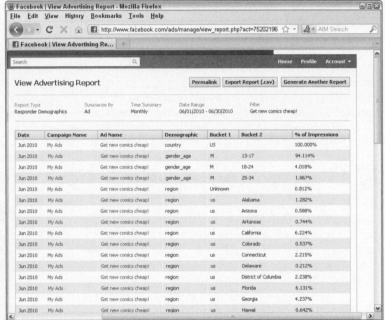

Figure 4-11: See what demographics are responding to your ad.

Adjusting as You Go Along

With data in hand from your Facebook Ads Reports, the next step is to apply your insights to your ad campaigns. There are several different ways to approach this, but to get started, here are some basic optimization tips to help you make the most of these new insights:

1. **Redefining your audience:** After running either the Responder Demographics or the Responder Profiles report, you could uncover certain groups of users who are clicking your ads more often than others. You can redefine your targeting filters by using the data from your reports for better optimization so that you can reach more of the most desirable audience for your ads.

2. **Reallocating your budget:** All the reports can help you understand which ads are performing well and which can be paused. Look for different ads or different groups of users that have been performing particularly well

for you and then optimize those to get the highest click through rates and conversion rates possible. Pause ads and campaigns that aren't performing well. (See the next section for information on how to pause a campaign.)

Because your budget is defined at the campaign level, any ads you pause in a campaign will reallocate your budget to the ads that are still running.

3. **Testing ad messages:** The data provided by your reports can also be used to test out different ad messages and their performance against one another with different types of users. For example, if you run a business that appeals to both males and females, you might run a couple of ads that each target both genders. Using information from the Responder Demographics report, you can identify any differences in how males and females respond to your ads. Certain phrases, images, or promotions might be more appealing to one group, and you can use this information to continue making changes to your ads. After you test these ads, you can try creating separate ads for men and women.

Pausing or Stopping a Campaign

While you're running one or more Facebook Ad campaigns, you might come across a situation where you need to pause, or temporarily suspend running a particular ad. You can pause a Facebook Ad campaign without deleting it, which allows you to preserve your ad and settings for possible future usage. So, when would you need to pause an ad campaign? There are several possible scenarios:

- ✔ **Time to study the results:** You want some time to study the data from the ad campaign or need others in your organization to study the existing data from the campaign without spending more money while your company is assessing the performance.

- ✔ **Technical issues:** Perhaps the Web server or computers that run part of your business are malfunctioning or need to be fixed, and you don't want to pay to send new potential customers to an unresponsive or broken Web site.

- ✔ **Inventory issues:** In a best-case scenario, your ad campaign was so successful that you're temporarily out of stock of your advertised product, and you don't have the ability to take rain checks or have a reliable date on when more product will be available. In a worst-case scenario, you could have problems with your supplier and be out of stock, missing a shipment, or unable to guarantee to your new customers that you can fill those orders.

- ✔ **Budget reasons:** Your advertising budget might have been spent much quicker than you expected, even with daily budget limits, and you need to discuss budget allocation within your company. By pausing a campaign, you can stop additional expenditures until new money is available.

There may also come a time when you are ready to permanently suspend, or delete, a campaign from your account. Perhaps it was an unsuccessful campaign that you do not want to risk an employee accidentally starting up again. Perhaps a product line (from a specific ad campaign) has been recalled and you are removing the entire line from your own inventory. You can easily go into Facebook Ads Manager and delete any campaign you want stopped for good.

Thankfully, if you need to pause or delete a campaign, Facebook makes it very simple. Just follow these steps:

1. **Bring up your Facebook Ads Manager screen.**

2. **Click the Campaigns link from the left-hand navigation bar to bring up the Campaigns page.**

   Next to the campaign name you need, you will see a green arrow next to the word *Active*, between the Ad Name and the Last Updated fields, and below the Export Report button.

3. **Click the green arrow to bring up a drop-down selection box. See Figure 4-12.**

4. **Change the drop-down selection from Active to either Paused or Deleted.**

5. **Click the Save button to either pause or delete the ad campaign.**

If you simply paused the ad campaign, it will remain in the list of campaigns, and all your performance data for that campaign is still available in Ads Reports. Whenever you want to resume a paused campaign, simply repeat the preceding steps, but in Step 4, toggle Paused back to Active.

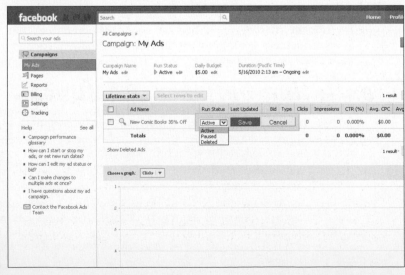

Figure 4-12:
You can
pause an
ad cam-
paign when
needed.

Chapter 5

Understanding the Types
of Ad Campaigns

In This Chapter

▶ Explaining the different kinds of Facebook advertisements

▶ Discussing the importance of images in a Facebook Ad

▶ Coordinating Facebook and external ad campaigns

▶ Scheduling multiple campaigns to run concurrently

*W*hile you're putting together your Facebook Ad strategy and running your first campaigns, start by discovering what options are available and what tools you have at your disposal when creating your overall Facebook advertising strategy and specific ad campaigns. Facebook has changed some of the names and labels for its ads, but the concepts have remained the same.

In this chapter, we illustrate some of the various ad types that Facebook offers to its advertisers. We walk through you some of the important elements, such as using images in a Facebook Ad, and then discuss the nature of multiple campaigns and using the Scheduling option to run your Facebook Ad during a specific period of time on the site.

Differentiating between Ad Types

In the past, Facebook used certain distinctions or labels for the different types of ads that it offered:

✔ **Engagement ads** offered viewer interaction, asking the viewer to click something, answer a question, or watch a video.

✔ **Social ads** took advantage of the Facebook platform and included information from a person's Friend list that influenced the ad or even determined whether the ad was going to be visible to someone.

Today, the two major categories of ads are those that promote

  ✔ An external Web site (similar to other ad systems like Google AdWords)

  ✔ A Page, Event, or other element within Facebook

Both categories of ads are available in the cost per click (CPC) and cost per impression (CPI, or CPM) bidding models. (You can read about these bidding methods in Chapter 4.) Facebook doesn't favor one category over another. However, we have seen through our professional experience that users do seem to favor ads that don't take them away from Facebook because the interaction is easier to complete and not as invasive or disruptive to the Facebook user experience.

Specifically, you can choose from several types of Facebook Ads:

  ✔ **External Web site ads:** These ads work like most online systems. The advertiser writes a title and ad message and displays an appropriate image. When the user clicks the ad, that user is taken to a page on an external Web site where the offer on the landing Web page should match the offer or description given in the ad. For example, a British Columbia tourist Web site promoting Vancouver is running ads for people who may want to visit Vancouver (see Figure 5-1), and the external Web site matches the ad completely.

  ✔ **Facebook Page ads:** Also known as *Fan ads,* these ads promote an existing Facebook business Page. The goal of the advertisement is to have the user Like or become a Fan of the promoted Facebook Page. If you're trying to build a following on Facebook, whether to raise your overall business awareness or to build an army of customers more predisposed to shop from you, running ads to promote your Facebook presence is the way to go. For example, an online time travel adventure series uses a Facebook Page ad (see Figure 5-2) to promote their Page. (See Figure 5-3.)

  ✔ **Event ads:** These ads allow you to raise awareness about an upcoming event, whether it's a fixed-time event or an announcement of something new. You can promote anything from an upcoming sale on your Web site to a free one-day giveaway (for example, Ben & Jerry's is running Event Ads to promote a Free Scoop Day at its ice cream shops) to the beginning of a charity promotion through a Web site (for example, Starbucks using Event Ads to promote days where a portion of its sales purchases went to charity). One additional feature of Event Ads is the ability for a user to see which Friends are also attending the event. (And as an advertiser, your users see this ad only until they click it, after which it won't be displayed to that user again.)

  Nike recently did a football campaign, in which we reviewed a teaser campaign for people to show off their best talents to Nike. (See Figure 5-4.) When we viewed the advertisement (as pictured), more than 10,200 users had RSVPed to attend.

Figure 5-1:
Promote
your own
Web site
with a
Facebook
Ad.

Figure 5-2:
The
Timeslingers
Facebook
Page ad.

Figure 5-3:
The
Timeslingers
Facebook
Page.

✔ **Group ads:** Similar to Facebook Page ads, you can create an ad to promote an existing Facebook Group where you are the Administrator. The goal of this kind of ad is to promote the Group and encourage new people to join the group and be an active part of the proceedings.

✔ **Application ads:** Similar to Facebook Page ads, you can create an ad to promote an existing Facebook application that you want to people to try and install on their profile. The goal of this kind of ad is to promote the installation and usage of a given Facebook app, like the ad for the TripAdvisor Cities I've Visited application shown in Figure 5-5.

As of this writing, only the creator of the application can generate a Facebook Ad campaign to promote the application.

✔ **Poll ads:** These ads allow your users to vote or express their opinion on a given topic that you choose. When clicked, Poll ads also redirect the voter to a page of your choosing. Not only can you gain valuable research information but you also encourage the user to participate actively in your brand and gain a sense of participation or ownership. Because you are asking a question (such as your extended golf export with a Burner club, as in Figure 5-6) and not pushing a particular immediate sale, your likelihood for interaction with Facebook users goes way up. This allows you to provide "entertainment" while gaining information as well.

✔ **Video ads:** These ads allow you to show the user a specific video when that user clicks the ad. A new window pops up to play the video associated with the advertisement, which basically allows you to air the "commercial" to your target audience. As of this writing, there is no restriction as to the length of the video selected. As shown in Figure 5-7, when the video is done playing, the window offers you the choice of Liking the brand (joining the Facebook Fan Page), sharing the video with someone else, or playing the video again. You will see video ads used by the movie studios to promote upcoming films, as well as consumer product companies like Gillette or Toyota promoting their newest offerings.

As of this writing, Poll and Video ads are available only to advertising clients with a minimum of $25,000 per month for Facebook Advertising who contact the Facebook sales team directly.

✔ **Branded Gift ads:** These ads (see an example in Figure 5-8) allow the viewers to interact with their friends and brands because it allows the viewer to decide on a charity and participate. These branded gifts display on your home page, and Facebook users can see which Friends have already sent gifts and what those friends said on people's Walls when they gave this gift. After the campaign is over, Facebook tells you how many gifts were sent, along with the demographic information of the people who shared and received the gift.

Figure 5-4:
You can turn a promotion into a Facebook Event to promote.

Figure 5-5:
Promote your Facebook application with an ad or two.

Figure 5-6:
Gain some insight from your audience with a poll ad.

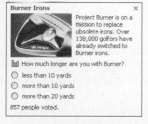

Figure 5-7:
You can add video to your Facebook Ads.

Figure 5-8:
You can
build a
Facebook
Ad about
giving gifts.

Using Ads with Social Attributes

One of the appeals of advertising on a social media network like Facebook is the ability for advertisers to use an implicit recommendation when those advertisers reach out to new consumers: the recommendation of a Friend from someone's network who is already a Fan or user of the advertiser's product. After all, numerous studies have shown that recommendations from friends or family are considered one of the top motivating factors to influence someone on buying a product. (See the sidebar, "The power of referrals.") With Facebook, an advertiser can include a social element to its ads to help catch a user's attention and leverage an existing Fan base.

You can see an ad with a social element in Figure 5-9. These ads retain the same format as any other Facebook Ad, but they include an extra line or two and reference at least one or two existing Fans of a given Facebook Page or people who RSVPed for that Event. The names are clickable and take the user to that person's Facebook profile when clicked. (By the way, that click would not count as an ad click.)

Figure 5-9:
Show new
users that
their Friends
like your
product or
Page.

When you want to include a social attribute to your ad, you simply want to target Friends of Your Connections as part of Step 2 (Targeting) in the ad-creation process. In the Targeting section of building your ad (as shown in Figure 5-10), do the following:

1. **Scroll to the bottom of that section.**

2. **Place your cursor in the Friends of Connections field.**

3. Start typing or pick from the prompted list of options.

Facebook prompts you with any Page, Event, Group, Application, or MarketPlace item for which you are Administrator and want to promote. Select the Facebook Page or Event that you're trying to promote and continue with the ad-creation process.

Figure 5-10:
Show your Facebook Ad to Friends of your Fans.

So, for example, say that you're viewing the ad for Vanguard Productions (as shown in the first image in Figure 5-11), a publisher of creative works like novels and music, and you see that two of your friends are already Fans of their Page. You click Like to join that Page, and the ad automatically updates itself by adding you as someone who likes Vanguard Productions (see the second image in Figure 5-11). When your friends look at your News Feed, they will see under Recent Activity that you liked Vanguard Productions, which could lead to more people being introduced to that page, which is an indirect benefit of a Facebook Ad with social attributes.

Figure 5-11:
Facebook Ads can show you what your Friends like, influencing what you might like.

The power of referrals

Advertisers have pondered just how powerful social media advertising can be, with the effects of user referrals on ad response rates and the like. The Nielsen Company (best known for its TV ratings) created a product called BrandLift to survey hundreds of thousands of Facebook users about their impressions and responses to 125 Facebook Ad campaigns that were conducted by 70 well-known brand advertisers. To test this product, Nielsen worked directly with Facebook to issue a special report, "Advertising Effectiveness: Understanding the Value of a Social Media Impression."

This report focused on 14 Facebook Ad campaigns that engaged users to become a Fan of a company's Facebook Page. Three types of ads were examined (as shown here) to gather statistics from those campaigns: namely, increase in recall, awareness, or purchase intent from:

1. A standard *Homepage Ad* (or *Engagement Ad):* A Facebook Ad that promotes a Page.

2. A *Homepage Ad with Social Context:* A Facebook Ad promoting a Page that targets Friends of Connections.

3. *Organic Ads:* Newsfeed stories are sent to Friends of users who became a Fan of that business' Facebook Page.

When average Facebook users saw the company's Homepage Ad, their ability to recall the brand, their awareness of the brand, and their purchase intent all went up. However, when Nielsen compared that group with the group that saw both the Homepage Ad and the Homepage Ad with Social Context, Nielsen saw a two-to-fourfold increase in several areas. The purchase intent went up further when the user saw all three types of ads.

Therefore, the study proved that what advertisers have always felt: Consumers trust their friends and peers more than anyone else when it comes to making a purchase decision. When a potential customer sees Friends already approve of a given brand, that customer becomes more likely to purchase or follow that brand themselves.

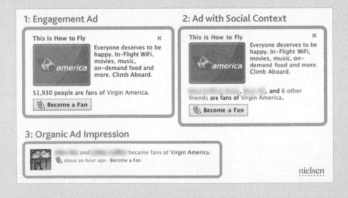

Understanding the Importance of Images

As we mention in Chapter 2, one of the unique features of Facebook advertising (as opposed to other ad systems, like Google AdWords) is the ability to include an image with your ad. You can see a variety of ad images used in Figure 5-12. Using images has proven to be a big factor in improving the success rate of many different Facebook advertisements, and using images should be a planned and thought-out element of your ad campaign. Taylor Pratt wrote an article for *Search Engine Journal* in March 2010 in which he showed that he could influence the click-through rate of a certain ad just by applying different images.

Take a look at this block of ads running on Facebook. Here are several options you can consider when picking an image for your own Facebook Ad:

Figure 5-12:
Facebook Ads use a variety of different images.

✔ **People matter.** In many ads, a picture of a person smiling or interacting with someone is an acceptable image. This picture helps bring out the right emotion to encourage interaction from a Facebook visitor. Of course, depending on the niche your ad is targeting, the type of person is important. For example, if you're trying to target Military Dads (as shown in Figure 5-13), your ad will make much more sense if the person in your ad image is a man in a military uniform. If you're advertising health insurance or a doctor's office directory (see Figure 5-14), an image of someone in a white lab coat will make a more authentic impact than just a smiling face.

✔ **You can include text in the image.** Although there are differing opinions about whether you should include text as part of your image, there are valid examples where text is part of your image and has an impact. In Figure 5-15, look for the words `free eBook` in the ad titled "IT Pros Ready for Change?" and `free evaluation` in the "Shop for Solar Panels" ad. Understand, however, that your image can be only 110 pixels wide by 80 pixels tall, so including an image with a lot of text (like the image for the ad "Sell Your Music Online") won't have a big impact because most of the text is unreadable to the viewer. Try to limit any added text to a few key words or phrases, or to highlight a specific price or date, for example.

✔ **Consider using an action shot in your ad.** If one of the goals of your ad is to evoke a sense of desire or interest in your product, your image can use an *action shot* or a shot of someone actively engaged in using your product or service, whether you're trying to promote a game, a social dating site, or a product to promote your health. You can see some examples of this in Figure 5-16.

✔ **Have several images ready.** If you can create or find multiple images to choose from, you can use more than one image in your ad campaign. You can test your ads (which we highly recommend to do; see Chapter 6 for more information on testing your ads) to see whether one image creates a better response than others or you can run multiple ads with different pictures (see Figure 5-17) to emphasize different elements.

Figure 5-13:
Your ad
image
should
correspond
with your ad
target.

Figure 5-14:
The people
in your
ad image
should
have the
expected
appearance
based on
the ad
message.

Figure 5-15:
Ads with
text in the
images.

Figure 5-16:
Use images
that show
people or
characters
in action.

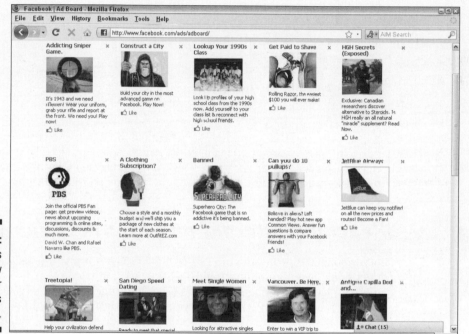

Figures 5-17:
You can
use multiple
images to
promote
one ad
campaign.

Multiple Concurrent Campaigns

Sometimes, Facebook Ads may be like (dare we say it?) those famous potato chips: One is not enough. Maybe you'll find that you need to run multiple Facebook Ad campaigns at one time, for a variety of reasons why. Perhaps you're not only building up your Facebook Page in terms of audience, but you have an upcoming event to promote. You could be selling two distinctly different products or categories with unique but separate campaigns. You could even use different types of Facebook Ads to bring attention to a big upcoming promotion that you're running, like the Nike Football as shown in Figure 5-18.

Figure 5-18:
Nike uses
more than
one type of
Facebook
Ad to
reach its
audience.

Reaching internal and external Web sites

If your goal is to promote your entire business — not just one aspect — you might consider running multiple Facebook Ad campaigns that promote not only your external Web site but also your "internal" Facebook Page. Because each Facebook Ad can point to only one target destination, you would need to create multiple campaigns to reach multiple destinations. (We discuss cross-campaigning in Chapter 6 as well.)

One way you can encourage consistency is to ensure that any promotional codes you create as part of your ad campaign work on both your Facebook Page and your external Web site.

Here's an example of what we mean. Wildchild is a street wear brand promoted on Facebook by its parent company, Wildchild Nation. WildChild has been a consistent advertiser on Facebook and maintains a robust presence on the site. One of its landing pages, Shop Now!, features Wildchild products for sale (see Figure 5-19) and has used a promo code that works on this page or on the Wildchild Web site. Given that the promo code (FACEBOOK5) is easy to identify, the Wildchild staff could tell that any use of that code was a result of their Facebook advertising, which helps them better judge the overall impact of their Facebook advertising.

Figure 5-19: Businesses can run Facebook promotions that are valid throughout their business.

Scheduling your Ad

You can create your ad campaigns at any time, picking the exact date and time you want your ad campaign to go "live" on Facebook. Here are some of the more popular reasons why you might want to consider scheduling your ads:

- ✔ You need to sync your Facebook Ad campaigns with other offline or online ad campaigns.

- ✔ You are waiting for the products to become available in your system before advertising them.

- ✔ You want to define the ad campaign in the system so someone else can review it (or make additions or changes) before it goes live.

- ✔ You are still running small tests to find the optimal ad combination, and you want to schedule your main campaign to run after you've had enough time to test all the elements of your ads.

- ✔ You want the ad campaign to run at a specific time of day when your audience is awake and using Facebook.

Scheduling your ad is pretty simple. When you are on the final step of creating your ad, under the header Schedule, look for these two options:

✔ Run My Ad Continuously Starting Today

✔ Run My Ad Only During Specified Dates

You want to pick the latter option (specified dates), which will bring up the start date and end date fields. as shown in Figure 5-20. Use the drop-down arrows to select your starting month, day, and year; and then select an appropriate end month, day, and year.

If you're unsure how long you want your ad campaign to run for, select a start date far in the future. You can always come back later to edit your ad after you have a better idea of how long the campaign will run. You can also pause or delete your campaign, as we referred to in Chapter 3.

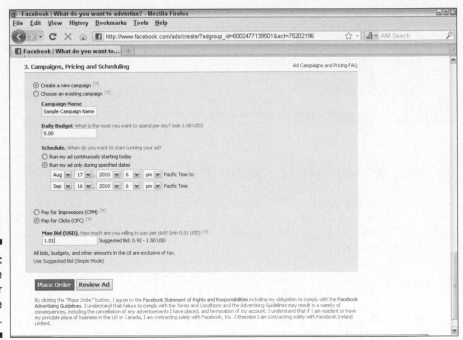

Figure 5-20:
Schedule
your ad for
a given time
period.

Chapter 6

Getting Set to Implement and Measure Results

In This Chapter

▶ Testing your Facebook Ads before a big launch

▶ Using Facebook Ad Sales representatives to plan your campaign

▶ Deciding on performance goals and targets for your ads

▶ Finding other ways to promote yourself on Facebook

▶ Expanding the reach of your Facebook Ads with other marketing initiatives

*J*ust like any other aspect of something you create for your business, you need a period of evaluation and analysis to make sure that this new effort is something that brings a positive effect to your business while justifying the cost or expense. Facebook Ads are no different: The best and most successful campaigns come from a careful monitoring and adjustment as the campaign goes on. Furthermore, the best Facebook Ad campaigns are those that co-exist within a business' larger marketing campaign — and, on occasion, help augment or feed off non–Facebook marketing efforts for your business.

In this chapter, we look at some of the final planning steps you should take before running your main ad campaigns, and then look at those planning efforts to do now to help you while you manage and update your ad campaigns. We also discuss alternatives to using the Facebook "self-service" ad system: namely, the Facebook Ads Sales team and other creative advertising options within Facebook.

Allocating Resources to Create and Monitor the Campaign

When it's time to start running your campaigns, you might need some collaboration or assistance from different parts of your business, unless you run a one-person enterprise where you have to wear many hats. (And where do you store all those hats, by the way? But we digress.) The various departments within your business need to know about these ad campaigns, and the appropriate people need enough time and resources to contribute their part effectively.

So, what types of resources do you need to consider? Here are a few:

- ✔ **Monetary/financial resources:** Facebook bills you on a daily or weekly basis when your ad campaign is running, so you need to make sure that those funds are available. As of this writing, Facebook Ads require that you have either a PayPal account or a valid credit card (like Visa or MasterCard). Depending on the size of your business, you might not have a company credit card at your disposal. If that's the case, go get one or work out a reimbursement system where your personal credit card is used and then reimbursed.

- ✔ **Technical expertise:** Unless you're a whiz at graphic design or you've already found the stock picture that's perfect for your ads, you'll probably need some assistance designing the images necessary for a successful ad campaign. As we discuss in earlier chapters, you might need different images for different purposes, and we highly recommend having those images ready before your main campaigns start running. Additionally, if you're offering, say, a free trial version of your software (like Clickable does in its Facebook Ad, as shown in Figure 6-1), have that trial version (or whatever item) created and available for download. And don't forget to set up the support structure (like a Web page or phone number that will facilitate the download) and any tracking codes in place before you distribute your offer.

- ✔ **Marketing expertise:** Some people think that because an ad message is only 135 characters long, it cannot be that difficult to write. Ask anyone who makes their living in marketing or sales, and they will tell you confidently that the reverse is true. You have to make every character count! Therefore, you're going to need an expert (or the closest person you have to a marketing expert) to help you write the appropriate messages and be available to refine those messages as you test your ads. If this is a scarce resource, do some work yourself, like researching existing Facebook Ads; looking at other marketing, ad, or sales campaigns that your business has run before; or seeing how other companies market the same products on the Internet using other ad systems like Google AdWords.

Check out the Facebook Ads Board (www.facebook.com/ads/AdBoard) to see an example of dozens of live Facebook Ads to see how other people write their advertisements.

✔ **Ongoing maintenance resource:** Nope, this isn't a janitorial issue. We're referring to the need for someone (and yes, that person could be you) to log on to the system and monitor the results of your ad campaign. This person not only has to be able to look at the results but should also have the authority or responsibility of making updates or changes to the campaigns based on existing results.

Running a Facebook Ad campaign is not something you build, release, and walk away from, but rather an ongoing effort you need to nurture and tweak as it goes along.

Figure 6-1: Make sure you have the resources to make your ad offer work properly.

Search Engine Management ✕

🔁 Clickable
search made simple

FREE TRIAL

Free 15-Day trial! Boost your ROI. Receive expert bid recommendations & manage all your accounts with a single login: Call 888-440-8049

👍 Like

On top of all these elements, you need to make sure that management and other appropriate departments are aware of the ad campaigns, specifically the target start date, possible end date, and the products or Web pages to be highlighted (or used as landing pages), so they can plan appropriately.

Depending on the size and complexity of your business, it might not hurt to send internal updates of the progress your ad campaign is having. This info could turn into anecdotes or statistics quoted by your sales department. For example, let's say in the first week of your ad campaign, the number of people who Like your Facebook Page increased by 100%. You can let your staff know that thanks to the recent ad campaign, you've doubled your Facebook Page member count in only one week.

Integrating Your Off-Line Campaigns

For you to get the biggest bang for your buck and have effective marketing for your business, you want to keep your online and offline marketing campaigns in sync so that you communicate one message to your customers, no matter where they go. Therefore, make sure that any Facebook Ad campaigns you put together are in sync with any other non–computer-centric advertising or marketing campaigns.

Here are some things to think about when planning your overall strategy:

- **Be aware of your "can't miss" and circulation dates.** When it comes to magazine, newspaper, or other forms of advertising, there is always a "drop dead" date by when your material must be submitted by or prepared to make a certain edition of that product. Make sure that your Facebook Ad campaigns are ready by the same time so they can run concurrently. In addition, make sure that your Facebook Ad campaign goes live around the time of the circulation date so that you get maximum exposure.

- **Don't forget to reuse images.** If you already have offline campaigns, odds are you have some sort of graphic or colorful font to accent your marketing piece and gather attention. Try to reuse (and resize, if necessary) those graphics to not only liven up your Facebook Ad but also to "brand" that ad the same as your offline marketing materials. After all, you want every dollar of your campaign to work in concert with each other rather than battle each ad medium.

- **Each medium should have its own tracking codes.** A *tracking code* is a specific word or term that is referenced or tied to a particular ad campaign, whether that ad is on Facebook or not. (You know those TV ads that say, "Call this 1-800 number and mention offer code TA01?" TA01 is a tracking code.) Some businesses want to put the same tracking or identifying code on different campaigns so that they can measure the overall effectiveness of every campaign. Instead, make sure that each campaign is individually tracked so that you can measure the effectiveness of each platform independently. You can always aggregate the data yourself later to get one overall number.

- **Put a notice on your offline marketing materials.** Don't be afraid to put a line to the effect of, "Hey, you can follow our business on Facebook" in your marketing materials (as shown in Figure 6-2). To help drive traffic, perhaps even mention that Facebook followers have a special introductory offer. The point of your marketing (besides building sales and a following) is to remind people using different mechanisms about you and your brand. You can even add Facebook buttons (or *badges*, as Facebook calls them) to your Web site by going to the Facebook Badges home page (www.facebook.com/badges) and clicking the type of badge you wish to install.

If you do give a shout-out to your Facebook Page on your offline materials, make sure that the Facebook Page is created and "live" *before* those materials are shipped out, or Fans will find nothing and get upset for wasting their time.

Figure 6-2:
Mention
your
Facebook
presence
in your
marketing
materials.

Facebook badge

Testing Your Ads

When you start creating your Facebook Ad campaigns, ask yourself whether you can make your ad more compelling. After all, you're paying to run these ads, so it's natural to be concerned about ad performance and whether you're getting the best value for your (or your company's) money. Facebook allows you to create multiple campaigns and track the results so you can test concepts against Facebook's user base to see whether changing any one factor makes a noticeable difference.

Creating test campaigns

When you start to create an ad campaign, don't assume that Facebook Ads have to look exactly a certain way or must include certain keywords or a particular wording. As you develop your ads, you'll see many ways to create an ad. Your audience might respond differently based on changing one or two words or your image, for example. Because there is no source for the perfect ad, try using different ads to find the one(s) that generate the most interest (and hopefully, the most responses, orders, and/or profit) from the Facebook user community.

The online advertising system of Facebook makes it very easy for you to get to the point of having a refined, well-positioned ad. You achieve this goal by creating *test campaigns* where you run different possibilities for advertisements.

Then you study the test results to see which ads produced the most clicks — and through conversion tracking, the most orders or actions taken.

The most common kind of test campaign is a *split ad campaign*. You create two virtually identical ad campaigns and run them with the same test ad budget, payment model, and ad copy, but you have *exactly one difference* between the two campaigns. Maybe you're trying to decide between two images to use (see Figure 6-3), or two titles, or two types of offers in your ad message. When the test period is over, you choose the ad with the higher success rate and then use that image/title/message in your main ad campaign.

Figure 6-3:
Split test your ad with two images to see which picture causes more clicks.

When running a test campaign, here are some tips to keep in mind:

✔ **Set a time limit.** You can test and test forever, but you'll run out of money and opportunity. Instead, set a period of time (one or two weeks, or one month) and be disciplined to finish a number of test campaigns in that time period and decide on the best ad elements from your test campaigns to use after your main campaign has started.

✔ **Change only one factor at a time.** If you really want to know whether one factor is making a difference, change only that factor and make sure that every other component of your ad is the same. If you're testing different images, use the same title, ad message, and landing page for your ad. If you're testing different ad messages, use the same title and image. This way, you can compare similar ads. If one has a higher click-through rate, for example, go with the better performing ad in your main campaign.

✔ **Don't forget about keywords.** You can run similar ads but use different keywords as targeting filters to see whether those words (which have to match someone's Likes and Interests) make a difference in terms of click-through rate or conversion rate.

✔ **You can test against different demographics.** You don't always have to change some element, such as your ad copy, to test effectiveness. Sometimes, you just have to present the ad to the right target audience. Simply use the same ad but use different targeting filters in your two ad campaigns. For example, say you're running an ad about a travel deal (see Figure 6-4). You run one ad campaign for people on the West Coast, and a second campaign for people on the East Coast. You might find that a targeting factor like location might influence the call of action more than other factors.

✔ **You can run multidimensional tests on your ads.** Because there are a number of factors behind your ad campaigns, you can choose to test multiple factors at the same time, especially if you only have a short period of time to accomplish your testing. Pick combinations of factors that make sense, and see which ad performs best.

Figure 6-4:
Run the
same kind
of ad to
different
audiences
and mea-
sure the
response.

Determining ad success

While you run your different ad campaigns, look for the ad or ads that stand out from the competition and create a higher response from the audience. Specifically, you'll be looking for the best words (whether in the title or as part of the ad message), the best offer or call to action presented to the viewer, and other elements like the most responsive images used in the ad.

This winnowing process can happen multiple times. You run a group of test campaigns and determine that factor A is important. Then you can run a new group of test campaigns, all with factor A, in search of other important or valuable factors that can improve your campaign. Your limit for running campaigns is really your available time and budget for refining ads.

Don't fall into the trap of going for the ad solely because of a high click-through rate. You could design an ad with every hot buzzword to attract attention, but if the people who click that ad don't respond to your call to action, you're wasting money on meaningless clicks.

And if two ads produce the same results (or, at least, results with a statistically negligible difference), keep one of the ads and then create a new ad that takes a completely different direction to see whether the new ad can improve your results from the original, or "control" ad.

Placing Ads through a Facebook Rep

If you're planning on running a big ad campaign, Facebook has a sales team of advertising representatives that can help you create, execute, and maintain your Facebook Ad campaign. Their job is to provide you with the widest variety of ad types possible, along with offering help in building the right reports and conversion tracking information so you have the best idea of how your campaign is doing. The Facebook sales team also offers suggestions on what you or your company can add to make your ad campaign even better.

If you decide to use a Facebook Ad Sales representative, you will enjoy several benefits beyond the higher amount of customer service:

✔ Sponsored Ads on Facebook users' home pages (that can include video or RSVP) are currently available only to advertisers who go through a Facebook rep and spend a certain amount of money.

As of this writing, you need to budget a minimum of $25,000 per month to use a Facebook rep to coordinate your ads.

✔ Ad campaigns coordinated through a Facebook rep can include a tracking code that you can use to identify the success rate of your ad campaigns.

✔ Facebook Ad sales reps can assist in optimizing the advertisement and will monitor the execution of your ad campaign. They work with you to identify and monitor the statistics you most care about (like click-through ratio, conversions, and so on), on a schedule you are comfortable with, and e-mail and phone you with updates and results.

Getting in touch with a Facebook rep

As of this writing, go through the Facebook Web site to contact the Ad Sales team to initiate contact with a representative.

1. **From the Facebook Ads page (`www.facebook.com/ads`), click the Contact Our Sales Team link along the bottom of the page.**

   You are taken to a simple Integrated Solutions: Contact Us form (as shown in Figure 6-5) where you can indicate your country of residence and estimated total budget that you plan on spending on Facebook.

2. **Click the Submit button.**

   • *If Facebook feels that your budget is significant enough to require a Facebook Ad sales rep,* an Advertiser Information form appears (see Figure 6-6) where you can provide your contact information.

   • *If Facebook feels your budget is not significant enough,* you see a message recommending that you try the Facebook Ads system directly, like we do in this book.

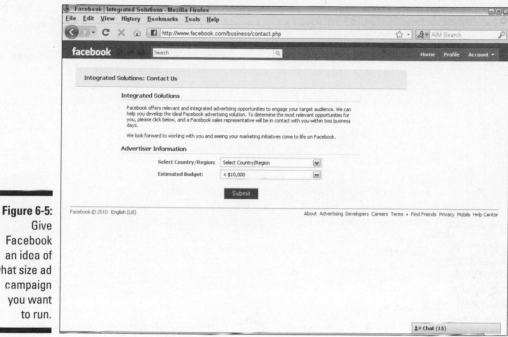

Figure 6-5:
Give
Facebook
an idea of
what size ad
campaign
you want
to run.

3. **Fill in every field in the form and click the Submit button.**

Your information will be transmitted to Facebook, and you should
expect a call from someone on the Ad Sales team soon.

Taking over a home page

One of the advantages of running a large ad budget and going through the
Facebook Ads Sales team is the ability to run sponsored ads on a Facebook
user's home page, like those shown in Figure 6-7. Only ad campaigns that
are managed by Facebook directly have the ability to run ads in this space
on a user's home page. (All advertisers can run ads in the Ad Space on other
Facebook Pages, which is the rightmost column on any Facebook Page other
than the home page.)

In addition to the obvious placement advantage, there are other advantages
to an ad being placed on the user's home page. Ads that run on the home
page can incorporate video into the ad (like the Nike ad in Figure 6-8) or poll
viewers with a question (like the Burner Irons ad in Figure 6-8). These added
technologies allow you to reach out to your audience via different means and
interact with your Fans and customers, not just advertise to them.

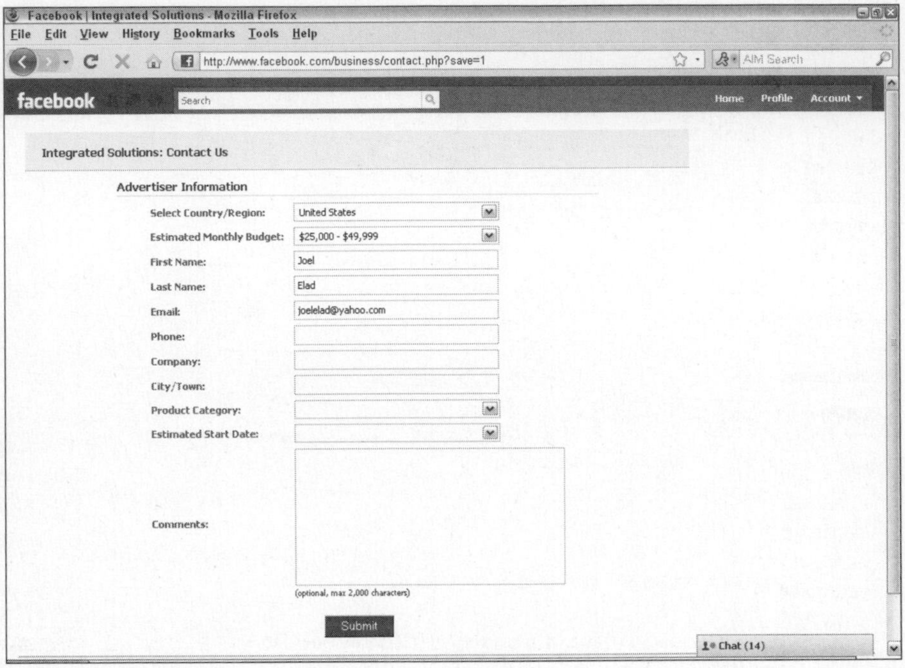

Figure 6-6:
Provide your
information
to Facebook
so a rep can
contact you.

Figure 6-7:
Get your ad
in front of
Facebook
users on
their home
page!

Sponsored ad

Figure 6-8: Sponsored Ads can include video (left) or social elements, like a simple poll (right).

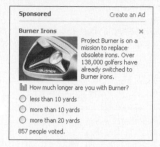

Developing Performance Objectives

Because you can track the performance of your Facebook Ad campaign down to the single ad impression, click, and conversion, you'll find it useful to establish objectives or target measurements that indicate your ideal goals for your Facebook Ad campaign.

The most important step is to set the objectives for your ad campaign. The easiest objective to measure is sales of a product or catalog of products from your Web site or Facebook Page, but you can have other objectives as well:

✔ **Gaining leads who request information:** Facebook Ads can be a great way to generate leads from people who are interested in your product or service, but need more information (and hopefully, a phone call from your sales or marketing department) and a personal follow-up from your business before a sale can be made. The ad can take your viewers to a page on your Web site where they have to provide more information, like the form shown in Figure 6-9.

✔ **Giving away a trial version of your product or service:** The best way to introduce your product or service to someone without requiring a full sale of that item is to give prospective users a trial version to use and test to help them decide whether they want to come back and purchase the full version of your product or service. Giving away a free item is usually an easier call to action than spending money, and all you have to do is create a landing page on your Web site that explains how to get the free version, like in Figure 6-10.

✔ **Encouraging attendance at a marketing event:** You can use Facebook to increase attendance at a marketing event or promotion for your company, and you can track the increase of RSVPs (or count the actual attendance at the event by asking those attendees how they heard about the event) by running an ad and pointing the viewer to the Facebook Event page asking for an RSVP.

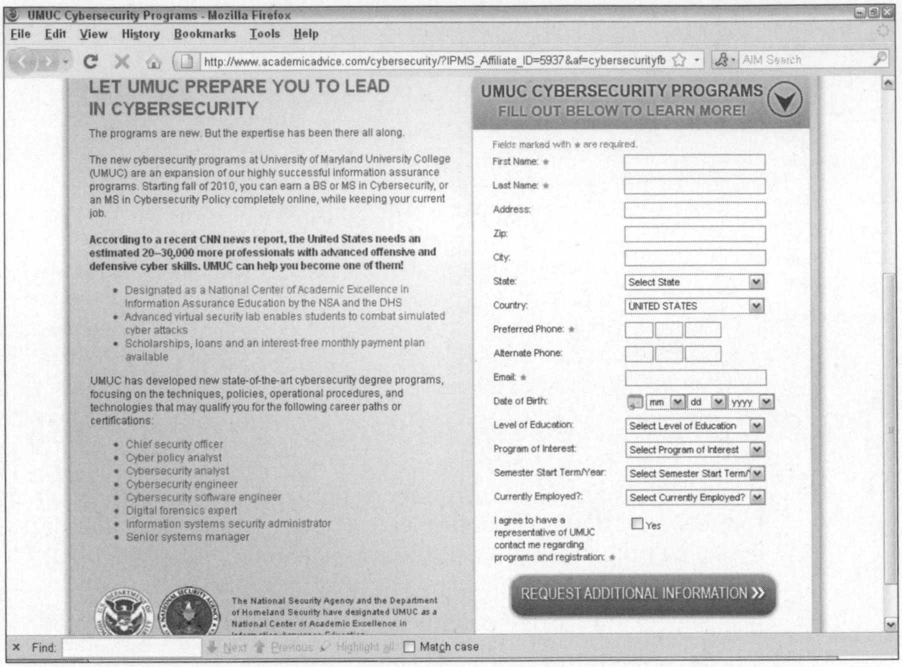

Figure 6-9:
Use
Facebook
Ads to gen-
erate more
leads for
your
business.

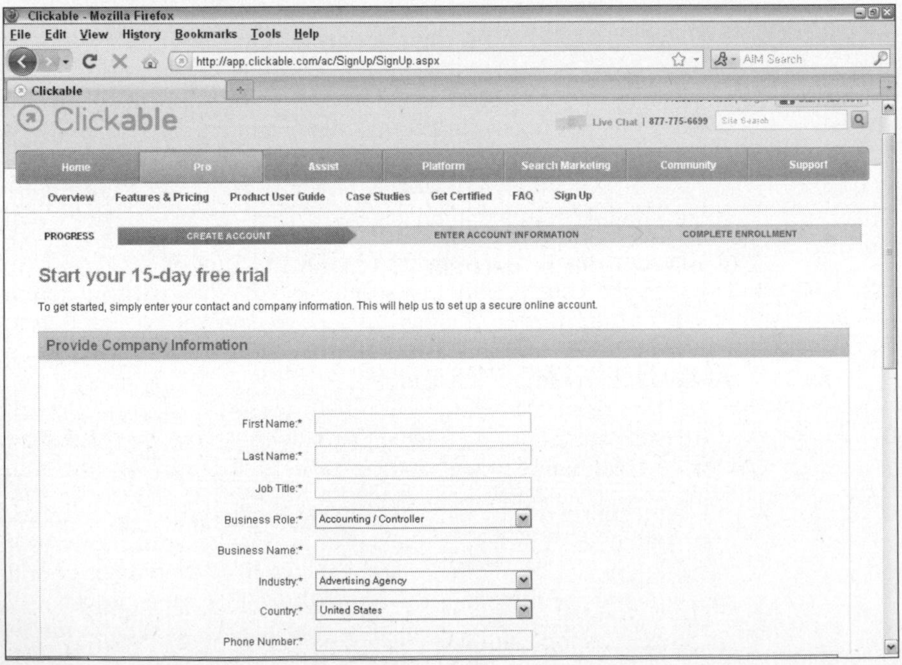

Figure 6-10:
Use
Facebook
Ads to give
away a
trial ver-
sion of your
product or
service.

Defining conversions

Because you might need to measure more than just straight product sales, you can consider using different measurements when monitoring the success of your Facebook Ads. Before you can fully test and implement your Facebook Ad campaigns, you need to decide what should be considered as a *conversion* (a positive, active response to someone viewing *and* clicking your ad).

Therefore, the most important criteria for evaluating what counts as a conversion are the objectives you set for your ad campaign. For example, if your goal is simply to build an active following on Facebook, a conversion could be counted as someone who clicks Like and becomes a Fan of your Facebook Page. Similarly, if your goal is to increase attendance at a future event (or promotion), someone who RSVPs for your Facebook Event could be counted as a conversion.

If your Facebook Ad campaign is designed to promote something on your Web site, your conversions should be defined by the actions viewers take when they click the ad and are taken to your Web site. Your conversion could be as simple or complex as

- Someone signing up for your e-mail newsletter or requesting information
- Someone creating an account on your Web site
- Someone creating an account and downloading a free or trial product
- Someone creating an account and buying a product or service from your Web site

If you've run ad campaigns on other Web sites using Google AdWords, your definition of a conversion can be the same for your Facebook Ads as it was for your other ad campaigns. Then again, because Facebook Ads are not as direct sales–focused as other ad systems, you might want to tailor your measurements differently with Facebook Ads, especially if your goals are more community- or brand-building than product sales.

Analyzing results

If you're running your Facebook Ads solely to increase sales for a given product or your Web site sales in general, determining the success of your ad is purely mathematical. You have to determine whether the cost of your ad campaign was less or more than the profit you gained from the additional orders that you got because of your ads.

Some of the data you need to determine success or failure can be found on your Facebook Ads Manager page, through the Ads Reports offered by Facebook. (We discuss Ads Reports in detail in Chapters 10 and 11.) The remaining data will be determined from your own Web site or store, the sales and access data from your online presence, and your customer database.

Exploring Alternative Facebook Advertising Options

If you're interested in presenting your company and brand to the Facebook community but you don't want to limit yourself to just Facebook advertising, you have some additional options. Because Facebook is all about the user community as well as the fun and games that go on among members, being part of the conversation can seem more genuine (and, because of that, more effective) than a blatantly obvious ad that sits on the right side of the page.

A new crop of potential advertising options on Facebook doesn't occur within the Ad Space. Sponsorships and paid placements are quickly becoming a favorite form of advertising, as more and more companies are taking advantage of these opportunities to gain a competitive advantage and increased brand awareness.

Advertising within applications (FarmVille, Mafia Wars)

One of the most popular forms of sponsorship or paid placements is coming from the wildly popular games available as Facebook applications. One of the most popular Facebook game developers is Zynga (see Figure 6-11), which is responsible for some of the most widely played games on Facebook today, including FarmVille, Mafia Wars, Treasure Isle, Café World, and Zynga Texas Hold 'Em Poker.

Zynga boasts a daily active user count of 70 million Facebook users, which gives the developer an enormous base to work with on behalf of its advertisers. This variety and wide scope of an audience allows Zynga to attract all levels of advertisers to their games, and Zynga currently offers two ways for advertisers to participate:

✔ In-game ads in the form of offer walls that appear within their game. (*Offer walls* are screens of targeted advertisements that game players can click in exchange for receiving credits for that particular game. An example of an offer wall inside the game Island Life appears in Figure 6-12.)

✔ Virtual currency offers, in which you can award viewers of your ads virtual currency points to be used within one of their games

Zynga has very detailed Advertising Guidelines that you can read online at www.zynga.com/about/advertisingGuidelines.php. Zynga will want to make sure that your ads are not "spammy or scammy," for example, so not every advertiser will be approved. There are prohibited categories of ads and prohibited content that cannot appear in the ads. The goal of all these guidelines is to make sure that Zynga does not accept an advertiser that might lower or damage their brand and image with their own customer set.

Figure 6-11: Zynga provides a multitude of Facebook Games that accept advertising.

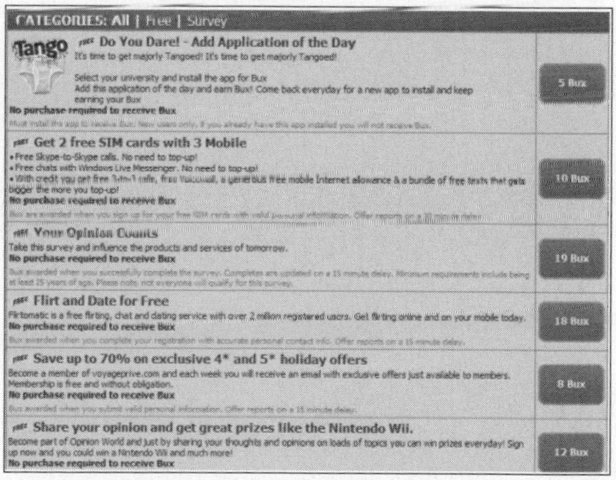

Figure 6-12: Offer walls contain special advertisements that can earn users points toward games.

In general, whatever application you choose to advertise in will require you to conform to general guidelines, such as Zynga's guidelines discussed earlier. Every application has their own brand and image to protect, and your ad will be a reflection on their brand and user experience, so be aware that any partner may require specific guidelines.

As of this writing, having virtual currency offers inside a Zynga game requires a minimum ad budget of $75,000. If you want to run Zynga in-game advertising, your minimum ad budget is $300,000.

Advertising by creating an application

You can leverage a popular Facebook application or platform (like Zynga) to place advertisements for your business, or you can go one step further and promote awareness by creating and distributing (or sponsoring) your own Facebook application. For example, Pei Wei, an Asian quick service dining chain, created its own Mango Harvest Facebook game (see Figure 6-13) to promote its restaurant, and encouraged adoption of this game by including a contest where participants could win cash and food prizes.

You have lots of choices about what kind of application you want associated with your business or brand. Understand, however, that your application doesn't have to be that complicated. Nevada Senate candidate Sue Lowden, for example, created an Online Yard Sign application (as shown in Figure 6-14) that simply adds an "online yard sign" to your Facebook profile. The goal of this application is purely an advertising and online support mechanism, but it can help Lowden build buzz and gain awareness, which are most likely the objectives.

If you think creating or sponsoring the development of a Facebook application is the way to go, you can approach a development company like InvolveSocial (see Figure 6-15) or go straight to the freelance sites like eLance.com or guru.com and hire your own Facebook application developer to write the application for you. Take a look at existing applications like FedEx's Launch a Package app to see how these apps can add value to your user community. If you're looking for ideas on what Facebook applications to create, take a look at the Facebook Application Directory by going to `www.facebook.com/apps/directory.php`.

Figure 6-13:
Promote your business with your own Facebook app.

Figure 6-14:
Write a
Facebook
application
to promote
your busi-
ness or
brand.

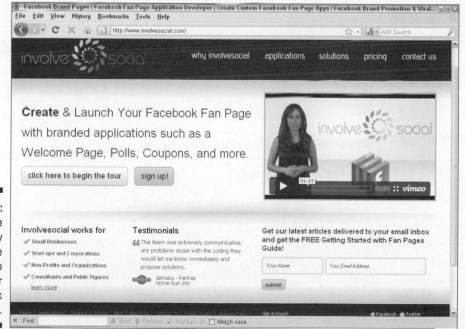

Figure 6-15:
You can hire
a company
like Involve
Social to
write your
Facebook
app.

Cross-Promoting via External Networks

If you're on Facebook and are working toward running ad campaigns on Facebook, we think the chances are high that Facebook isn't the only way you plan to promote your company or brand. So, if you're using multiple avenues to communicate with prospective (and current) customers, why not consider doing some cross promotion and share the marketing effort among multiple platforms?

Cross-promoting with blogs

If you maintain or operate a blog for your business or brand, you should definitely consider using some cross-promotion between your Facebook Ad campaigns (and Facebook Pages) and your blog. Some ideas that come to mind include

- ✔ Creating a blog post to announce a new Facebook Page, Event, or application

- ✔ Adding your Facebook Page to the set of links mentioned in your blog

- ✔ Create a Facebook Group that has a common interest with the focus of your blog

- ✔ Encourage your blog readers to post comments on the blog or Facebook Page

You can also connect Facebook with your blog by installing a *widget* (a piece of computer software that runs on a Web site) on your blog that displays a box of information from your Facebook Page. The free Facebook Like Box plug-in (shown in Figure 6-16) can be installed to appear on your blog (or your Web site) to show the stream of status updates from your Facebook Page along with summary information and a list of the Page's current Friends.

1. Go to `http://developers.facebook.com/docs/reference/plugins/like-box`.

2. Fill out the fields:

   - *Facebook Page ID:* When you create a Facebook business Page, Facebook assigns a unique Page ID to each Page that has been set up. If you are logged in to Facebook when completing these steps, Facebook will automatically fill in the Page ID for the first Page that you administer. If there is more than one page that you administer, you will need to pull up that Page and look at the very end of the URL in the address bar. For example, the end of the URL of one of Joel's pages for the So Cal Comic Con reads like this:

   `.../pages/So-Cal-Comic-Con/134310759943641`

The Page ID in this situation is that last number, 134310759943641.

- *Width:* Because you will be putting this Like box on your own Web site, you can set the Width of this box in terms of pixel size. Pick a width that will not disrupt the rest of the objects on your Web site.

- *Connections:* You can provide a sample of users that Like your Page by setting a sample number of users in this field.

- *Stream:* If you want the Like box to contain the stream of Wall Posts and comments, check this box.

- *Header:* If you want the box to contain the Header "Find us on Facebook," click the box. Otherwise, uncheck the box and your Like box will start with your Page name.

Figure 6-16:
Promote
your
Facebook
Page on
your blog
using a
widget.

3. **Click the Get Code button.**

A new window appears in the middle of your screen, like in Figure 6-17. You can copy the HTML command that appears in the iframe window. (If you already have the JavaScript SDK installed on your Web site, you can also copy the text from the XFBML window). The HTML command from the iframe window looks like this:

```
<iframe src="http://www.facebook.com/plugins/likebox.php?id=1343107599
        43641&amp;width=292&amp;connections=10&amp;stream=true&amp;
        header=false&amp;height=555" scrolling="no" frameborder="0"
        style="border:none; overflow:hidden; width:292px; height:555px;"
        allowTransparency="true"></iframe>
```

Figure 6-17:
Get the
HTML com-
mand for
your Like
box by
copying the
text from
this window.

Your Like Box plugin code:

iframe

```
<iframe src="http://www.facebook.com/plugins/likebox.php?id=1343107599436 41&
amp;width=292&amp;connections=10&amp;stream=true&amp;header=false&
amp;height=555" scrolling="no" frameborder="0" style="border:none; overflow:hidden;
width:292px; height:555px;" allowTransparency="true"></iframe>
```

XFBML

```
<fb:like-box profile_id="134310759943641" header="false"></fb:like-box>
```

XFBML is more flexible than iframes, but requires you use the JavaScript SDK.

[Done]

4. Embed that command within your blog page where you are allowed to insert your own code.

One of the hidden benefits of the Like Box widget is that your blog readers can click a link from that box and become Fans of your Facebook Page instantly, without having to go to Facebook. We discuss other Facebook plug-ins in Chapter 12.

Cross-promoting with e-mail blasts

One of the best ways for a business to keep in constant communication with current customers or a user base is to send out e-mail *blasts* (communications with their customer list) to keep them informed and connected with the business or brand. Integrating your Facebook activities with your e-mail blasts are a great way to expose your marketing efforts to a larger and established audience in one shot for no extra money. You can

✔ Encourage your e-mail subscribers to stay informed of your activities and post comments and communicate with you via your Facebook Page, like how Lynn Dralle is announcing to her Queen of Auctions mailing list. (See Figure 6-18.) She set up her link in her e-mail to take viewers to her Facebook Page directly, like this:

```
<a href=http://www.facebook.com/TheQueenOfAuctions>here.</a>
```

✔ Integrate your contests and promotions with your Facebook Page, like how Wendy's did with its Frosty campaign (see Figure 6-19). The contest helps encourage ongoing usage of Wendy's Facebook Page.

✔ Extend your Web site functionality by creating a Facebook Page and applications that promote your brand on Facebook, and announce it to your e-mail list, like Redbox did (see Figure 6-20).

Figure 6-18:
Help your customers follow you on Facebook.

Figure 6-19:
Announce Facebook promotions in your e-mail newsletters.

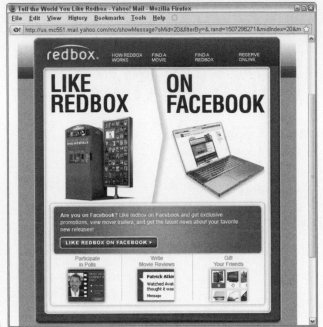

Figure 6-20:
Get your
e-mail
subscribers
to promote
you on
Facebook.

Part III

Managing Your Facebook Advertising Campaigns

The 5th Wave   By Rich Tennant

BANK MGR

"Our customer survey indicates 30% of our customers think our service is inconsistent, 40% would like a change in procedures, and 50% think it would be real cute if we all wore matching colored vests."

In this part . . .

After you do all the work to develop and launch your
Facebook ad campaigns, you might think the rest
can be left on autopilot. Unfortunately, this running
campaigns requires dedicated attention. You need to
know how to react and incorporate incoming responses
and feedback.

In this part, we discuss ways how you can monitor and
improve your ad campaigns. We go over how to create
specific pages within your Facebook business Page, and
how those specific pages will help to convert lookers-on
into customers. We go into more depth regarding testing
and optimizing your ad campaigns, and spend some time
discussing what happens when you get a lead and want to
convert that person into a real customer.

Chapter 7

Creating Pages for Your Campaign

In This Chapter

▶ Choosing between internal and external landing pages

▶ Creating a new tab on your Facebook Page as an ad landing page

▶ Installing the FBML application for creating custom Facebook Page tabs

▶ Adding a form on your Facebook Page to gather user information

*I*n online marketing, a *landing page* — sometimes known as a *lead capture page* — is the page that appears when a potential customer clicks an advertisement or a search engine result link. Such a page typically displays content that's a logical extension of the advertisement or link and also that is optimized to feature specific keywords or phrases for indexing by search engines.

Specifically, for cost per click (CPC; or PPC [*pay per click*]) campaigns, your landing page can be customized to measure the effectiveness of different advertisements. And by adding a parameter to the linking URL, marketers can measure advertisement effectiveness based on relative click-through rates.

In this chapter, we discuss landing pages and their usefulness for your Facebook Ad campaigns. We cover landing pages that reside as part of your business' online Facebook Page as well as landing pages on your Web site or a third-party Web site. We go over how to install the FBML special programming language, which you use to build special landing page tabs within your Facebook Page. Finally, we show you how to introduce some common marketing elements, such as a user information form, to your Facebook Pages to capture viewer and potential customer data.

Choosing a Landing Page

In the world of online advertising, there are typically two general categories for landing pages that people see after clicking an online ad. The two categories most online advertisers are familiar with are known as *reference* and *transaction landing pages*. Specifically, these two types of pages can be summarized as follows:

✔ **Reference landing pages:** These landing pages focus on providing a reference to the viewer of the brand, organization, or business that is sponsoring the ad. Therefore, on such pages you typically see information, pictures, tools, and Web links that matter to Web viewers who are interested in knowing more about a particular company instead of a specific product. For example, the Merrill outdoor community Facebook Page uses a reference landing page (see Figure 7-1) to introduce new members to the different parts of their Facebook Page.

Businesses who advertise on Facebook can receive a lot of value by pointing their ad viewers to a reference landing page, since Facebook is a community building site more than a transactional site, and a reference page can offer value and resonate with a user more than a pitch for a one-time sale. For example, Viking Grills has a special tab within its Facebook business Page full of content and interactivity that would appeal to potential Viking customers (see Figure 7-2).

✔ **Transactional landing pages:** These landing pages keep the viewer's focus on the transaction proposed in the advertisement. Such pages guide viewers to complete the sale of a product, download a trial version of software, or receive a free report for joining the membership list of a business or group. A common transactional landing page is a contest page, where the viewer has to enter the required information (such as name, address, phone number, e-mail address, date of birth, or other demographic data) and either click a check box or Web link to enter the contest, or complete an additional step to be registered to win. As an example, Viking held a contest through its Facebook Page (see Figure 7-3) where people could sign up to win a grill via a transactional landing page.

Figure 7-1: Associations can provide a reference landing page for new members.

Figure 7-2:
A business can use a reference landing page for its brand.

Figure 7-3:
You can use a trans-actional landing page to promote a contest.

When a visitor, after clicking an online ad, completes the call to action or does the desired action on a transactional landing page, the advertiser can now count this new visitor as a *conversion.* Many advertisers then calculate and measure the *conversion rate,* which, simply put, is the percentage of visitors (based on everyone who clicked the ad) who fully completed the intended action. This rate is very important and carefully watched because the conversion rate can determine whether an ad campaign is profitable or successful. We discuss conversions again in Chapter 9.

There is another type of landing page that is used in the world of online marketing, especially in the discipline of direct marketing. This page is known as a *squeeze page.* These squeeze pages are very targeted and focused transactional landing pages, whose only goal is to encourage, push, or convince the viewer to complete the call to action and be counted as a conversion. If you've ever seen a very long Web page that tries to explain in great detail why product X is the cure to all your problems, you've been on a squeeze page. Because squeeze pages are seen more on product-focused ad campaigns, which are not as effective in Facebook's community environment, we do not recommend them or cover them here.

You have two choices for your landing page location when someone clicks your Facebook Ad: a page hosted internally on Facebook (most likely on your Facebook Page) or on an external Web site not hosted by Facebook. In the following sections, we are going to discuss the advantages and procedures for pursuing either option.

Opting for an internal Facebook landing page

When you're trying to promote your Facebook business Page, or an Event, Group, or Application, you will need an internal Facebook landing page. Technically, building an internal landing page is much easier and less work than building an external landing page. Having an internal Facebook landing page offers you many other benefits as well:

✔ **You create a seamless experience.** As we mention throughout this book, Facebook Ads allow you to interact with your potential customers through ads that don't require them to leave Facebook to respond to your call to action — and that increases the likelihood of their response. When hosting your landing page within Facebook, your viewers will see your landing page as a part of their Facebook activity. When we take a look at Ventegy's internal landing page (see Figure 7-4) we see a clear explanation of what they offer within their Facebook Page.

✔ **Your content is seen as more organic or authentic.** When an Internet user clicks an ad and is taken to a new Web site, the mindset immediately changes to respond to the new environment. When your internal landing page loads as a part of the screen within Facebook, though, you benefit from a subconscious linking between Facebook and your business because the viewer starts to associate your business as part of their Facebook interactions, which is usually a positive experience.

✔ **Your new Facebook Friends help you advertise.** When you redirect potential new customers to your Facebook Page and they end up Liking your Page, for example, their action is broadcast to their Friend's News Feeds, at no extra cost to you. (*Note:* Each Facebook user *can* choose to block that News Feed entry, but most users allow the posting.) This results in extra exposure, which can take off as you build a following on the site.

Later in this chapter ("Creating a separate tab for your campaign"), we discuss some of the necessary steps to build an internal landing page as a custom tab on your Facebook business Page.

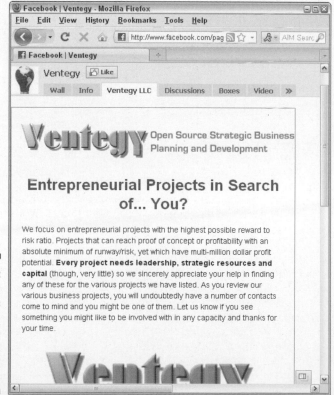

Figure 7-4:
Provide a seamless experience with an internal landing page.

The cost of this easier, natural internal landing page is control. You will have to rely on Facebook's Insights program to see any usage statistics from the visitors who come to the page. You cannot introduce these visitors to the power and complexity of your own Web site when they use an internal landing page. It's harder to run complex tools or features on your internal landing page as well. If some of these points are important to you, then perhaps you need an external (Web site) landing page, which we cover in the next section.

Opting for an external Web site landing page

Using an external Web page as your advertisement landing page has its advantages.

And when we say "external," we mean external to Facebook. This can be a Web page on your own Web site or a Web page on a partner or third-party Web site. If you've run advertisements on other online sites (such as Google), you're used to having your ads point to a specific Web page tailored to match the offer in your ad and designed to encourage any viewer to respond to the call to action from your ad. For example, when Marriott's Fairfield Suites ran a Facebook Ad campaign to promote their Small Business Road to Success challenge, they used an external landing page on Marriott's Web site (see Figure 7-5 below) to promote the contest.

Figure 7-5:
You can use an external landing page for your ad visitors.

Here are the distinct advantages to using an external Web site as your landing page:

- ✔ **You have more control over your landing page.** Although Facebook offers you the ability to almost replicate one of your Web pages on its site, you have full control over any page hosted on your Web site. Your Web site traffic logs will capture all the incoming data, and you can use any programming languages or Web applications you like, which means you can give the user a more rich experience. And you can fully track your visitor's activities when they're on your Web site. This is important to marketers who are trying to build traffic to their Web site, and it is important to marketers who have a lead nurturing platform under their Web site and can track and predict what the next page or offer should be sent to this visitor.

- ✔ **You can fully optimize your external page for the search engines.** When you control and host your own landing page, you can optimize that Web page to take advantage of search engine optimization (SEO) and be read by the search engines to gain a high placement on the search engine results screen. As of this writing, internal Facebook Pages won't see a benefit from optimizing those pages for high search engine results (at least not yet!)

- ✔ **You might not have to build a new page.** In some cases, your landing page is already an existing Web page within your site. This means that you can design your ad and then simply give the existing URL to have your Facebook Ad redirected when it is clicked.,

- ✔ **You don't have to worry about any rule changes.** When you're building pages on another Web site (like Facebook), you're limited by the rules and user agreement of that Web site, and those rules can change over time. You're not fettered by such restrictions when you use your own Web site to host your landing page, as long as the landing page displays the offer clearly stated in your Facebook Ad.

If your external landing page asks for too much information upfront or doesn't correspond with what your Facebook Ad is offering, Facebook reserves the right to reject your ad campaign and not run your ads.

When you use an external landing page for your Facebook Ads, rest assured that Facebook will review the landing page to make sure that the page is appropriate and complies with Facebook standards. To help prevent Facebook from deciding that you might be asking for too much information upfront, some advertisers employ a *two-step close* system with their landing pages:

1. They build what is known in the Internet marketing world as a *jump page,* which is a page that continues discussing the offer the user sees in the initial ad he clicked, with a new hyperlink at the bottom of this page.

2. When a user clicks the new hyperlink at the bottom of the jump page, he is taken to a second page that collects the user information and allows the person to take advantage of the offer.

Using this technique, the landing page is accurate and complies with Facebook standards, and you (the advertiser) have ample opportunity to sell your new customers on why they should respond to your call to action.

As an example, when golfstakes.com used Facebook to advertise its mobile golf scoring program, users were redirected to an external landing page that spoke about the free offer to score their golf games (see Figure 7-6). When users clicked the link at the bottom of that page, they were taken to the sign-up screen, as shown in Figure 7-7), where they could register for the service.

Of course, an external landing page is not free of worries, either. You are shifting the user's focus away from the Facebook environment, and that change may influence their interest in participating. With today's instant gratification and short attention spans, any external Web page, especially a two-step close process, can lose more new viewers than intended, and cause a profitable ad campaign to become unprofitable or unsuccessful.

Figure 7-6:
Present your offer and get the potential buyer to respond.

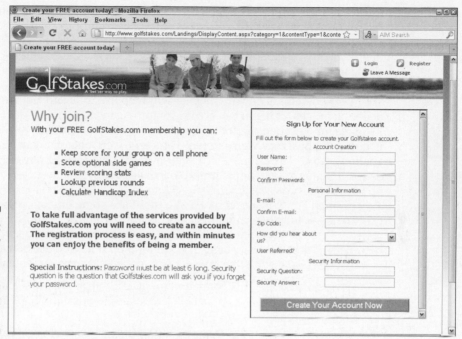

Figure 7-7:
Once they
indicate
interest,
ask for the
relevant
information.

Creating a Separate Tab for Your Campaign

After you choose which type of landing page best fits your needs, it's time to build one. If you use an external Web site, you can find myriad books and tutorials on how to build an individual Web page that you can use to build your external landing page. Here, we cover building an internal landing page that's part of your Facebook Page.

Specifically, we cover what is known as a custom tab, or a page that you are building from scratch that will be accessible as a tab within your Facebook Page. Understand that some people simply use the existing Wall tab within their Facebook Page as their internal landing page. If that is the case, then you do not need to create something extra. However, many campaigns choose to create a separate tab to guide their viewers to their call to action.

Using FBML to create a custom tab

To build an internal landing page, you currently use the new computer language, Facebook Markup Language (FBML). *FBML* is the Facebook version of *HTML,* the language used to write Web pages. For the most part, a working knowledge of HTML is all you need to use the Static FBML application, also created by Facebook. You add the app to your pages, and then you can create a "Web page" within a tab or box that you can attach to your Facebook business Page. This process sounds more complicated than it really is, but we'll walk you through it, so don't worry.

Using FBML pages allow you to add a rich, Web-like look and feel to your Facebook presence. If you can create something in HTML (a product page, catalog page, or a product finder tool), odds are that you can do it in Facebook. Compare the Best Buy Web site (see Figure 7-8) and one of its custom Facebook tabs (see Figure 7-9) You can see that using FBML allows any company to seamlessly extend its brand to its Facebook presence.

And although FBML is based on HTML, there are some custom commands you can use to fully take advantage of this new language:

✔ `<fb:google-analytics>`: This command tells Google Analytics to pay attention to this tab like it was a Web page on your own Web site.

✔ `<fb:bookmark>`: This command creates a button that lets a user bookmark your application. When clicked, a link to your application will appear on the user's profile.

✔ `<fb:create-button>`: This command allows you to render a Create button on your tab that allows user-generated comment to be entered on that tab.

Figure 7-8:
Best Buy's
Web site.

Figure 7-9:
Best Buy's
Facebook
presence.

As of this writing, Facebook has alerted their user community that FBML will most likely be removed as an option as soon as early 2011. If this occurs, you will need to create landing page tabs using iFrames, which is discussed in more detail in *Facebook Application Development For Dummies* by Jesse Stay.

Installing FBML on your Page

When you're ready to install FBML, just follow these steps:

1. **Go to the Facebook Apps Directory at www.facebook.com/apps/ directory.php. In the Search box under the All Applications header (on the left side of the screen, that should say 'Search apps' inside), enter** FBML**, and then press Enter.**

   This brings up a results screen like that shown in Figure 7-10.

   One big mistake that some people make is searching from the main Facebook Page instead of the Apps Directory for Static FBML. Searching from the main Facebook Page brings up the Static FBML *Page* instead of the *application*. And if you Like that application, it won't actually install FBML on your business Page, so be careful.

Figure 7-10:
Find the
Static FBML
application.

2. Click the Static FBML link or the Arrow graphic to go to the Static FBML application page.

This brings you to the Static FBML home page, as shown in Figure 7-11.

Even though this is an application, you can Like the page to follow any announcements made by the FBML developers.

3. Click the Add to My Page link (top left of the screen).

You see a pop-up screen asking which Facebook Page you want to add this application to, even if you manage only one Page, like in Figure 7-12. Click the Add to Page button for every Facebook Page you are maintaining.

4. Click the Close button in the pop-up window.

That's it! You added Static FBML to your Facebook Page, and when you go to that Page, you will see a new tab titled FBML.

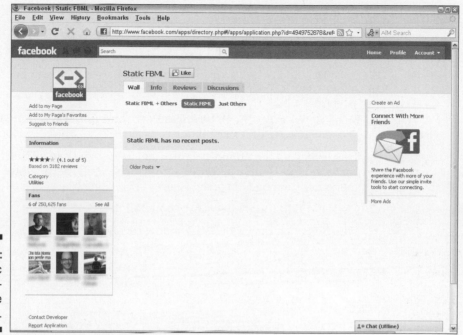

Figure 7-11:
The Static
FBML appli-
cation home
page.

Figure 7-12:
Add FBML
to your
Facebook
Page by
clicking the
button.

Building a custom FBML tab on your Facebook Page

When you're ready to build a custom landing page within your Facebook Page using FBML, follow these steps:

1. **Bring up your Facebook business Page, and underneath the Page photo, click the Edit Page link.**

   This brings up the Administrator page, where you can edit all the different functions associated with your business Page. Scroll down until you see the section on FBML (see Figure 7-13).

2. **Click the Edit link underneath the FBML header.**

   This brings up the Edit FBML window, as shown in Figure 7-14.

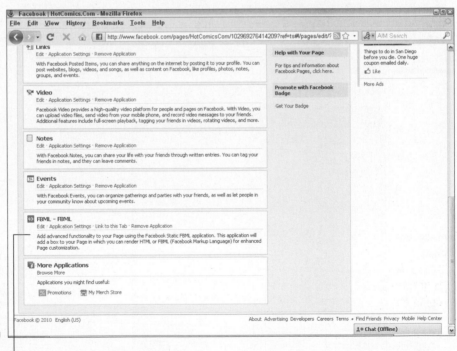

Figure 7-13:
Look for the FBML Edit section.

FBML section

3. **Fill in the appropriate information in the boxes provided, and then click the Save Changes button to save your work and exit.**

- *Box Title field:* Enter the name that you want to appear as your Tab title (and hopefully, you will pick a title shorter than the default placeholder Your FBML Tab Name Goes Here.)

- *FBML field:* Enter your FBML commands, which (as we mention earlier) are very similar to HTML commands for any given Web page.

  For example, if we wanted to write up a sample list of dealers who would be attending the So Cal Comic Convention, we might write the following code:

```
<title>Preliminary list of dealers to attend the So Cal Comic Con:</title>
<ul>
<li>Terry's Comics</li>
<li>R&K Comics</li>
<li>Sky High Comics</li>
<li>Southern California Comics</li>
<li>More to be added!</li>
</ul>
```

  You are taken back to your Facebook business Page's Wall page. (The Wall page shows all the status updates and comments associated with that page.) Along the list of tabs should be a new tab with the title you just gave for your custom page (see Figure 7-15).

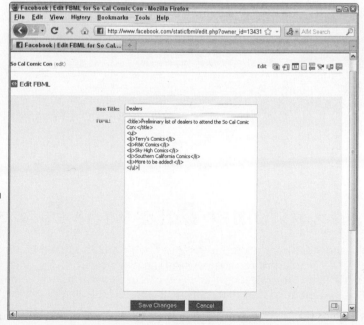

Figure 7-14:
Design your custom Page from the Edit FBML screen.

You can add as many FBML pages as you want. To do so, simply repeat the steps we describe previously.

If you want to make this tab the default landing page for anybody viewing your Facebook Page, go into your Wall Settings to edit your Page. There, from the Default Landing Tab for Everyone Else list, choose the name of your newly created FBML tab (in our example, it is Dealers), like in Figure 7-16.

New FBML tab

Figure 7-15: Your Page now has the new FBML tab.

Figure 7-16: You can set up your new FBML page as the default for any viewer.

Capturing Customer Data with Forms

One of the most important purposes of having a customized landing page is the capability to allow (and encourage) new or potential customers provide you with some information, which you can use to market to them on an ongoing basis. Hopefully, that marketing will lead to future sales or opportunities.

How much is a Fan really worth? $3.60?

Vitrue, a social media marketing platform company, recently tried to estimate the "value," or return on investment, of each Fan of a Facebook Page. Its findings, published in the April 2010 edition of *Adweek,* estimated that the value could be somewhere around $3.60 per Fan, per year, based on a CPM cost of $5. (Read all about CPM in Chapter 3.) This figure is based on Vitrue calculating that an average consistent Fan base of 1 million Facebook users will generate approximately $3.6 million worth of media value over a one-year period.

Vitrue based their findings on the number of impressions that were generated in the Facebook News Feed (or stream of the most recent updates from various users' Facebook friend networks.) Vitrue looked at the sum of all Facebook data generated from all their current clients, which was a total of approximately 41 million Fans. Their conclusion was that each client received approximately $3.60 in value from every user who clicked Like and became a Fan of that client's Facebook business Page.

Understand that these particular numbers might not apply to any individual client of Vitrue. Furthermore, these numbers should not be assumed to apply to any company on Facebook, as Vitrue's study was limited to only their current clients who had at least 1 million Fans who liked their client's Facebook Page. Therefore, even Vitrue's clients who have fewer than 1 million Fans may have different results.

Let's examine these proposed figures with a Page containing 1 million Fans. Suppose that a company posts two updates on their Page each day in a month. This action would generate 60 million impressions for the company per month (1 million Fans see 2 posts for 30 days, or $2 \times 30 \times 1$ million). Vitrue assumed that the cost of 1,000 impressions was $5. The cost of generating 60 million impressions in 1 month, using this cost statistic, would be $300,000 (= 60 million $\times$ 5/1000). On a yearly basis, this cost would soar to $3.6 million ($300,000 $\times$ 12). Therefore, it is reasonable to conclude that the company is "receiving $3.60 in value" for each of their 1 million Fans ($3.6 million/1 million Fans).

Any company that uses Facebook as an online channel to promote their products or brand is very interested in knowing their Fans' "return on investment". Obviously, for some companies, the return could be greater if Fans share their posts with their friends, or actively comment on the company's update posting, which is often described as "viral marketing."

Since you need the users' basic information, like name and e-mail address, in order to market to them, you will need to capture that information. The easiest way to collect the user's information is to add a form to your Facebook Page. Accomplishing this is basically a two-step process:

1. Create a new custom landing page using FBML.

   See how in the earlier section, "Using FBML to create a custom tab."

2. Insert HTML code that presents a simple form in the FBML page.

If you're already using an opt-in form on your Web site, you can simply copy the HTML code from that Web page and insert it into the FBML page. Not only does this make your life easier but it also keeps your Facebook Page consistent with your Web site.

Here is a sample opt-in form that collects a person's name and e-mail address and mails it to someone in your company:

```
<form action="MAILTO:someone@company.com" method="post" enctype="text/plain" >
Your name: <INPUT type="text" name="name"><br>
E-mail address: <INPUT type="text" name="email"><br>
<INPUT type="Submit" value="Submit">
<INPUT type="reset" value="Clear">
</form>
```

You can insert this code, with some alternation to put in your specific use information, into your FBML tab to present viewers with an input form they can complete to get more information or take advantage of the offer in your ad.

You can see an example of an opt-in form on a Facebook Page in Figure 7-17.

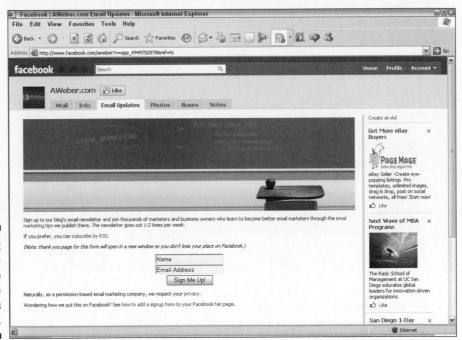

Figure 7-17:
Use an opt-in form to gain future customers and Fans.

The key to remember with any information gathering, like an online form, is to gather enough information to make it worth your efforts, but not too cumbersome where the user is not deterred to fully participate. Some experts say there is an inverse relationship between data gathered and participation: The more information you require someone to provide in order to get their prize or entry, the less amount of participants you will find that complete the process.

Chapter 8

Testing and Optimizing Your Ad Campaign

In This Chapter

▶ Looking at your Facebook Ads Reports

▶ Making changes or updates to your ad campaigns

▶ Gaining insight from Facebook Insights reports

▶ Drawing conclusions from your ad campaigns' effect on your pages

Sure, there may be 50 ways to leave your lover, but there are also many ways to make a successful Facebook advertising campaign. And with all the information and tracking capabilities available, you can strive to improve your ad campaign through testing and optimizing your ads so you get the biggest amount of response — and, hopefully, the most profitable or beneficial response you can generate from your ad campaign dollars.

In this chapter, we delve into the reporting options available in Facebook. We show you what to look for in your test campaigns so you can make better decisions on how to revise or update your ads before you run a major campaign with lots of advertising dollars. We walk you through Facebook Insights, where you can see how the reaction is going to your Facebook business Page and the traffic generated from sources like your ad campaign. We discuss Ads Manager and Ads Reports again in Chapters 10 and 11 because these tools help you understand how your main campaigns are performing. We illustrate them here because they are important in helping you verify how to test and optimize your ad campaigns before you start spending the big dollars on your main campaign(s).

Using Facebook Reporting Data

Facebook provides a plethora of reporting data you can use to help gauge your ad's performance. Our feeling is the more testing, the better. When you run a test campaign, you're getting actual responses from real Facebook users, not a group of testers sitting in some building. Those decisions and actions of the viewers of your ad campaign should be indicative of your ongoing ad performance.

Understand that any reporting data from your test ad campaigns, such as click-through percentages and cost per click (CPC), will probably change when you run your main ad campaigns. (Like the disclaimers you see in a financial commercial's fine print: Past performance is not a guarantee of future behavior.)

The idea is to use the test campaigns to identify the most popular or most likely elements for success compared with other options you've tried in your ads.

In this section, we cover some of the reports offered through Ads Manager, so you know what to look for as you design your main ad campaigns and make the final decisions. We cover Ads Manager and reporting in more depth in Chapters 10 and 11. For now, you can reach Ads Manager by going to this Web address: www.facebook.com/ads/manage.

The Advertising Performance report

The most common report to review is your Advertising Performance report, which is available from your Reports screen within Ads Manager. When you are looking at your Ads Manager screen (www.facebook.com/ads/ manage), click the Reports link from the left navigation menu, and select Advertising Performance from the first drop-down menu selection. This report, as shown in Figure 8-1, shows you all the major statistics — such as click rate and cost per click (CPC) — for any ad campaign you've run. As you review your campaign, look for results that stand out or give you an idea of what stood out among the various tests you may have run, such as a higher click rate than normal, or a CPC or CPM (cost per thousand) rate that is lower or higher than Facebook's suggested range.

When you are testing or optimizing your initial ad campaigns, you need to refer to several values that can be found in the Advertising Performance report. These values help you decide which test campaigns are better or worse than others, or which test ads generate the results you are seeking. In the next few sections, we are going to talk about these different numbers and what lessons or trends you can infer from your initial ad campaign results.

Impressions

This statistic within the Advertising Performance report doesn't show the number of times you can mimic your favorite comedian or singer. This type of impression is actually the number of times your ad was shown to someone on a Facebook Web page. Before you jump straight to other figures (like click rate), spend a minute and take a look at the number of times your ad was run on the site, regardless of the eventual success or failure of that ad. This number gives you a view into the reach of your ad.

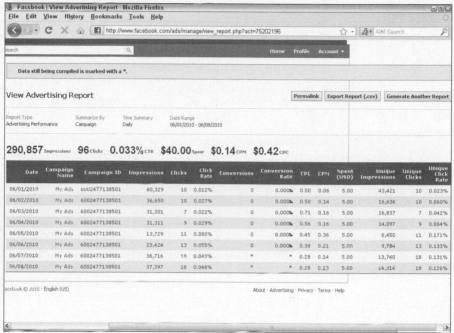

Figure 8-1:
Your
Advertising
Performance
report has
all your
major
statistics.

When you look at the amount of Impressions, you need to keep in mind how your initial amount of impressions will affect your campaign. Questions to ask yourself here include the following:

✔ Is the number of impressions enough of a good sample size to make a valid decision? Are you getting 20 impressions? 200? 2,000? A good sample size is one in which one single extra click or conversion won't double or triple your click rate, for example.

✔ What changes, if any, should I make to my ads if I see a big change in the number of impressions received on a given day or week?

✔ Are my ads generating a consistent amount of impressions per day, week, or month?

Click rate (or the click-through ratio)

The click rate, also known as the click-through ratio (or CTR) is probably the most important ratio in determining the performance of your ad. By looking at the percentage of click-throughs for every impression, you will see what ads are performing the best from your entire set.

Questions to ask yourself here include the following:

✔ Are the highest-generating click rates significantly higher than the other click rates to indicate a genuine preference for one of your test ads? In other words, is one of your test ads an "obvious choice" because that ad's click rate is far and beyond every other click rate you have? Or is a group of test ads scoring higher than other test ads?

✔ Are the highest click rates good enough to justify a bigger investment in Facebook Ads? In other words, are you getting enough of a return from your click rates to justify the expense?

✔ If you made changes to your test campaigns while they were running, are the daily click rates after the change significantly better or worse than before the change?

Cost per click (CPC)

Regardless of the payment model you chose to run your test campaigns on Facebook Ads, Facebook will calculate what your resulting average cost per click (CPC) was for those campaigns. So, say you chose to pay for Impressions under a CPM model. (Read about cost per millions, CPM, in Chapter 4.) If you received 100,000 impressions for $500 (at a $5 CPM, or $5-for-1,000 impression rate), and those 100,000 impressions resulted in a 1% CTR of 1,000 clicks, your average CPC would be the Amount Spent divided by the Number of Clicks: $500/1,000, or $0.50 per click.

Knowing your average CPC gives you an idea of bidding ranges where your campaign will perform optimally. In the previous example, if you're getting an average CPC of $0.50 through a CPM payment model and you're paying more than $0.50 if you run a CPC payment model, perhaps you should consider changing your payment model going forward to take advantage of the CPM model.

The Responder Demographics report

If you're more interested in the types of people who are looking at and responding to your ads, the Responder Demographics report is more of what you want. Facebook groups your ad viewers based on two of the filters you used when targeting your ad. (Read how to set ad targets in Chapter 2 and how to run the Responder Demographics report in Chapter 4.)

So, for example, you can pull up a report that shows you the responders to an ad or ad campaign based on gender/age, and then location by country or state. Here's how:

1. **When you are looking at your Ads Manager screen (`www.facebook.com/ads/manage`), click the Reports link from the left hand navigation menu.**

2. **Select Responder Demographics from the first drop-down menu selection.**

   In the example shown in Figure 8-2, we ran an ad targeting male comic book fans, age 18+, in the United States. The report shows the amount of impressions, the number of clicks, and the click rate for each demographic segment. (A *segment* is a range of users, such as *males age 18–24,* or *males living in Florida.*)

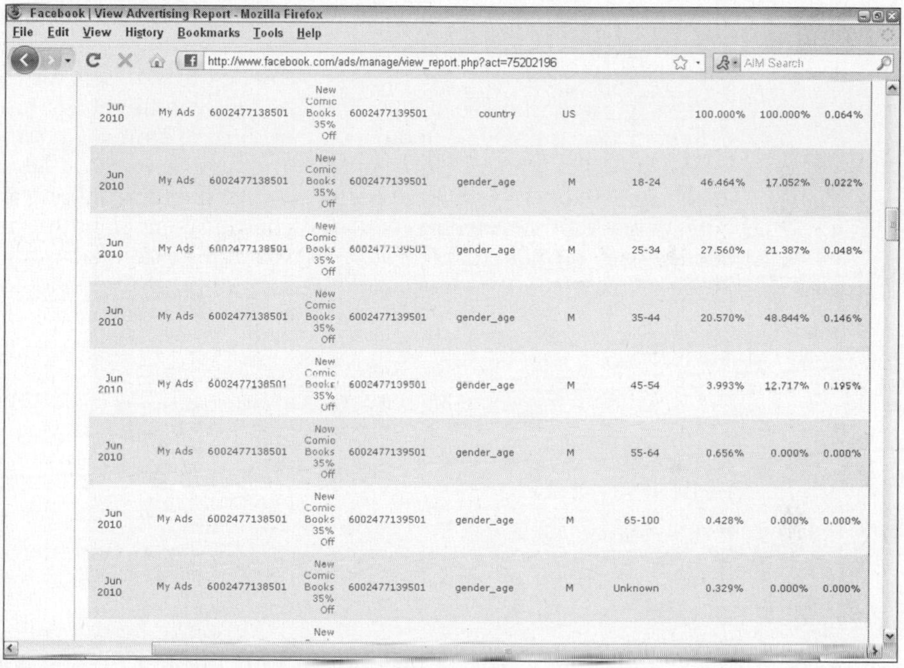

Jun 2010	My Ads	6002477138501	New Comic Books 35% Off	6002477139501	country	US		100.000%	100.000%	0.064%
Jun 2010	My Ads	6002477138501	New Comic Books 35% Off	6002477139501	gender_age	M	18-24	46.464%	17.052%	0.022%
Jun 2010	My Ads	6002477138501	New Comic Books 35% Off	6002477139501	gender_age	M	25-34	27.560%	21.387%	0.048%
Jun 2010	My Ads	6002477138501	New Comic Books 35% Off	6002477139501	gender_age	M	35-44	20.570%	48.844%	0.146%
Jun 2010	My Ads	6002477138501	New Comic Books 35% Off	6002477139501	gender_age	M	45-54	3.993%	12.717%	0.195%
Jun 2010	My Ads	6002477138501	New Comic Books 35% Off	6002477139501	gender_age	M	55-64	0.656%	0.000%	0.000%
Jun 2010	My Ads	6002477138501	New Comic Books 35% Off	6002477139501	gender_age	M	65-100	0.428%	0.000%	0.000%
Jun 2010	My Ads	6002477138501	New Comic Books 35% Off	6002477139501	gender_age	M	Unknown	0.329%	0.000%	0.000%

Figure 8-2: See Responder Demographics for your Facebook Ads.

There were some very interesting results from our example report as well as some very interesting lessons you can take away from this report that can help you with your main campaigns:

- **Which segments give you the best click rates?** Although comic books might skew to a younger audience, the best click rate in our example occurred for the 35–44 age range (0.146%, more than three times the 25–34 percentage and almost seven times the 18–24 percentage). The second-best campaign came from the 45–54 age range. Although this age range saw about 4% of all impressions, these viewers responded with a 0.192% click rate, which is the best click rate we have seen in this report and higher than average. Therefore, we might want to now test an ad that specifically targets 35–55-year-old males.
- **What expected segments perform better or worse than expected?** You will likely have preconceived ideas about what age ranges should be your best and worst customers, for example, but your reports might

show you a different theory. For example, we ran an ad campaign for Team Terrapin, a sailing team that took part in the biennial Newport to Bahamas race. The age breakdowns for the initial ad campaign are shown in Figure 8-3. The highest CTR rates were achieved with men ages 45 and older, but there was a decent response from females ages 35 and older, and that group had a better CTR than younger men (age 18–35). So, if you wanted to have custom age ranges, you might pick males and females age 35 and older.

✔ **What unexpected segments show promising results**? You can sort your entire report by a field like CTR so that you can see a list of your highest CTRs for a campaign, like that shown in Figure 8-4. This way, you can see segments that are high performers that you might not have included in your big campaigns. In our example, certain states like Kansas and Alabama had better CTRs than any other age or location filter. When you see an unexpected segment perform well, consider running additional tests just on those segments to see whether you can harness that audience or determine that the success was more of a fluke.

Figure 8-3: Pick the demographics of people who pick your ad.

Date	Campaign Name	Ad Name	Demographic	Bucket 1	Bucket 2	% of Impressions	% of Clickers	CTR
Jun 2010	Team Terrapin	Team Terrapin	country	US		100.000%	100.000%	0.311%
Jun 2010	Team Terrapin	Team Terrapin	gender_age	F	18-24	20.238%	3.465%	0.052%
Jun 2010	Team Terrapin	Team Terrapin	gender_age	F	25-34	9.722%	4.290%	0.133%
Jun 2010	Team Terrapin	Team Terrapin	gender_age	F	35-44	7.164%	6.434%	0.270%
Jun 2010	Team Terrapin	Team Terrapin	gender_age	F	45-54	7.840%	12.601%	0.483%
Jun 2010	Team Terrapin	Team Terrapin	gender_age	F	55-64	3.498%	3.217%	0.277%
Jun 2010	Team Terrapin	Team Terrapin	gender_age	F	65-100	0.739%	1.340%	0.546%
Jun 2010	Team Terrapin	Team Terrapin	gender_age	F	Unknown	0.269%	0.000%	0.000%
Jun 2010	Team Terrapin	Team Terrapin	gender_age	M	18-24	18.495%	12.064%	0.196%
Jun 2010	Team Terrapin	Team Terrapin	gender_age	M	25-34	11.024%	10.188%	0.278%
Jun 2010	Team Terrapin	Team Terrapin	gender_age	M	35-44	7.612%	12.064%	0.477%
Jun 2010	Team Terrapin	Team Terrapin	gender_age	M	45-54	6.802%	16.890%	0.747%
Jun 2010	Team Terrapin	Team Terrapin	gender_age	M	55-64	3.681%	13.673%	1.117%
Jun 2010	Team Terrapin	Team Terrapin	gender_age	M	65-100	1.100%	3.753%	1.026%
Jun 2010	Team Terrapin	Team Terrapin	gender_age	M	Unknown	0.248%	0.000%	0.000%
Jun 2010	Team Terrapin	Team Terrapin	gender_age	Unknown	18-24	0.672%	0.000%	0.000%
Jun 2010	Team Terrapin	Team Terrapin	gender_age	Unknown	25-34	0.287%	0.000%	0.000%
Jun 2010	Team Terrapin	Team Terrapin	gender_age	Unknown	35-44	0.282%	0.000%	0.000%
Jun 2010	Team Terrapin	Team Terrapin	gender_age	Unknown	45-54	0.233%	0.000%	0.000%
Jun 2010	Team Terrapin	Team Terrapin	region	Unknown		0.753%	0.000%	0.000%

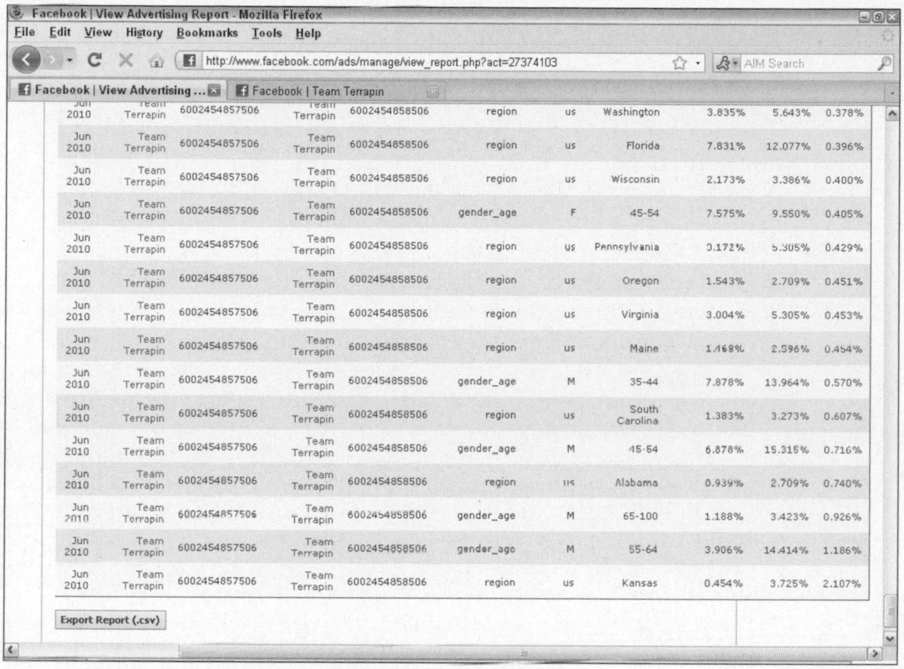

Figure 8-4:
Find out whose "hidden gem" segment groups who like your ad.

Facebook | View Advertising Report - Mozilla Firefox

File Edit View History Bookmarks Tools Help

http://www.facebook.com/ads/manage/view_report.php?act=27374103 — AIM Search

Facebook | View Advertising ...   Facebook | Team Terrapin

Date	Team	Account	Team	Account	Type	Country	Value	%	%	%
Jun 2010	Team Terrapin	6002454857506	Team Terrapin	6002454858506	region	us	Washington	3.835%	5.643%	0.378%
Jun 2010	Team Terrapin	6002454857506	Team Terrapin	6002454858506	region	us	Florida	7.831%	12.077%	0.396%
Jun 2010	Team Terrapin	6002454857506	Team Terrapin	6002454858506	region	us	Wisconsin	2.173%	3.386%	0.400%
Jun 2010	Team Terrapin	6002454857506	Team Terrapin	6002454858506	gender_age	F	45-54	7.575%	9.550%	0.405%
Jun 2010	Team Terrapin	6002454857506	Team Terrapin	6002454858506	region	us	Pennsylvania	3.172%	5.305%	0.429%
Jun 2010	Team Terrapin	6002454857506	Team Terrapin	6002454858506	region	us	Oregon	1.543%	2.709%	0.451%
Jun 2010	Team Terrapin	6002454857506	Team Terrapin	6002454858506	region	us	Virginia	3.004%	5.305%	0.453%
Jun 2010	Team Terrapin	6002454857506	Team Terrapin	6002454858506	region	us	Maine	1.468%	2.596%	0.454%
Jun 2010	Team Terrapin	6002454857506	Team Terrapin	6002454858506	gender_age	M	35-44	7.878%	13.964%	0.570%
Jun 2010	Team Terrapin	6002454857506	Team Terrapin	6002454858506	region	us	South Carolina	1.383%	3.273%	0.607%
Jun 2010	Team Terrapin	6002454857506	Team Terrapin	6002454858506	gender_age	M	45-54	6.878%	15.315%	0.716%
Jun 2010	Team Terrapin	6002454857506	Team Terrapin	6002454858506	region	us	Alabama	0.939%	2.709%	0.740%
Jun 2010	Team Terrapin	6002454857506	Team Terrapin	6002454858506	gender_age	M	65-100	1.188%	3.423%	0.926%
Jun 2010	Team Terrapin	6002454857506	Team Terrapin	6002454858506	gender_age	M	55-64	3.906%	14.414%	1.186%
Jun 2010	Team Terrapin	6002454857506	Team Terrapin	6002454858506	region	us	Kansas	0.454%	3.725%	2.107%

Export Report (.csv)

Optimizing Your Campaign

After you run some test campaigns and gather initial data about how your Facebook Ads are performing, you can improve your overall results by going over this information and optimizing your campaign to try and get the biggest bang for your buck. This is known as *optimizing your campaign.* Your goal in optimizing your campaign is to increase your click-through rate or generate more sales or responses to your call to action by picking from your test ads the elements of your campaign that elicited the greatest response. Although, of course, you're not guaranteed a specific number of clicks or impressions based on your optimization, you should be able to improve your ad effectiveness through these steps we discuss in this section.

Refining bid range pricing on your ads

One of the big discussions we've had with Facebook advertisers is coming up with an appropriate bid for your CPC campaigns. Facebook has its estimated bid ranges when you create an ad with targeting filters, but Facebook will consider ads with lower bid prices, especially for words or areas that are not heavily used or represented in their database and therefore have little to no competition from other advertisers. For example, ads that appeal more to an older audience, such as for nursing homes or medical devices, would probably cost less to run as an advertisement than something that matters to Facebook's core youth audience, such as soda pop, skateboarding, or Japanese animation.

As you run your test campaigns, pull up reports to see what bids are being accepted. For example, in one of our CPC test campaigns for a Facebook for Business ad, we were given a bid range of $2.44 to $3.53 per click, but we decided to try different (lower) bid prices to test that effectiveness. Remember, in Facebook Ads, you get to pick the bid price that you are willing to pay based on the bid model you chose, either a bid price per click received on your ad or a bid price to show your ad 1,000 times. (We discuss bids and pricing in more depth in Chapter 4.)

During our first week, when we had put in lower bids, we got several clicks below $1 per click, as low as $0.39. (See the Avg. CPC ($) column in Figure 8-5.) We raised our bid to $1 and then $1.25. Within a couple of days at each bid level, we were seeing the same CTR and number of impressions with a low daily budget. No matter that we were raising our bid price to as high as $1.50, we were only getting 4–5 clicks per day, which resulted in an average CPC of $1 to $1.25. (See Figure 8-6.)

Unfortunately, when we raised our bid price, we didn't see the corresponding jump in actions taken — although, to be fair, we used a low daily budget so the sample size wasn't that large. In this particular example, we then took a look at a test campaign using a CPM pricing model. We had put in a bid of $0.20 per 1,000 impressions, figuring that we would get as many as 25,000 impressions per day with a $5 sample daily budget. Our results for the first week showed a lower CPM than we were expecting, averaging $0.11 on most days, resulting in an average of 45,000 impressions per day, as you can see in Figure 8-7.

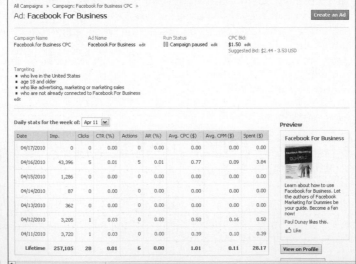

Figure 8-5:
We tested
our click-
through rate
at low ad
bid prices...

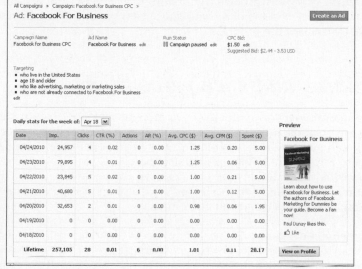

Figure 8-6: and higher bid prices that were still below the recommended range.

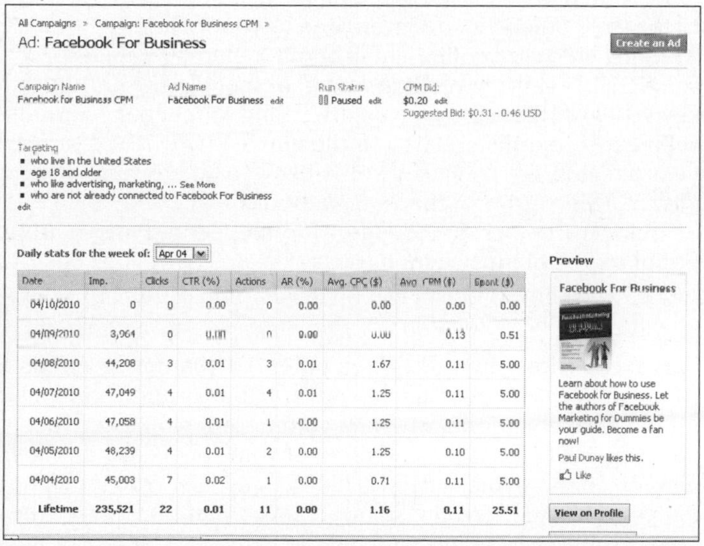

Figure 8-7: We looked at our ad performance in a CPM model.

Our results also showed that our CTR from this pricing model was more than $1 per click, averaging $1.25 per click for this week, and we were achieving a click-through rate of 0.01%. However, the number of people who took action beyond clicking the ad was much better in this campaign than the previous CPC example. In total, we grew the "Facebook for Business" Page to almost 1000 fans, which doubled the audience for this Page ad, with a small investment of dollars using Facebook Ads.

Therefore, going forward, we would probably adopt a CPM pricing model for our main campaigns of this ad. These are the kinds of decisions you can make by tracking the progress of your initial test ad campaigns.

Gaining audience perceptions

Your interactions with potential customers on Facebook is more like an ongoing conversation, where the dialogue can last for a long or short time, and your audience will build their impression of you over time. Therefore, you need to be aware of how your audience perceives you when you run your ad campaigns and maintain your business Page on Facebook. This can be done not only by watching your Ad Reports but also by looking at your Page statistics and comments from your customers.

As you build out your presence using Facebook Ads to gain and maintain your customer base, here are some tips to keep in mind:

- **Stay relevant to your customers.** As you use your targeting filters to reach out to potential customers, keep in mind that you might want to target people who are interested in your brand but don't mention it by name on their profile. Think about including similar products and services in your keyword targeting, or include the activities or lifestyle keywords of the audience you are trying to reach. For example, if you're selling merchandise related to the movie _Twilight_ and targeting 13–18 year old girls, try using keywords like "Team Edward" and "Stephanie Meyer" (the author of the _Twilight_ books). Then, keep an eye on your Responder Demographics report for unexpected information, such as a popular type of music among a clear majority of your customers or perhaps your responders all like the same television show, like _Family Guy_ or _The Vampire Diaries_.

- **Stay fresh with your ads.** When potential customers or Fans see the same ad over and over again, you and your brand can appear stale and unimpressive, and this will hurt your conversion rate. Therefore, consider updating at least one aspect of your ad every few days, even if it's just the color or image used. This is especially true if you notice declining performance with the same ad over time. Don't stray too far from the colors you use to brand yourself and your company. Perhaps use subtle shades, or change the wording instead of the colors or image.

- **Try an unconventional approach (think outside the box).** Try something you might not expect to work. For example, reach out to potential users by picking keywords or filters that might not seem obvious at first but have some relevance. For example, you might start marketing your chocolates or flowers to men who update their status to "In a Relationship" because now they are more likely to need those items for their new girlfriends. It's a little cliché, but perhaps if you target people who like a new movie about spirituality to try your spirituality Web site, you are feeding off something else that has opened your potential customer's horizons (for example, targeting people who liked the movie *Ocean's Eleven* or *The Hangover* to take a trip to Las Vegas).

Any keyword on a user's Facebook profile is something that person identified and added to his profile voluntarily, so it's got a lot more weight than some random keyword automatically typed into a search engine box, for example. .

✔ **Consider an appropriate call to action.** With other ad systems, like Google AdWords, you know your audience is already searching for something, so you can go for the direct sale and gear your ads toward product sales. With Facebook, though, you're creating and maintaining a conversation, but you also shouldn't be afraid to ask for something, like their name and e-mail address for your mailing list. Give away something for free to pique interest and encourage participation, like the ads shown in Figure 8-8. You may think that you have to "take things slow" to build the audience trust, but never neglect some form of the call to action.

Figure 8-8:
Use free information or products to create a compelling call to action.

As you run different campaigns, and if you're promoting a Facebook Page or Event, consider using Facebook Insights to get a better picture of how your Fans and customers are interacting with your Facebook elements. We discuss Facebook Insights in depth in the upcoming section, "Measuring Insights with Facebook Insights."

Maximizing results

As you run test campaigns and gain insight into the "buying public" that you hope to interact with on Facebook, your goal is to maximize the results of your overall Facebook Ad campaign. The way to do this is to run test campaigns and then make judgment calls based on the results of the efforts you've done so far.

One of the greatest advantages of Facebook Ads as opposed to other platforms is the ability to target your ads to a very specific demographic, so your ads display only to the group you specify. As you refine your ads, you can work toward refining your campaigns, so only the best matches to your ad are going to be shown that ad impression, which should improve your click-through ratio and number of actions taken.

As an example, look at a test ad campaign we ran. Initially, we targeted all males between ages 13–34 for a specific campaign for "young males." After running the campaign for a test period, we can see from the Responder Demographic report (shown in Figure 8-9) that more than 94% of the people receiving the ad are between the ages of 13 and 17. Therefore, we can refine the targeting filter to target males age 13–17 to maximize our reach to this demographic, which seems to be the ideal segment given our other factors.

Data from this report also showed us that we should also write a new ad to target the 18–34 year old males specifically, and try to improve our percentages for that demographic. Obviously, you don't want to dismiss a targeting factor based on one campaign, but rather start clean or use a different approach with segments you are not reaching effectively with current campaigns.

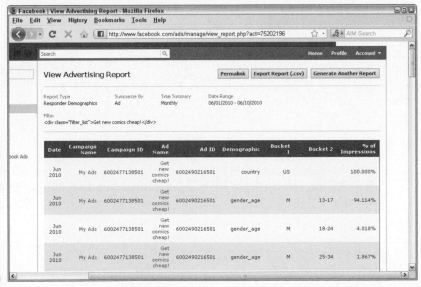

Figure 8-9:
Use responder information to highly target your ads.

Another way to maximize your results is to run some test campaigns to see what new information or insight you gain from those campaigns. You then use that information to redirect or focus your campaign to go after a greater or more targeted audience. For example, if you run a test campaign with your initial targeting factors, you can then run the Responder Profiles report (see Figure 8-10) to see actual interests, books, movies, and so on that are part of the profiles of people who clicked your ad. After you know these specific keywords, you can add them to your campaigns going forward and perhaps relax some of your existing targeting filters to try and reach a larger, but more focused, audience.

You can also tailor your ads to directly match the stated interests of your audience. If people clicking a comic book ad have Iron Man as an Interest, write an ad that targets Iron Man fans instead of just comic book fans. Either add targeted keywords into your title or rewrite your ad to match the stated interest. Even better, you can create a split ad test where you have one ad with the new keyword inserted into the title and one ad without the keyword in the title. If the ad with the new keyword performs better, you know to use that ad going forward.

Therefore, pay attention to your audience, whether they are potential customers or existing fans of your brand. Facebook makes it easier to keep track of your audience, and now you can directly measure your current audience with Facebook Insights.

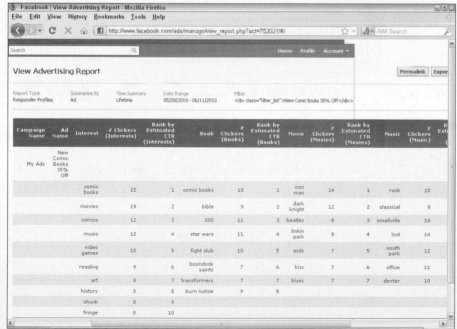

Figure 8-10:
Use responder profile information to refine your ads.

Measuring Insights with Facebook Insights

When you create your own Facebook business Page or set up your own Facebook Event for people to RSVP, you're also setting up the capability to track the usage of that Page or Event through the Facebook Insights program. This program is designed by Facebook to give you "insight" into how your Facebook Page or Event is being seen and used by their users, along with hard data that can prove useful when optimizing an ad campaign to increase traffic to these objects. You would use Ads Manager when you need statistics specifically about your ad campaigns, and Insights for usage statistics on how your Pages or Events are being seen by Facebook users.

Facebook Insights separates the information into two main areas:

- Fans
- Interactions

The Fans section contains more information about the active Fans on your business Page, and the Interactions section covers the feedback left by your Fans and the activity on the various tabs within your Facebook business Page.

When you are ready to access Facebook Insights, follow these steps:

1. **From your Facebook home page, click the Ads and Pages link along the left side of the screen.**

2. **Once you get to your Ads Manager home screen, click the Pages link along the left side of the screen.**

   You are taken to a summary of the Facebook Pages where you are an administrator, like in Figure 8-11.

3. **Click the View Insights link below the Page header that you wish to study.**

   In our example, we would click the View Insights link below the So Cal Comic Con header to view that Facebook business Page.

Users who Like your Page

Once you have pulled up the Insights report for your Facebook Page, you will notice two sections: The Users graph and the Interactions graph. Click the Details link for your Users report to first see the activity report for your Users, like in Figure 8-12. You will see the statistics for

✔ Daily Active Users

✔ Daily New Likes

✔ Total Likes (running count)

Figure 8-11:
You can
view
Insights
from your
Pages
screen.

View Insights link

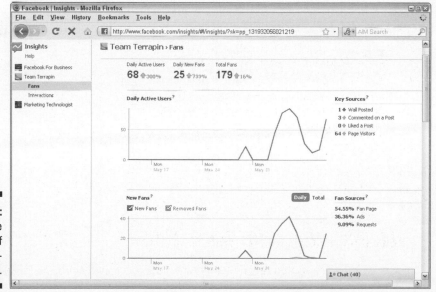

Figure 8-12:
See the
usage of
your busi-
ness Page.

You will also see a Key Sources list to show you the number of people who performed certain actions (like Commented on a Post or Liked a Post) associated with your business Page. Look at the up or down arrows to see whether this level of activity is higher or lower than recent data, which gives you a real-time view on whether activity is on the rise or decline, in a function list display.

Below the Daily Active Users graph, you can view the graph for New Likes to your Page over a given time period. Most importantly, to the side of the graph is the list of Sources, which indicates the page or source where each person decided to Like your Page, and each sources' overall percentage. In the given example, almost 55% of new Likes clicked the Like button from the business Page itself, and more than 36% of new Fans clicked the Like link from a targeted Facebook Ad.

When running test campaigns, you can see over time whether the percentage of new likes from your ads is going up or down, which can indicate whether the ad is a success or not. Keep in mind that if someone clicks the title of your ad to view your Facebook business Page first, and then clicks the Like link, the source for that user will show up as your Facebook Page. The click will still register in your Advertising Performance report, so you can measure progress with that report.

Click the Total link next to Sources to see a graph of your total User base to get a clear trend of how much your base is improving, stagnating, or decreasing, as shown in Figure 8-13.

Figure 8-13:
See the trend for your overall Fan base on Facebook.

User demographics

You might have sales or survey data to back up your idea of your business's target groups and markets, but one way to verify who is interested in your business is to look at your Facebook Insights that measure user demographics and see whether those statistics sync up with your knowledge of your customer base.

After you click the See Details from your Users section, scroll down until you get to the Demographics section, as shown in Figure 8-14. Here, Facebook breaks down the Users base from your Facebook Page into age and gender ranges, along with a short list of the top countries, cities, and languages represented in your user base.

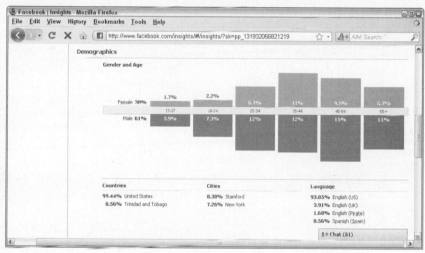

Figure 8-14: Discover the demographic composite of your Facebook Page user group.

As you look over the demographics, here are some questions you should ask yourself that might affect your campaign:

- ✔ **Am I targeting a user segment that isn't interested?** You can present your ad to a targeted niche of users, but if they keep getting presented the ad and don't click to Like your page, perhaps they are the wrong target. One of the best clues is your Fan demographics, which could show that regardless of how they found your Page, certain user segments aren't interested in Liking you.

- ✔ **Am I ignoring a user segment that might want to be Fans?** This is the opposite of the previous point, as here the question is, should I be targeting a user group with my ads that seem to like my business Page? Perhaps your demographics show that a user segment that you are *not* targeting is still a measurable percentage of your user base because they're finding your Page through other means. If you see support for this user segment that isn't bolstered by advertising, consider running a campaign going after more of these potential users.

✔ **Should I consider an international campaign?** A number of small businesses run initial campaigns that target only their home country, like the United States. However, your Fan base might indicate that your Page has international appeal, which would cause new members from overseas to sign up when they see something they like on a U.S. friend's Facebook Page, for example. When you see your demographic base begin to get global, consider running some international test ads to see what happens.

User Page Views

After you get someone to Like your Facebook Page — the first test — the real test comes in a user's ongoing, regular use of your Facebook Page, which comes into view specifically with the Page Views Activity graph within Facebook Insights. This graph (see Figure 8-15) breaks down the amount of Page Views (and amount of Unique Page Views) per day. You can see the day-by-day count of Page Views and Unique Views in the chart, and more importantly, the list of which tabs within your Facebook Page attracted the most attention. Typically, your Wall is your highest viewed tab because that's what users see upon default (unless you set another page as your default, which we discuss in Chapter 7) when they go to your Page.

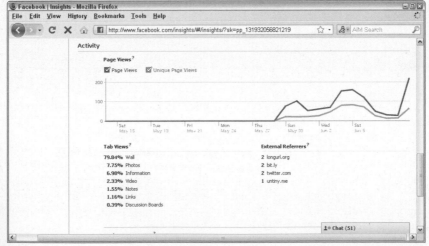

Figure 8-15: See which pages your users are viewing.

Pay attention to the other tabs your users are going to, especially if you see these numbers going up over time. Perhaps one of your test campaigns redirected users to a new tab on your Page. That tab might make an excellent landing page for your main campaigns, especially if that tab enjoys a sustained amount of usage after you end the test campaign.

The other list of value in this section is the External Referrers list, off to the right side of the Tabs View list. This list shows you the Web sites of the top referring domains that your Fans are coming from when coming to your Page. This list can give you a good idea whether your other ad campaigns (Google AdWords campaigns; or other marketing initiatives, such as banner ads, blog posts, or articles) are sending traffic directly to your Facebook Page.

Media consumption

The last part of the Users Details section is meaningful to those of you who incorporate media (photos, audio clips, or video clips) into your Facebook Page. Facebook has a separate measurement for the amount of *media consumption:* that is, video and audio clips played as well as photos viewed on your Facebook Page. You can see this by scrolling to the bottom of the page to view the Media Consumption chart, as shown in Figure 8-16. Facebook breaks apart the three different media views available on your page so you can view each category separately.

Like the other charts we discuss in this chapter, you're looking for any consistent trends, like an upward tick in the number of viewers for a given category. Perhaps you uploaded a series of video clips on your business Page and you want to see whether your current and new Fans are viewing those clips.

Figure 8-16: See how much media your users are viewing on your Facebook Page.

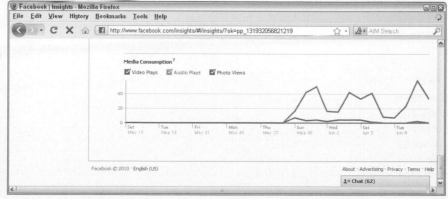

Story and discussion feedback

For those of you who are engaging your Facebook Page users, click the See Details link for your Interactions report within Facebook Insights to get a better idea of how those users are responding to you and each other within your Facebook Page. The details for the Interactions report shows a number of helpful pieces of information, as you can see in Figure 8-17.

Every time you post a story on your Facebook Page, your users can see it in their News Feed, and they can interact with it in a few ways, which Facebook tracks with this report. Specifically, they can

- ✔ **Like** your story, by clicking Like after the story mention
- ✔ **Comment** on your story, by clicking the Comment link and writing their comment underneath
- ✔ **Unsubscribe** from your page, which removes any future stories from their News Feed

You can see an individual day's number for any category by rolling over the data point with your mouse until a black box appears with the daily data, as shown in Figure 8-18.

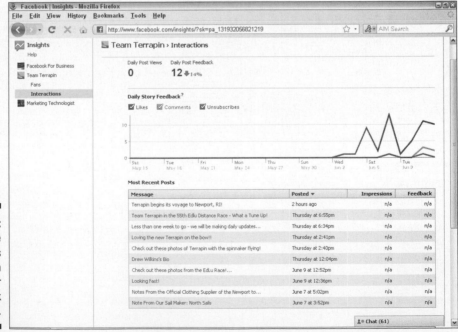

Figure 8-18:
Use your
mouse to
detect daily
interaction
numbers.

Underneath your Daily Story Feedback report are the most recent posts to
your Facebook Page, along with the time you posted to your Facebook Page.
In some cases, you see the number of Impressions each post got, along with
the amount of feedback generated by each post.

Page Activity (Mentions, Reviews, Discussions, Videos, Photos)

The other part of the Interactions Detail report is the graph showing the
amount of Daily Page Activity your Fans are generating on your Page. Unlike
the Daily Fan Views graph, this chart (see Figure 8-19) shows you how many
times your Fans performed an action on one of your Page views, whether
they wrote on your Page Wall, uploaded their own photo or video to the Fan
Photos section, wrote reviews (if you enabled that feature), created posts on
your Discussion Board (if you enabled that feature), or wrote a mention of
your Page in their own Status Update or Wall posts to their friends.

Figure 8-19:
See how
many
actions your
Fans are
taking with
your Page in
this report.

Chapter 9

Tracking Conversions to Sales

In This Chapter

▶ Defining and categorizing your lead conversion

▶ Turning a lead into a sale

▶ Calculating your Return on Investment

▶ Tracking your conversions

*B*y now, your Facebook Ad campaign should be off and running. It's time to shift gears a little and talk about what happens after viewers start showing up at your Web site or your Facebook Page. At this point, the Facebook Ad has done the first few parts: It introduced your product or service to a new user, piqued that user's interest, and enticed the user to click the ad to learn more. Now it's time to complete that process with conversions and sales.

In this chapter, we discuss the concepts of conversions, leads, and actual sales (or actions, depending on your ultimate goals); and we describe the best ways to lead as many customers through the cycle as you can. We discuss actions and processes that don't necessarily require Facebook — but, don't worry, because Facebook can be an assistant in these steps as well.

Setting Up a Process to Convert a Lead to a Sale

After you get someone interested, naturally the next question is, "Now what?" As you use Facebook Ads to collect leads, you will want to guide people to the end of your sales cycle. However, this means different things for different people. For some people, the end of the sales cycle means ordering products from your business (and maybe even becoming repeat customers of your business), and for others, it might simply be joining a mailing list and remaining active on the mailing list by not unsubscribing and/or responding to offers from the list owner.

Defining a conversion

Before you take any customer down a road, you first need to map it out. Nothing confuses a customer more than a business that isn't sending a consistent message. Therefore, you (and your business) need to decide what constitutes a *conversion,* or the transformation of a lead to a customer, member, or user. Typically, a conversion occurs when this lead responds to your call to action by performing that action. Different levels of conversion include when some people take the full action offered (like ordering a product), while others can take another action that doesn't have the same financial impact but still converts them from a lead to a user (like joining a mailing list without ordering anything).

Being able to measure conversions lets you know whether your Facebook Ad campaign is successful, based on comparing the costs of the campaign against the effect you see from conversions. This process also lets you know whether to spend more or less in your campaigns, or perhaps whether you need to change something (perhaps a target or keyword) in your campaigns. After all, if you're spending $10 to get $5 worth of benefit, that's a sure-fire way to go quickly into debt. Then again, based on the long-term or lifetime value of a new customer, spending $10 to gain a lead could simply be considered a simple investment called the *customer acquisition cost,* which many businesses are used to paying.

What constitutes a conversion depends on your normal business processes and how Facebook, in general, factors into your business model. So how should you define a conversion? Here are some questions you should think about to help you figure that out:

✔ **What is your average lead time between getting a lead and converting that lead?** In other words, on average, how long is the interval between someone finding out about your business and then taking action? For ordering a product online, the lead time can be almost instantaneous. The user sees the offer and decides right away that he has to order the product — maybe because you throw in a few free gifts if the order is made right away. Other businesses (like those businesses that operate as a B2B, or Business to Business sales) focus on building a list of people and then sending them weekly or monthly e-mails with newsletters or product offers. Here, the lead time might be quick, or it might be 6 to 12 months until their first big order. For service companies, the lead time could be months or almost a year until the user needs that particular service. Say that you advertise carpet cleaning: A customer might see your ad but not take advantage of your services until her next carpet cleaning, which could be months away.

✔ **What is the specific call to action in your Facebook Ad?** In other words, what is your specific offer to the customer? If you're giving away a free product, like a white paper or a demo version of your software (like eVoice's transcription service, as shown in Figure 9-1), a conversion occurs when a user accepts your free product. At that point, the job of further converting that person from free user to paying customer is completely up to you, seeing as how the ad in question did its job. If your call to action is for someone to join your Facebook business Page, any conversions after that point are attributable to your business's normal processes, not the initial ad campaign.

✔ **Is there a specific action that a user needs to perform on your Web site?** In other words, is the customer performing the correct steps on your Web site to be counted as a conversion due to your ad? It's not enough that the customer responded to your call to action. Perhaps that customer has to complete each step properly so you can count them properly. In some cases, businesses make a special offer "for Facebook subscribers" that requires them to enter a special code on the business's Web site. (For example, MyPartyShirt.com offers a 10% discount if you enter its Facebook Ad code, as seen in Figure 9-2.) Here, you could consider a conversion only those orders that use the special code, or you could consider any order that came from that initial click as a conversion. Then again, if your main goal is exposure rather than sales, the user arriving at your Web site might be your conversion.

Figure 9-1:
Your conversion can be defined by your specific offer or call to action, like a free trial.

Figure 9-2:
Use a unique offer code to track conversions from your Facebook Ads.

If you do other forms of online advertising, you might consider your conversions using Facebook Ads to be similar to whatever you established as your conversion using those systems. In some cases, especially if you're trying to build up a Facebook following, it might not be fair to compare your Facebook Ads conversions with those of your other online campaigns. For example, a conversion from another platform, like Google AdWords, could be the sale of the advertised product, or an immediate download of a free product.

Understanding the types of conversions

Many different types of businesses use Facebook to advertise, and because of that, you can find lots of different types of conversions there. When we take a look at the Ad Board from one of our profiles, we see all sorts of businesses, services, platforms, products, and people. Each of these ads has a different conversion, and some ads offer more than one type of conversion.

Some of the most common types of conversions from Facebook Ads are the following:

- **Membership:** A user becomes a member of your Web site or a Fan of your Facebook Page. The user's basic profile information becomes available to you, but there is no explicit promise of regular, upcoming communication. In many cases, the user chooses to get more involved by joining specific lists, or by reading about and responding to an offer. When users are members of your Facebook Page, they implicitly agree to receive your updates and see those posts on their Wall, and have the option to use the tabs within your Facebook Page. As an example, when General Mills was looking to build a Chex Mix Fan base on Facebook, it ran an ad campaign encouraging users to join the Facebook Page where people discuss . . . yes, you guessed it, Chex Mix! (See Figure 9-3.)

- **Mailing list:** Users sign up for a free newsletter or other customer list, with the explicit understanding that they are agreeing to receive future communication from you, most often with a specific theme or subject in mind (such as upcoming tips for weight loss). This is different from membership because, in the case of being on a mailing list, the owner of the list typically communicates in a one-way fashion with the list members. In a membership situation, the conversation is two-way, as members are active and talk with each other and the membership site owner.

- **Contest/mailing list:** Users respond to a contest or promotion, where they provide their basic information in hopes of winning a prize, like the Pala Play & Stay giveaway shown in Figure 9-4. They are either automatically added to a mailing list and can opt out, or they can opt in to a mailing list with the expectation of future communication. You can track the number of contest entries resulting from a Facebook Ad promotion.

✔ **Become a lead:** Users respond to your ad by completing a form stating their full contact information; answering any initial questions you may have; and granting permission for you to send them information regarding a product or service, and, in some cases, granting the advertiser the right to contact them specifically to give them additional information about the offer (such as, for example, when a user wants an application packet to apply to graduate school or wants to be a franchisee of your business).

✔ **Trial customer:** Users sign up for a free download of your product or a trial membership on your paid membership site (like Clickable's 15-day trial, seen in Figure 9-5), or they can receive an e-mailed version of your product. The user understands that this item is free for a limited amount of time or usage, and will be prompted to make a full version purchase at the end of their trial. In some cases, especially for service businesses like restaurants, the trial could be a coupon for a discounted or free item (like Pick Up Stix's $5 chicken combo with drink, as shown in Figure 9-6), which the customer must remit at your place of business.

Figure 9-3:
The Chex Mix Facebook Ad gathers Facebook users to talk about their favorite snack mix.

Figure 9-4:
A Facebook Ad contest promotion.

✔ **Paying customer:** Users place an order on your Web site or through your Facebook Page, typically with a special promotion or offer they saw on your Facebook Ad, like a percentage discount or free shipping. The users are added to your customer database and can expect to receive communication not only about their order but also upcoming promotions and offers on your Web site.

✔ **Paid membership:** A user decides to join your paid membership service (typically on a monthly basis) immediately after clicking your ad, or buys a product with a recurring monthly subscription cost, like a cell phone or online game accounts. The user is added to your customer database and provides a billing method that is kept on file by your business to process the recurring charge.

Figure 9-5:
Clickable
uses
Facebook
Ads to
promote a
15-day trial
of its
software.

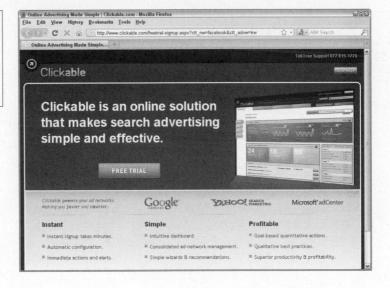

Figure 9-6:
Give away
discount
coupons to
bring people
into your
local busi-
ness.

There are, of course, other types of conversions, as people find new and interesting ways to use Facebook Ads to fit their needs. (See Chapter 15 for ten nontraditional ad campaign ideas.) The bottom line is this: In order to properly measure and track your conversions, you need to know what you're measuring exactly. After you figure that out, you're ready to move on.

Converting a lead

Regardless of whether you are in sales, you should always be thoughtful and deliberate when working with new leads to help convert them from users to customers. In some ways, the sales process is like dating someone, so you'd better be careful and respectful and get to know the person before you try to take the relationship to the next level.

Because you gathered this lead using Facebook, it's usually a good idea to consider the relationship marketing arena instead of direct sales, for example. Some companies have their "secret sauce" or "patented methods" for closing a sale and converting a lead into a customer — and if that's you, great! If that's not you, well, don't worry; there are general business and sales concepts to consider using for your business, such as the following:

- ✔ **Listen to your customer.** This is a very clichéd saying, but there's a reason why it's a cliché. With Facebook, you actually have the power to listen because your users can leave comments; make Wall posts; and in some cases, upload pictures, video, and other media to be part of the conversation. Reward your active prospects with attentive service, previews of upcoming products, and easy access whenever possible. Many companies use their Facebook presence (as well as Twitter and Web site presences) to handle customer service concerns as quickly and responsively as possible. It's best to end potentially harmful squabbles before things escalate. One great example is Coca-Cola, which regularly replies to customer issues (see Figure 9-7) through its Page's Wall and discussion board. (That's part of the reason why Coke has millions and millions of Facebook Fans.)

- ✔ **Be consistent when you communicate.** If you told a user that she's signing up for a monthly newsletter, don't send her a weekly newsletter. The opposite situation is just as true. Deliver what you say you're going to deliver so you're not overwhelming or underwhelming your users. If users are signing up for a newsletter or any regular communications, don't just send out product sales sheets. If you can't provide some original or useful content, don't just send out anything. You can't expect users to accept whatever you send out.

- ✔ **Make the offer enticing.** People respond to a good offer, especially if it makes sense to them. At this point, the user has already demonstrated some interest, and your ad campaign has used targeting to make sure the user is a better fit than just an average consumer. Because you're dealing with a better prospect than average, don't be afraid to sweeten the deal a little. Odds are good that your conversion rates will be higher with an interested audience.

✔ **At some point, ask for the sale.** You can be nice, open, friendly, and helpful forever, but you will never survive if you don't ask for the sale. There's a good reason why so many sales offers have time limits. You have to put the consumer in a position to make a decision right here and now. Although you might be afraid to ask for a sale, there's most likely a point where keep an offer alive costs more money than you'll earn if your customer says yes. Obviously, at that point, either get the sale and move on, or get out and go work on someone else. Magic Bullet has a full-featured Facebook Page, but there's also a clear Buy the Bullet button, which takes the user to an order form (see Figure 9-8) to commit to buying it.

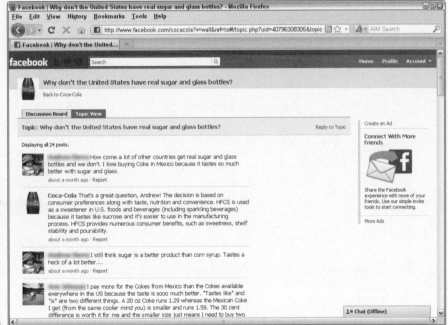

Figure 9-7: Coca-Cola responds to its customer inquiries using Facebook.

Figure 9-8:
Don't be
afraid to
present your
offer and
ask for the
sale.

Following Up with Your Leads

Ah, communication. You're sitting on a pile of customer leads, but of course, your business doesn't live on leads (unless perhaps you're a temp agency), does it? It lives on customers, orders, active participating members, and sales. Therefore, it's time to move those leads down the sales cycle and see how many of them will answer the call . . . to action, that is.

The easiest way to make this part as smooth and manageable as possible is to come up with a process for handling all these new leads on a continual basis. After the lead-generation train begins moving through the Facebook Ad campaign, it's not going to stop until the money runs out (or you shut it down). Then again, if your campaigns always outpaced your growth, you wouldn't run out of money, and the train would never stop. But hey! That could be a high-class problem to have.

In this section, we walk through some of the most routine or important points to consider in this part of the process.

Verifying a lead

So, you have your lead, and you're thinking about the best ways to convert this person to a customer, member, or user. However, converting this lead shouldn't be your only concern. You should stop and consider whether you can define this prospect as a lead.

First things first. You have to make sure that the lead meant to click the ad and respond the way they did. It may seem obvious, but sometimes mistakes are made. For example, kids sometimes use their parents' Facebook accounts and click around where they shouldn't. Or someone got someone else's user ID and password and did a lot of mischief. It happens.

The most important question you need to ask is this: How much information or data do I have on this lead? Do you just have a name and e-mail address? Do you have their address, phone number, or any other contact method for them? Do you simply have a John Doe on the list, or a 37 year-old male named John Doe who lives at 123 Easy St in Anytown and works as a Project Manager at IBM? The data you have will depend on how the lead was obtained and what information this person has already provided to get to this stage. If you're relying on Facebook for contact information, you will need to see what contact information has been marked private by the lead. If you got the initial lead through a Facebook application that your business developed, you have access to their Facebook profile data when they allowed your app, so you can look there for identifying criteria. Otherwise, you will be reliant upon whatever information that person will provide for you.

Next, you should verify the lead's interest in you and your business. Did that person actually Like your Page or RSVP to your Facebook Event? Does that qualify him or her to be contacted? Did that person fill out your Web site form connected to your ad? Did he opt in properly? Did he provide valid data for contact or follow-up? These are but some of the questions you will need to ask yourself, and the data, when figuring out which leads are worth your business' time and resources.

The most common way that a business verifies a lead is by using verification e-mail messages. If you've ever registered for something online and were told to confirm your registration by clicking a link in an e-mail, you were using a verification e-mail message. You don't need to question every user who joins your Facebook Page by clicking Like — "Hey, did you mean to click Like? Are you sure?" Users will figure out quickly enough whether your Page is the right fit for them. But when they're registering for something on your Web site, it wouldn't hurt to use a verification e-mail to make sure the right person is signing up, for the right reasons.

You can also run your data through an *address verification program,* which sifts through your data to make sure the address given is legitimate. Typically, these programs are available only for addresses in, say, the United States, but check around to see whether someone in a foreign country doesn't offer the same service for their citizens.

You can use an address verification service like Jigsaw (www.jigsaw.com), a popular service for marketers, to verify addresses and e-mails for millions of people.

Calling on a lead

When it's time to start contacting your leads, you won't need to put on your best three-piece suit and go knock on doors. Today, there is a plethora of ways to communicate personally with your leads without using the door-to-door technique.

Of course, your form of contact is limited by the amount of contact information you have about the leads in your databases. If all you have is a name and e-mail address, then e-mail is all you can use until the user provides further contact information, perhaps by completing an order or filling out a contest entry form. If all you have is a connection via Facebook, where the user Liked your Facebook Page, you can communicate either with messages directly or by posting information on Facebook for that user to see. In the latter case, it is really a "one-to-many" technique, but it's still communication between two parties.

Depending on the information you have, there are several ways to contact your lead:

✔ Facebook messages/posts (see Figure 9-9)

✔ E-mail messages

✔ Instant Messages (IMs) or chat sessions

✔ Phone calls

✔ Regular mail letters or postcards

When you contact your lead, make sure that the communication looks and sounds like it is coming from your business. This means using a corporate e-mail address; corporate letterhead or stationery; or, when contacting someone online, a corporate ID. You should also keep track of this communication (see the next section, "Tracking leads in a CRM system," for more information on why and how to do this) and remember that approaching a lead is a means to convert that lead into a customer or user.

Tracking leads in a CRM system

One of the quickest ways to a business failure is to contact a person multiple times about the same issue or to repeatedly send the same e-mail text. If you've already moved the lead into becoming a paying customer, don't keep sending e-mails or messages that treat the person like a non-user. One of the surest ways to make sure that your communication with the client is consistent, clear, and organized is to use a form of a customer relationship management (CRM) system.

A customer relationship management (CRM) system is a system that helps you keep track of all your communications and interactions with your customers. (Hence the "customer relationship" in the title.) CRM systems are very popular with sales, marketing, and customer service departments because these systems can show someone everything they know about a customer, from their demographic and personal information, to their last ten orders, to the last time a sales rep called on them, the day and time that call was placed, and the results of that call. Systems like these help companies know when it's time to call on a customer again, when it's time to back off a customer, or when it's time to fix a customer's problem quickly because of their extensive history.

The advantage of using a CRM system is that you can keep notes on your customers and partners, so every time you talk with them, you can have your notes and the company profile right next to you, especially if your boss or co-worker is 3,000 miles away working via teleconference and needs access to the same information at the same time. Furthermore, you can judge the number of interactions you've had with each customer and decide whether you need to increase or decrease the amount of communication, or use different offers or a different pitch the next time you call them.

Figure 9-9:
Respond to
your leads
with a message via
Facebook.

Examples of smaller CRM systems that any size company can use include

- **Salesforce.com (`www.salesforce.com`):** One of the most recognizable CRM brands for small business, Salesforce.com is your online solution to keeping track of your customer's information and interactions. Whether you have 1 or 1,000 employees, Salesforce.com has a solution for you. (See Figure 9-10.)

- **Microsoft Dynamics CRM (`http://crm.dynamics.com`):** Whether you want a solution integrated with Microsoft Outlook, or a purely online solution, Microsoft Dynamics CRM helps you keep track of all your customer interactions.

- **ACT! (`www.act.com`):** This solution started as a simple contact management system to help you keep track of your customers' or contacts' addresses and phone numbers. From there, the program grew to help keep track of sales calls and other important information.

- **Oncontact (`www.oncontact.com`):** This mid-market solution offers both a hosted (they maintain the software and data) and an on-premise (you support everything as part of your computer systems) solution. They offer a fully customizable solution and can offer "on-demand" pay as you go service. The winner of many awards, like the ISM Guide Top 15 CRM systems of 2009 award, OnContact is a fully featured, budget-friendly solution.

Salesforce.com is integrating Facebook and Twitter into their platform so you can keep track of your prospect's activity on these sites, giving you a more complete picture of their activity, especially if you want to monitor their interaction with your Facebook Page. You can find out more about Salesforce.com by reading *Salesforce.com For Dummies* by Tom Wong.

If you're starting off small, you can keep notes yourself in your own system. For example, if you use Microsoft Outlook, you can add all of your leads as contacts, and use the Notes section for each contact to record phone calls and interactions with that person.

If you decide to implement a CRM system to track your leads, the biggest piece of advice we can offer is this: Use that system. That means you or your company need to track every single interaction you have with your customers, whether it's an e-mail blast, a Facebook message, or a direct mailer being sent. Make sure every incoming phone call is logged in that contact's record, with time, date, person(s) they spoke to, and the purpose of the call. Also, any decisions or special offers for that person should be logged in the system so that the next time that person calls your business, you (or another employee) will know immediately what you can and cannot offer them. You can even use systems like Xobni (`www.xobni.com`) that can pull in social data about your lead based on his e-mail address, which can help you make sales and promotion decisions.

Figure 9-10:
Consider
using CRM
systems like
Salesforce.
com.

Converting a lead to a sale

There are thousands of books out there on how to "make the sale," "close the deal," or whatever terminology you like to use. Our goal is not to try and replace any of them but offer some key tips and guidance that may help you guide that lead toward your business's desired goal. Facebook is in your corner on this one, actually, because having a business Page and building a relationship with your leads is part of the relationship marketing you will need to practice to reach these goals. As you add more information through your Facebook Page, your leads get exposed to information about your organization in a way that is quiet and consistent — and probably more favorably received than junk e-mail or unsolicited phone calls.

At this point in the sales cycle, you should have a qualified lead who's heard at least part (if not all) of your presentation. Now you should

✔ Make your full offer presentation.

✔ Address any concerns from the customer.

✔ Reduce the customer's fear or apprehensions.

✔ Close the sale.

Your sales cycle does not have to be a rigid process. You can incorporate a lot of these key factors into your daily interactions with your leads via your Facebook Page and communication, so you gradually convert a percentage of your base all the time. The key here is not just go for the immediate sale, but be knowledgeable and communicative about your product line, and be available to answer questions so that people will begin to see you as an expert and a resource.

As you share your knowledge, you shouldn't be afraid to make some special offers, especially targeted offers available, for example, only to your loyal Facebook followers. When people see the information you provide on a constant basis and begin to trust you as their expert resource, like the knowledgeable guy behind the counter in their favorite local hardware store, they are much more open and receptive (and likely) to make the purchase from you instead of just some random guy with an ad.

Search for mentions of your brand on Facebook and try to answer any concerns someone is having about your products, either through a direct message or a comment underneath their post. Many companies are doing this "online customer service" on sites like Facebook, and it shows consumers that you care about answering their questions without receiving anything in return.

Viking Range Corporation's Facebook Page, for example, combines a contest to win a Viking Smoker with an entire How To section full of downloadable videos showing how to cook various food items (see Figure 9-11). Viking Range also provides recipes, product information, dealer information, and a vibrant Wall where fans discuss Viking Range products and the art of cooking with representatives from the company.

If you're trying to sell your business more than just individual products, Facebook is great for getting customers involved in your business so they have a sense of ownership and belonging. Companies can learn a thing or two from some of the biggest brands on the planet, who use robust Facebook presences to connect even more with their existing and new customer bases.

Tracking the ROI

The last step of any process like this is to step back, assess your costs and efforts, and see what your return on investment (ROI) was. Depending on the length and complexity of your sales cycle, keeping track of the ROI might not be something you can implement right away, but you should always be aware in general whether you're spending too much money without enough of a result; or whether you've found an inexpensive way to increase revenue, profits, and your business status.

When you want to track the ROI of your conversion process, you need to calculate these figures:

✔ **Profit per customer:** If your business already knows its average order size, in terms of monetary value, per customer, you can use this figure to help you calculate the average profit per customer, which is the revenue per customer minus the costs per customer. (The costs per customer is equal to the cost of the goods sold + fixed costs per order + variable costs per order.) Take into account your revenue and cost of goods sold and decide which fixed or variable expenses are part of each order from a customer. For example, if your average order size is $50, you pay on average 40% of retail price for the cost of the goods (or $20 for $50 worth of goods), and your fixed and variable costs of doing business for each order is $6 per order, then your average profit is $50 – ($20+$6), or $24 average profit per customer. If you haven't tracked these figures yet, then be able to look at a customer order and derive the approximate profit from that order, or devise a lifetime value for a customer who you've just converted to a mailing list or database. *Lifetime value* means the estimated profit you will receive from one customer for as long as the customer does business with you.

✔ **Cost of ad campaign:** You can run Facebook Reports to get your advertising costs from Facebook. (See Chapter 11 for more information on how to run Reports to get this information.)

✔ **Cost of follow-up:** Don't ignore your other costs, such as employee costs to handle follow-up inquiries, mailing out packets, and so on. Also, include some fixed costs like marketing materials, postage, and anything else related to your follow-up efforts.

✔ **Total costs:** Add up your cost of the ad campaign and any follow-up costs directly related to the ad campaign.

Figure 9-11:
Be the authoritative source of information and become the "expert."

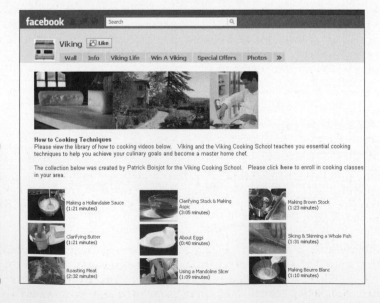

Your basic return on investment is this formula:

(Profit per customer * Number of new customers) – Total Costs / Total Costs

So, if you spent $100 to make $500 in profit, your ROI is 5 × investment, or 500%. There are a number of programs like Adtester CX (see Figure 9-12) that can help you monitor your ROI for any ad campaign, including Facebook Ads. Make sure you can calculate your profit (or approximate lifetime value or customer value) per customer or conversion, or you won't be able to compute ROI with any piece of software.

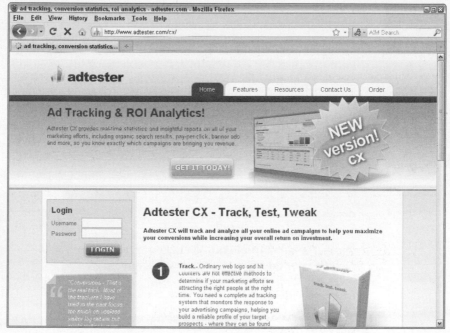

Figure 9-12: You can use programs like Adtester CX to monitor your ROI.

Tracking Your Conversions

At some point, you will want to know how your conversion efforts are going (when your boss is calling, say, asking to know the latest figures). For now, you have to track conversions by hand, but Facebook is working on technology to help you out.

As of this writing, Facebook is working on a Conversion Tracking tool that allows you to place a "tag" on your Web site pages to track the number of conversions you receive, along with the time it took a user to go from either seeing or clicking the ad to completing the call to action to be counted as a conversion. Because this tool was not ready by the time we went to press, we cannot comment on the specifics or functionality of this tool. We can only recommend that you check the Facebook Ads Manager page or go to the Facebook Help Center and search for "Conversion Tracking" to see the latest offerings.

If you want a great discussion of what analytic tools are available, check out *Web Analytics For Dummies* by Pedro Sostre and Jennifer LeClaire.

Metrics to track

Here are some of the metrics you will need to keep track of in your system:

- ✔ **Unique user identifier:** To keep track of any particular user, you will need to have some form of unique ID number or tracking element. An identifier like this allows you to follow each user and see exactly how far he or she went in the conversion process. For unique identifiers, you can use e-mail addresses, IP addresses, or unique ID numbers generated by Facebook that tie to users' profile IDs.

   If you're going to be tracking conversions from other sources, such as search engine ad campaigns or blog postings, you should definitely invent a new identifier code, like "FB01", here to represent that the user came from your Facebook Ad campaign and not from another source, so you can properly track the value of your Facebook Ad campaign.

- ✔ **Number of clicks:** Think of this as your starting base — the number of clicks your Facebook Ad received.

- ✔ **Number of unique clicks:** More important than just the raw number of clicks, the number of unique clicks represents individual people who clicked your ad and got started. This metric ignores additional clicks from individual users. Facebook Reports distinguishes unique clicks from total number of clicks.

- ✔ **Number of conversions:** This represents the number of people who went through the entire process and successfully answered your call to action.

- ✔ **Conversion ratio:** This is the number of conversions divided by the number of incoming people, or unique clicks.

- ✔ **Timestamps of click and conversion:** If you want to keep track of the amount of time it took a user to answer your call to action, you will need to keep track of two distinct timestamps: the date and time when the ad was first presented to the user, and the date and time that the user completed the call to action and reached the destination page.

If your conversion is defined as a user Liking your Facebook Page, then tracking the average time of conversion might be skewed because many users click the Like link within the ad itself and are instantly converted into Fans of your Page.

The easiest way to track a conversion is to place some form of a tag or marker (which can be a snippet of HTML code or an instruction to load a hidden graphic file, for example) on the final, or destination, Web page on your Web site that loads only when the user has fully completed your call to action and can be counted as a conversion. Some examples of this are the verification page a newsletter subscriber sees after verifying an e-mail address, the confirmation page shown after someone registers for your site (like the bidcactus confirmation shown in Figure 9-13), the order confirmation page a paying customer sees after placing an order, or the download confirmation page shown after a user downloads a free trial product.

Figure 9-13:
Put a marker or tag on pages like this to keep track of conversions.

When this marker loads, you may need to associate it with the unique ID identifier for your user, especially if you're tracking the length of time needed for the conversion. Sometimes, you can pass the identifier value in the URL as you link from page to page. Other times, you can hide the value as a form value that gets passed from page to page. You can also assign a cookie on each user's computer to help track these values. In the end, your Web site, shopping cart, or analytics program should be keeping a log of which unique identifiers are being passed along when the marker is being loaded, and you will have your list of users who can be counted as a conversion. See the next section, "Optimizing conversions," for more information on the steps needed to accomplish this.

If the Facebook Conversion Tool is not available, we recommend talking to your Web site hosting provider to see what analytical tools are available for your Web site or shopping cart. You may be able to assign these numbers and track your activity today.

Optimizing conversions

After you know your conversion ratio, your next goal may be to improve that ratio because more conversions lead to a short-term or long-term gain in revenue and (eventually) profit.

One way to optimize your conversions is to determine where in the ordering process the average customer is stopping progress or choosing not to buy your product. To determine this, you need to set up your system to keep track of each customer's actions so you can help pinpoint the reasons why users leaving without ordering. If you notice that a sizable percentage of people make it only to a certain step in your ordering process, you can use this information to examine that particular step and try to determine what might be the cause for people abandoning the process.

When you want to set up your tracking process to study your ordering process, follow these steps:

1. **Set up a unique name identifier for every single page in the ordering process.**

   Start with the home page for your Web site, any landing page your ad campaign might divert traffic to, the product detail page, the shopping cart page, the billing or payment page, the confirmation page, and any other page not mentioned here. This involves simply making something up, and writing down a specific string of numbers and/or letters to be associated with each page. So, for example, you could write **Home1** for the home page, **Landing1** for your first landing page, **Detail1** for your first product detail page, **Detail2** for your second product detail page, **Cart1** for your first shopping cart page, and so on.

2. **Make sure that each page in the ordering process transmits their unique name identifier when the page is loaded into anyone's Web browser.**

   Depending on how your e-commerce system and Web site are put together, there are different ways to embed your unique name identifiers. Check out more information on how to accomplish this through books like *Web Analytics For Dummies* or the documentation for your shopping cart software.

3. **Go to your tracking system, count the number of unique identifiers that get reported, and sum them up based on the identifier.**

   This way, you will see the number of people who reached each step of your process. If there is a step that has a number of followers, but the next step has almost no audience, then you might have found the step where people have an issue.

At this point, it will be up to you to figure out what could be in that step in the process that's sending people away. If you have the e-mail addresses of potential users, you could send out a random survey asking only the people who didn't complete the process why they didn't take the offer and place the order. You could put together a focus group and ask participants to walk through your process and give you their thoughts as they look at and process each page.

Part IV
Minding Your Metrics

The 5th Wave   By Rich Tennant

" Look-what if we just increase the size of the charts? "

In this part . . .

After you've run at least one ad campaign on Facebook, you might wonder, "Was it worth it?" Thankfully, in today's online world, you can track a number of activities so that you can know, in clear math, whether your ad campaign was worthwhile. You can even track individual behavior (don't worry, no privacy was compromised in the making of this book) so you will know whether the profit generated from a specific online ad was more than the cost of that ad.

In this part, we discuss how to review the data from your ad campaigns to understand the success and/or profitability of that ad campaign. This is important because it not only justifies your immediate expenses, but the *metrics* (measurable statistics) of your ad campaign, give you ideas for future campaigns, as well as the experience of knowing what didn't work. We discuss how to use Facebook Ads Manager and Reporting screens to pull the information you need from its database. We then discuss how to "extend" Facebook to your own Web site so you can track those results as well.

Chapter 10

Checking Out the Data

In This Chapter

▶ Exploring the Ads Manager interface

▶ Understanding the Lifetime Stats

▶ Viewing ads data as a graph

▶ Changing the settings for Ads Manager and your campaigns

After you set your Facebook Ad campaigns in motion, keep an eye on them to make sure that your budget is being spent wisely and also that your ads are still converting enough people to make the campaigns worth your while. Thankfully, Facebook has Ads Manager, which makes statistics and editing just a click or two away.

In this chapter, we review the Ads Manager interface, starting with the main screen, and show you how to read the summary reports and see the various graphs of data. Then we drill down to the individual campaigns where you can make changes to your ad settings or see the status of your campaign or particular advertisement. Finally, we talk about how to receive notifications from Facebook for important product updates and other news.

Getting to Know Ads Manager

Facebook Ads Manager allows you to perform administrative functions on your various Facebook Ad campaigns. This tool shows you the status, as well as the statistics, for all your Facebook Ad campaigns, and gives you the ability to coordinate your campaigns, set budgets and bid levels, and study results from one user interface. Ads Manager also comes with several graphs that allow you to see certain results data in a graph format.

If you want more detailed statistic information, you will either have to drill down by clicking campaign or ad names, or clicking the Reports link to go to Ads Reports. (We discuss Ads Reports in more detail in Chapter 11.) You also have the ability from Ads Manager to export the statistics to your computer in a comma separated values (CSV) file.

To get to Ads Manager, you have two options:

✔ From your Facebook home page, click Ads and Pages along the left side of the screen.

✔ Go directly to the Ads Manager at `www.facebook.com/ads/manage`.

You should see the Ads Manager home page screen like the one shown in Figure 10-1. The Ads Manager home page shows you a number of items:

✔ **Notifications:** The page includes a summary list of the recent notifications that Facebook sent you regarding your ad campaigns.

✔ **Daily Spend:** Based on the daily budgets you set on your various ad campaigns, Facebook will show you the amount of money you spent on all your campaigns for the past five days.

✔ **Table of Campaigns:** You should see a list of your most recent ad campaigns in a table format. By default, you see the Lifetime Stats for each campaign, but we talk about how to show different statistics in this same table in the section "Reviewing weekly stats on your ad campaigns" later on in this chapter.

Notifications   Daily Spend

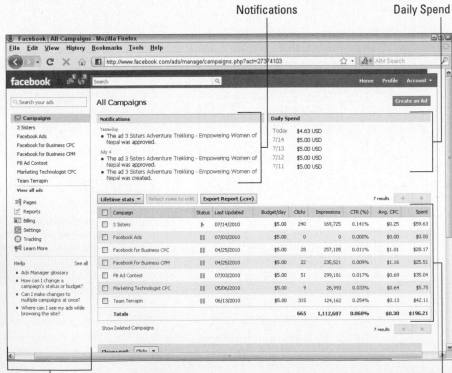

Figure 10-1: The Facebook Ads Manager home page.

Navigation bar   Table of Campaigns

✔ **Graph:** Although not visible in Figure 10-1, below your table is a graph of your various ad campaigns; the default view shows the number of clicks for each campaign in the past two weeks or so. Just like with the table, you can update this graph to show you different statistics for your campaigns.

✔ **Navigation bar:** Along the left side of the screen, you should see a list of your active and paused campaigns, along with a View All Ads link. Clicking that link takes you to the All Ads page (see Figure 10-2), which shows the active and paused campaigns and ads as well as any stopped or disapproved ads.

You have many choices of what to do next:

✔ **Review:** Review any ad campaign by clicking the Name of that ad campaign, either in the table or from the navigation bar.

✔ **Sort:** Sort the table by clicking any of the field column headers in the table. Click any column header to sort in decreasing order, from highest to lowest; you can toggle the sort in ascending or increasing order by clicking the same column header again.

✔ **Rename:** Click next to any campaign name in the table to rename the campaign and then click the Save button next to the campaign name you just entered in order to save your change and rename the campaign.

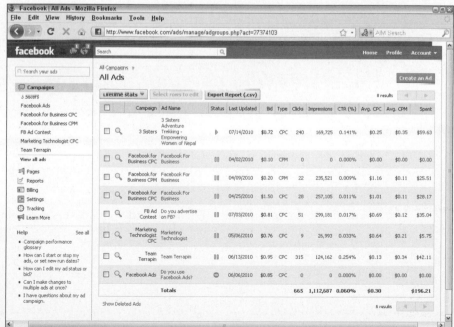

Figure 10-2: View all your ads within Ads Manager.

✔ **Change status:** Click the icon in the Status column to change the current status of any ad campaign to one of the valid options: Active, Paused, or Deleted.

✔ **Download:** Click the Export Report (.csv) button to download a version of the Lifetime Stats table as an Excel file that you can import into your home computer. (See Figure 10-3.)

At this point, you should use Ads Manager to either make updates or changes to any of your ad campaigns, or click existing campaigns to study the results more carefully. You can export any of the ad campaigns' statistics to do further analysis on your computer; or pause, delete, or resume any of the ad campaigns in your account.

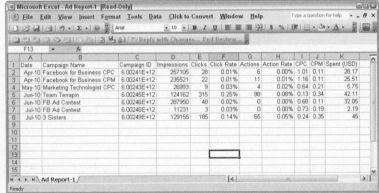

Figure 10-3:
Export statistics of your ad campaigns into Excel.

Understanding campaign notifications

Although Facebook Ads is mainly a *self-service solution* — meaning that you can create, manage, and stop advertisements yourself using Facebook's Web site at any time of the day — there is a channel of communication that needs to occur between you and Facebook so that Facebook can review and then approve or reject your ad. This channel is *campaign notifications,* which Facebook sends to you via a Facebook Message and by e-mail. Mainly, these notifications occur because Facebook still reviews all the ads that go on its site based on its Advertising Guidelines, and then informs potential advertisers whether an ad has been cleared for posting on Facebook or needs additional revision to be brought to acceptable standards.

Here are notifications you can expect to see on a regular basis:

✔ **Ad Created:** After you finish setting all your options for starting a new ad in Facebook Ads, Facebook sends you a notification e-mail that the ad has been created and exists in the system. At this point, the approval process begins, as the information is sent to Facebook for approval.

✔ **Ad Approved:** When Facebook reviews your new ad and determines that it complies with Facebook Advertising Guidelines, Facebook approves the ad, which means that ad will start having impressions on the site. Facebook will send you a notification e-mail that the ad has been approved.

✔ **Ad Disapproved:** When Facebook reviews your new ad and determines that the ad does not comply with Facebook Advertising Guidelines, it sends you a notification e-mail stating that the ad was disapproved (see Figure 10-4), with the following elements:

- A link to the ad in question

- An example of the ad's headline and message

- The Ad Disapproval Reason(s), quoting sections of Facebook Advertising Guidelines

- A link to review the ad that's been disapproved

- Links and Web addresses to contact Facebook if you have questions

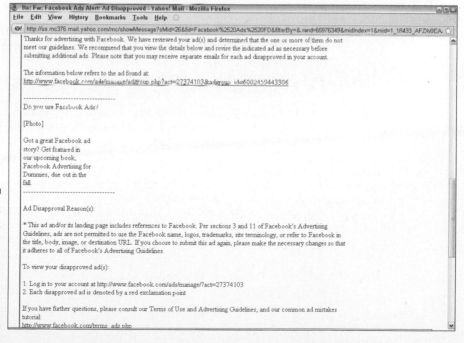

Figure 10-4: Facebook sends you a notification e-mail if your ad was not approved.

✔ **Account Charged:** Typically, Facebook charges you for each billable day you run ad campaigns. When Facebook bills you through one of its valid payment methods, Facebook sends you a notification e-mail that your account has been charged. This notification has the following details:

- Payment amount

- Date(s) of Facebook Ads that this payment covers

- Your Facebook Ads account number

- Transaction ID of the payment made to Facebook

- Method of payment

   As of this writing, Facebook accepts credit cards like Visa, MasterCard, and American Express; certain branded debit cards; and PayPal.

✔ **Daily Budget Change:** If you update the daily budget for any of your Facebook Ads, Facebook sends you a notification to confirm that you changed the daily budget and will include the new amount in your notification.

✔ **Additional Notifications:** Occasionally, you might see additional notifications based on your situation, including the following:

- *Ad Requires Editing:* In some cases, Facebook recommends suggested edits to your submitted ad. Facebook then allows you to go back to the ad and accept the suggested edits so your ad can be approved.

- *Coupon Expiring:* If you use a coupon code to get credit toward your Facebook Ads account, and that coupon is about to expire, Facebook notifies you that the coupon is about to expire and that it will start charging your defined payment method instead of using the coupon credit.

   Even if you use a coupon credit to start your Facebook Ads account, Facebook requires you to define a valid payment method such as a credit card as well before your Ads account is fully active.

- *Coupon Budget Low:* Similar to the Coupon Expiring alert, Facebook notifies you if your credit from an Ads coupon is about to be used up. When your coupon credit goes to $0.00, Facebook uses your defined payment method to charge any additional amount spent for that day and all days going forward.

If you don't want to get e-mails of these campaign notifications, simply click the Settings link from the Ads Manager home page and scroll down to clear and turn off any or all of the campaign notifications. (See Figure 10-5.)

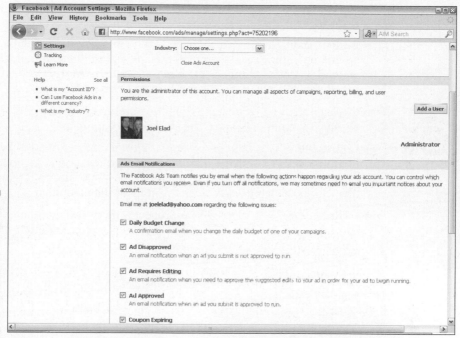

Analyzing Lifetime Statistics

From the Ads Manager home page, you can easily see the Lifetime Statistics for your different Facebook Ad campaigns, because by default, Facebook displays the Lifetime statistics for each ad campaign when you load the Ads Manager page. These numbers give you a high-level overview of how each campaign is performing on Facebook. You can click any Campaign name to bring up all the ads within the campaign to examine the details further. Up-front, however, you get a basic view of what has transpired so far.

When you look at the Lifetime Statistics, you should see the following data fields:

- ✔ **Status:** This is represented by a graphic, either (4) to indicate an Active campaign, (;) to indicate a Paused campaign, or (y) to indicate a Deleted campaign.

- ✔ **Last Updated:** This field reflects the last date you made any changes to the ad itself (like the title, image, message, or destination URL) or settings within the campaign.

- ✔ **Budget/Day:** This is your current setting for how much Facebook should spend, on your behalf, to run all the ads within this campaign for any given day. If you changed this number after the campaign has started, this field will reflect the current budget per day.

- ✔ **Clicks:** This field represents the total number of clicks on all the ads within this campaign since the start of the campaign.

- ✔ **Impressions:** This field represents the total number of ad *impressions* (an impression is when your ad is displayed once on a Facebook user's page; we discuss impressions in more depth in Chapter 2) from all the ads within this campaign since the start of the campaign.

- ✔ **CTR:** *Click-through rate* (CTR) represents the overall campaign click-through rate, and is calculated by dividing the total number of clicks by the total number of impressions. (We discuss CTR in more depth in Chapters 2 and 4.)

- ✔ **Avg CPC:** This field represents the average cost per click (CPC) that you paid for this campaign, regardless of whether you chose CPC or CPM (cost per thousand impressions) as your payment model. This field is calculated by the total number of clicks by the total amount spent. (We discuss CPC and CPM in more depth in Chapter 4.)

- ✔ **Spent:** This field represents the total amount of money spent on all ads within this campaign since the start of the campaign.

When you look at the Lifetime Statistics for your ad campaigns, you might want to change the view so you can study a particular time period: Perhaps a range that doesn't include split tests or other refinements to the campaign (we discuss split tests and optimizing your campaign in more depth in Chapter 8), or a part of the campaign that features a new promotion or a dramatic shift in your ad message. If you click the drop-down arrow inside the Lifetime Stats button, you can change the time period to Today, Yesterday, Last Week, or Custom (which allows you to define your own range; see Figure 10-6 to see the statistics for each campaign for the time period between July 8, 2010 and July 15, 2010, for example) to see the overall statistics.

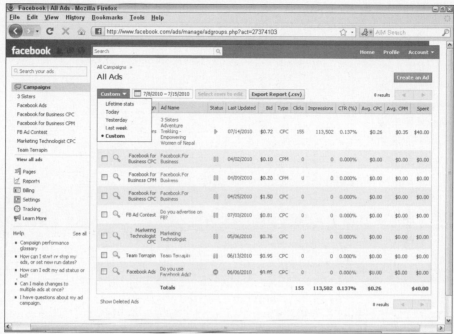

Figure 10-6:
See the
campaign
statistics for
a custom
period of
time.

Viewing graphs

Whether you're on the Ads Manager home page viewing All Campaigns or studying an individual Facebook Ad campaign within Ads Manager, Facebook allows you to view the ad data as a graph, as shown in Figure 10-7. Each campaign is represented by the overall daily numbers for the campaign, laid out in a line graph, with multiple lines representing different ad campaigns under the same account. The graph is drawn automatically, with emphasis put on the most recent week, although you can adjust the graph for any time period where you ran an ad campaign.

These graphs allow you to visually identify not only the high and low points for the campaign, but also when there were trends, shifts, and stabilization of the data within each campaign. You can also change the type of graph displayed. When you click the drop-down arrow in the box next to Choose a Graph, as in Figure 10-8, you can select one of three options to display the graph of your Ad campaign data:

✔ Clicks

✔ Impressions

✔ Click-through rate- (CTR)

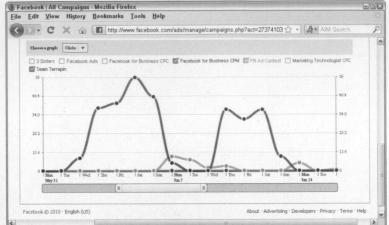

Figure 10-7:
Compare your Facebook Ad campaign data in a graph.

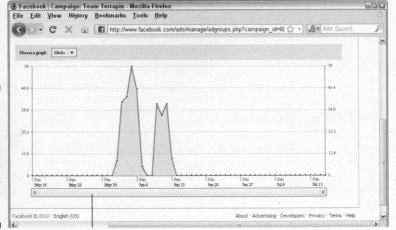

Figure 10-8:
Choose which data point you want to compare, using a graph.

The slider or bottom bar along the bottom of your graph determines how many data points are represented along the horizontal part of your chart. Each end of the bottom bar is represented by something resembling a tab with ridges. You can click each tab and drag it to stretch the bottom bar from left to right. When the bottom bar isn't stretched from end to end, you're looking at only a specific range somewhere between the start of your ad account and today.

As an example, compare the same graph with different settings along the bottom bar. When the bottom bar for a certain campaign is stretched, you see that the campaign was active for only a few weeks near the middle of that time range. Click and drag the bottom bar so that it's stretched for only a particular date range (see Figure 10-9), and you can see more detailed statistics because Facebook doesn't have to map out everything proportionally.

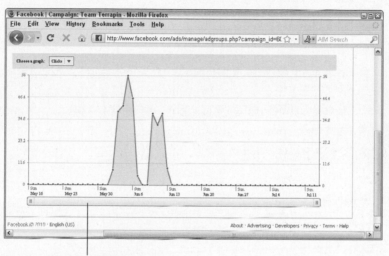

Bottom Reference bar

Figure 10-9:
Compare a graph of data for the entire time length of your account (top) and the same graph optimized for the active dates of the campaign (bottom).

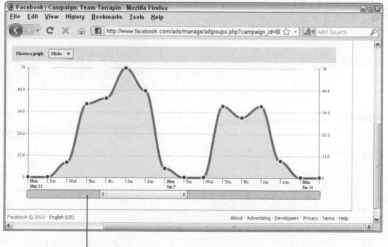

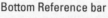

Bottom Reference bar

Reviewing multiple campaigns

As we mention, you can review any campaign by clicking the campaign name and reviewing the ad(s) inside the campaign. But what happens when you need to review more than one campaign, perhaps to compare the effectiveness of two campaigns? Facebook allows you to review and even edit multiple campaigns at the same time.

When you want to edit the status or daily budget of multiple campaigns at the same time, just follow these steps:

1. **Go to your Facebook Ads Manager home page at** `www.facebook.com/ads/manage`**.**

2. **Click the rows of the campaigns you wish to edit.**

   The Edit X rows button becomes enabled, as shown in Figure 10-10.

Edit X Rows button

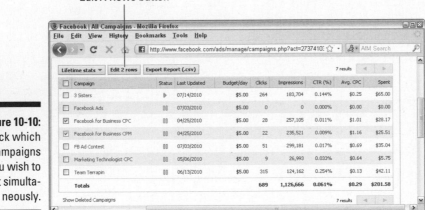

Figure 10-10:
Pick which campaigns you wish to edit simultaneously.

3. **Click the Edit X rows button.**

   The Campaign, Status, and Budget/day fields are now editable (see Figure 10-11), so you can rename the campaign, change the status, or change the amount of money you are willing to spend per day on that campaign.

4. **Click the Save button, which appears where the Edit X Rows button used to appear.**

   This saves your changes to the ad campaigns. You can also click the Cancel button to save no changes and exit this mode.

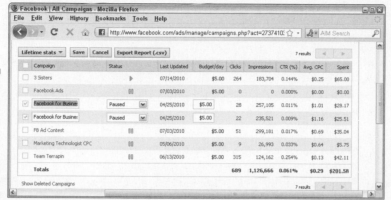

Figure 10-11:
Make changes to more than one campaign at the same time!

	Campaign	Status		Last Updated	Budget/day	Clicks	Impressions	CTR (%)	Avg. CPC	Spent
☐	3 Sisters	▶		07/14/2010	$5.00	264	183,704	0.144%	$0.25	$65.00
☐	Facebook Ads	❚❚		07/03/2010	$5.00	0	0	0.000%	$0.00	$0.00
☑	Facebook for Busine	Paused	▾	04/25/2010	$5.00	28	257,105	0.011%	$1.01	$28.17
☑	Facebook for Busine	Paused	▾	04/25/2010	$5.00	22	235,521	0.009%	$1.16	$25.51
☐	FB Ad Contest	❚❚		07/03/2010	$5.00	51	299,181	0.017%	$0.69	$35.04
☐	Marketing Technologist CPC	❚❚		05/06/2010	$5.00	9	26,993	0.033%	$0.64	$5.75
☐	Team Terrapin	❚❚		06/13/2010	$5.00	315	124,162	0.254%	$0.13	$42.11
	Totals					689	1,126,666	0.061%	$0.29	$201.58

To change the CPC or CPM setting for any ad, click the name of the campaign and go through the individual ad to make changes. At the time of this writing, multiple changes to ad values cannot be done in any Facebook campaign.

Reviewing weekly stats on your ad campaigns

When you need to get more specific data about your ad campaigns, click the campaign name to see the ads within that campaign. The campaign screen looks very similar to the overall Ads Manager home page, with the same statistical information like clicks, impressions, and CTR, but you see the ads data within only that specific campaign.

When you need to see how any given ad is performing, click the Ad Name from the campaign screen to go to the weekly data screen for that ad campaign, as shown in Figure 10-12. You can see the last week's data in a daily summary view, along with the Lifetime Statistics of that ad along the bottom of that table, with the ad preview along the right side, and the targeting filters above the statistical data.

From this screen, you have several options:

✔ **Adjust your CPC or CPM price for your ad.** Click the Edit link at the top right of your screen, beside the CPC Bids header. Facebook will continue to show you its suggested bid range for your ad.

✔ **Change any field of information directly without editing the rest of your ad.** Click the edit links near Ad Name, Run Status, or Targeting.

✔ **Pick another date to see any previous week's worth of statistical data for this ad.** Click the drop-down arrow next to the Daily Stats for the Week Of header.

✔ **Change the ad message or targeting filters.** Click the Edit Ad Creative button near the bottom right of the screen.

When you make any changes to your ad, the ad will stop running until Facebook has an opportunity to review your changes and approve the edited ad.

✔ **Start a new Facebook Ad with all the fields pre-populated with the information from your previous ad.** Click the Create a Similar Ad button. This button is especially handy when you want to split-test an ad and need to make one only change, or you want to take a high-converting ad and try it on another product or service offering.

You can scroll to the bottom of this page and view the graph for the ad campaign, and study either the clicks received, impressions of your ad, or the CTR of that ad over time.

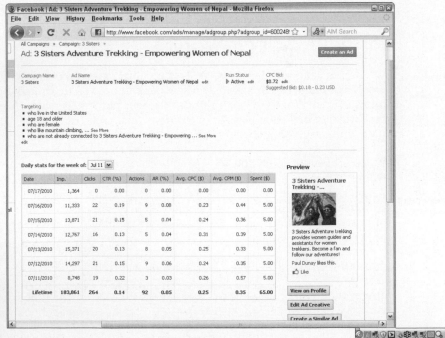

Figure 10-12: Study a week's worth of statistics for a campaign on one screen.

Adjusting Account Settings

Your Facebook Ads account is basically an extension of your Facebook account. Therefore, when you set up your Facebook profile, you're providing Facebook with a lot of the information used for your Ads account as well.

To adjust your Ad Account settings, click Settings from the navigation bar on your Ads Manager home page to access the Settings page like that shown in Figure 10-13.

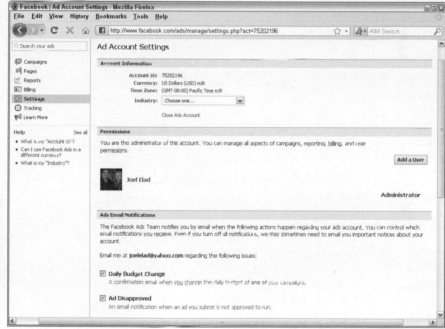

Figure 10-13:
Change the settings for your Facebook Ads campaign.

As of this writing, the only settings you would adjust from Ads Manager are

✔ **Your Industry affiliation:** You can choose an Industry to affiliate your account with, but this is mainly used by Facebook to get an idea of its advertiser base.

✔ **The user list of people who can access your ads account:** You can add another user to your Facebook Ads account to help manage your Facebook Ad campaigns.

a. *Click the Add a User button.*

This opens the Add a User to This Ads Account window, as shown in Figure 10-14.

b. *Enter the name or the e-mail address of the person you wish to add, and decide whether that person has general user access to the ad campaigns or can view only reports.*

No matter what level of access you give a user on the ads account, that user will never have access to your personal Facebook profile.

Anybody to whom you want to grant access to your Ads account must be a current Facebook user, so make sure that person signs up for Facebook first before you try to include him on your Ads Account user list.

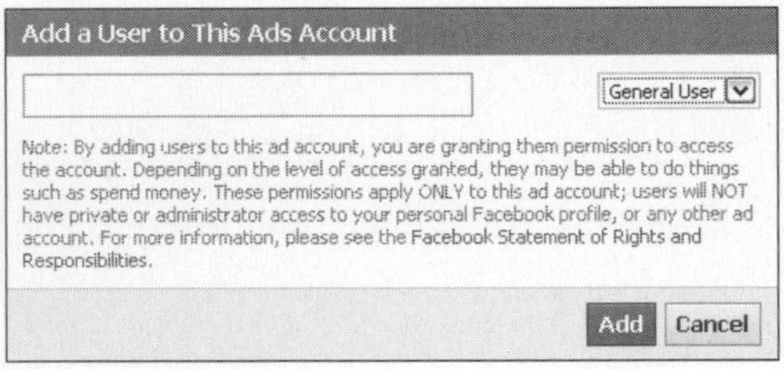

Figure 10-14:
Add another user to your Ads Account, either for everything or reports only.

> **Add a User to This Ads Account**
>
> [_____]   [General User ▾]
>
> Note: By adding users to this ad account, you are granting them permission to access the account. Depending on the level of access granted, they may be able to do things such as spend money. These permissions apply ONLY to this ad account; users will NOT have private or administrator access to your personal Facebook profile, or any other ad account. For more information, please see the Facebook Statement of Rights and Responsibilities.
>
> [**Add**] [Cancel]

✔ **The settings regarding how Facebook communicates with you during the ads process:** You can choose which ad alert notifications (besides Payment Completed, which you can set through a link in the Account Charged e-mail) you want to receive by selecting any (or all) of these check boxes:

- Daily Budget Change

- Ad Disapproved

- Ad Requires Editing

- Ad Approved

- Coupon Expiring or Running Low

- Opt-in Newsletters and Product Updates

We recommend receiving Facebook Ads newsletters and updates. These newsletters (see Figure 10-15) come with new product announcements, actual stories from existing Facebook advertisers, and tips and tricks from the Facebook staff on how to run a better ad campaign.

Figure 10-15:
Get the
scoop from
Facebook
in the Ads
News-
letters.

Chapter 11

Creating Reports

In This Chapter

▶ Running reports from the Facebook Reports system

▶ Analyzing interactions between you and customers

▶ Exporting ad performance data to your own system

▶ Creating a dashboard to monitor campaign activity and success

*W*hen you're looking to review the basic statistics on your Facebook Ad campaigns, typically Ads Manager (see Chapter 10) will have all the major data points you would want. However, you might need to dig a little deeper to find more detailed information regarding individual ads or campaigns. In these cases, turn to Facebook Reports to help you figure out profitability, prepare a summary report, or make a decision regarding a new campaign.

In this chapter, we walk you through the basics of Facebook Reports. We discuss how to get reports, interpret the results within each report, export that data to your computer for further analysis, and pull out demographic information as well as the likes and interests of your audience. We also look at Facebook Insights, which gives you a lot of detailed information on your Users and interactions when it comes to your Facebook presence. We finish by discussing a concept known as *dashboard management,* where you can monitor and maintain your Facebook Ad campaign by looking at a *dashboard,* or a customized set of measurements and ratios that change based on your campaign's performance. Dashboards give you a quick idea whether your ad campaigns are going in the correct direction or you need to consider a course correction.

Introduction to Facebook Reports

Facebook has developed a separate section for its Reports, which provide more detailed information than you can get in Ads Manager. To access Facebook Reports, go to your Facebook Ads Manager: `www.facebook.com/ads/manage`.

From the Ads Manager screen, you can access Facebook Reports by clicking the Reports link on the left side of the screen (see Figure 11-1).

This takes you to your Reports main screen, from which you can generate any of the main reports. (See Figure 11-2.)

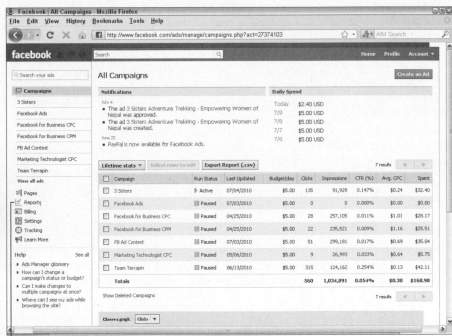

Figure 11-1: Access Facebook Reports from your Ads Manager.

Reports link

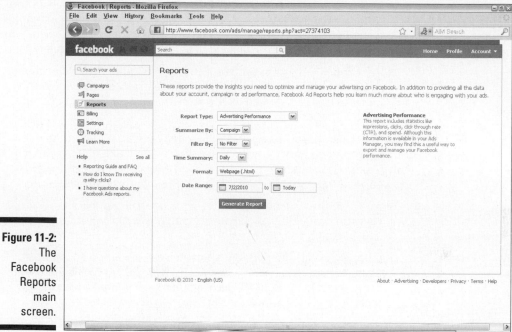

Figure 11-2:
The
Facebook
Reports
main
screen.

Generating Reports

The three available types of reports are

- ✔ **Advertising Performance:** Basic performance information for your ad campaign

- ✔ **Responder Demographics:** Information regarding the demographics of the people who view, click, or take action on your ads

- ✔ **Responder Profiles:** Additional information about the people who view your site, giving you some common data about users' Likes and interests without compromising any particular user's privacy rights

We discuss each report type in the following sections.

When you're ready to generate any of these reports, you have to set some options to customize your report:

- ✔ **Summarize By:** Determine how your reports data is grouped:

  - • *Account:* Groups data across every ad in every campaign you have in your account (like in the top image in Figure 11-3). With this option, you see just one summary line for each day, week, or month specified.

- *Campaign:* Groups data across every ad in a campaign (like in the bottom image in Figure 11-3), and shows a summary line for each campaign in the reports. If you have more than one campaign, you see a different summary line for each report in your account.

- *Ad:* Groups data from each ad within each campaign. On each line of the report, you see the name of the overall campaign and the name of each ad, as well as the statistics for each line that apply only to that ad.

✔ **Filter By:** This option comes into play when you have more than one campaign running under your account. Here, you can decide to filter your results by campaign or by ad, so you can select the campaigns or ads you wish to appear in your report. You have three options:

- *No Filter:* Every campaign under your account appears in your reports, provided that the ad campaign was active and running in the time summary selected.

- *Campaign:* With this option, you see a list of campaigns in your account (see Figure 11-4). Just select the check box beside the campaign(s) you want to see in your report to make those campaign's statistics appear in the report you generate.

- *Ad:* Similar to Campaign, selecting this filter presents a list of ads underneath the header, and you can select the ads whose statistics will appear in the report you're generating.

The Filter By option is really useful when you want to select two ads or two campaigns and then compare their statistics to see which one performed better.

✔ **Time Summary:** Tell Facebook the time units you want to use to group the reported statistics. Obviously, the shorter the amount of time, the more detailed information you are going to see because, for example, a daily report shows you data in 24-hour chunks while a monthly report summarizes all the statistics for any given month. You have three choices here:

- *Monthly:* Group data on a calendar month basis, regardless of when you started or stopped the ad or campaign during the month. As long as there are valid statistics for any day within a given month, you see an entry for that month in your report.

- *Weekly:* Group data on a calendar weekly basis from Sunday to Saturday. When the report mentions the date, it refers to the first day in the week whose statistics have been grouped for the week. So, for example, if the report covers "Week of 06/06/10," that means the week of June 6–12, 2010.

- *Daily:* Groups data on a daily basis between 12:01 a.m. and 11:59 p.m. each day based on your time zone, as defined in your Facebook Profile.

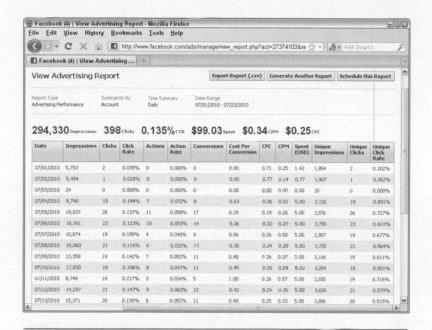

Figure 11-3:
You can summarize data by your account, campaign, or singular ads.

✔ **Format:** Tell Facebook how to format the requested report. The data inside the report doesn't change regardless of which format you select. The Format option is also known as the Export Format option because this is the option to use when you want to download the information to your computer. You have three options here:

Figure 11-4:
Filter your reports by selecting the campaigns you wish to analyze.

- *Webpage (.html):* Displays the report onscreen, using a regular Internet Web browser.

- *Excel (.csv):* Generates a comma-separated values file that you can open or save on your computer to read in Microsoft Excel or other spreadsheet program. We discuss how to export your data in more depth in the upcoming section, "Exporting data."

- *Multilanguage Excel (.csv):* This option is very similar to the preceding Excel option, but this option preserves multilanguage information, which is useful when using different languages in your campaigns.

✔ **Date Range:** Select the date ranges, or the start and end dates, of the reported statistics for your ad campaigns. Click the red and black calendar buttons next to each date to display a calendar in which you can click the specific day you want, as shown in Figure 11-5. Navigate the months by clicking the arrows on the top of the pop-up calendar.

When generating reports on a Monthly time summary, you see drop-down list boxes for the months and years that you want instead of the calendar buttons shown in Figure 11-5.

As you set the various options for your report, understand that a few reports don't have these options. The Responder Demographics report, for example, displays data only in a Monthly time summary, and the Responder Profile report shows data only from the past 14 calendar days for any ad or campaign.

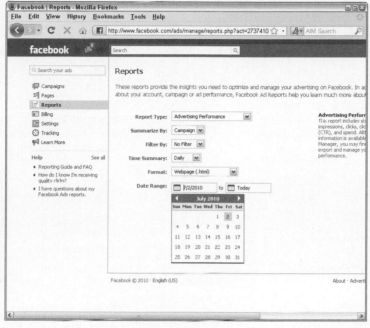

Figure 11-5:
Use calendar options to pick the start and end dates for your report.

Creating an Advertising Performance report

When you're looking for basic performance information for your ad campaign, generate an Advertising Performance report. This is the most comprehensive report available to you as an advertiser when you want to study how many times your ad was displayed, clicked, and acted upon by users.

To generate an Advertising Performance report, follow these steps:

1. **Go to the Reports screen within Ads Manager.**

2. **Make sure that Advertising Performance is selected for the Report Type.**

   Typically, this is the default option when you bring up Facebook Reports.

3. **Choose your customization options, such as Summarize By, Filter By, Time Summary, Format, and Date Range.**

4. **Click the blue Generate Report button.**

   If you selected the Webpage format option, your Advertising Performance report appears onscreen, like that in Figure 11-6.

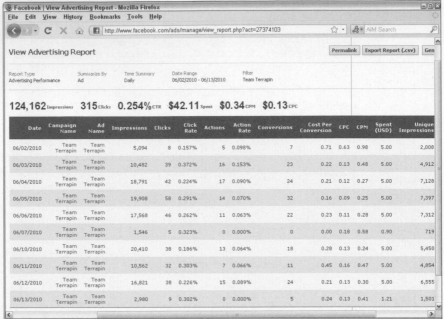

Figure 11-6:
An
Advertising
Perform-
ance report.

As you review your report, notice the following elements:

- **Ad name and filters:** These appear at the top of the report.

- **Summary line:** This appears at the top of the report data, which aggregates the data from the table into a big, bold, and easy-to-read line of summary data for that ad or campaign. The summary line should include

  - Total number of impressions

  - Total number of clicks

  - Click-through rate (CTR; total number of clicks divided by the total number of impressions)

  - Money spent on this ad or campaign for the date range of the report

  - Cost per thousand (CPM; the cost of 1,000 impressions of your ad, or money spent divided by total number of impressions)

  - Cost per click (CPC; the cost of one person clicking your ad, or money spent divided by total number of clicks)

✔ **Report table:** This appears below the summary line and displays the same information as the summary line, but is broken down into the time unit (daily, weekly, or monthly) that you choose. While the fields below are not visible in the previous figure, they are present in the table. You also see additional fields of information for the following:

- *Unique Impressions:* How many different individuals were shown your Facebook Ad. This number is different from total impressions because one person could see the same ad multiple times.

- *Unique Clicks:* How many different individuals clicked your ad. This number can differ from the amount of clicks because the same person can click your ad more than once. For example, if your ad is shown to someone two times and she clicked each ad, your ad would register two clicks yet only one *unique* click.

- *Unique Click-Through Rate:* The number of unique clicks divided by the number of unique impressions. Some people consider this number to be a more accurate representation of their ad performance because it removes any duplicate responses from any particular individual's actions.

- *Actions:* If your Facebook Ad includes the option to Like a Facebook Page or to RSVP to a Facebook Event, the Actions field in this report will represent the number of people who clicked Like or RSVP-ed Yes or Maybe to the event, indicating a positive response to your ad.

Any actions performed by a user (Liking a Page or RSVP-ing) will also be counted as a click in the Clicks and the Unique Clicks categories.

- *Action Rate:* If your Facebook Ad has an action associated with it, the Action rate is simply the number of actions divided by the number of impressions.

- *Conversions:* If you're using the Facebook Conversions tool to track conversions on your Web site, or you have an action associated with your Facebook Ad, this field is the number of people who count as a conversion or who positively responded to your ad.

This number could be different than the number of actions because if someone first clicks the headline of your ad and then later becomes a User or RSVPs to the event, that person would be counted as a conversion but not as an immediate action to the ad.

- *Cost of Conversion:* If you have an ad for which you're tracking conversions, this field is simply the number of conversions divided by the money spent for this unit of time. This field is sometimes known as *cost per lead,* or in certain cases, *cost per sale* or *cost per action.*

Your report table is sorted, by default, by using the Date field. You can re-sort the data based on any column in the table by simply clicking the name of the column in the blue header bar of the table.

If you click a column name once, it sorts the data within that column in ascending order. For example, if we sort a report by Click Rate, it will show the same data but in ascending (lowest-to-highest) order, with the lowest Click Rate as the first row, and the highest Click Rate as the last row, as shown in Figure 11-7. A little up-arrow appears next to Click Rate to indicate the new sorting order.

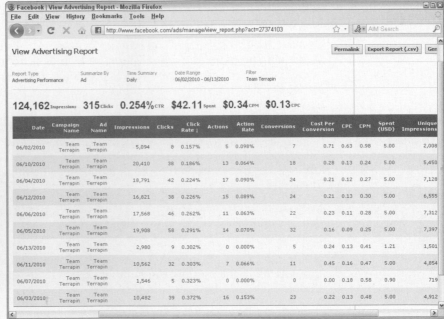

Figure 11-7: You can list the data in any column of your report in ascending order.

If you click the same column name twice, it sorts the data based on that column in descending order, or highest to lowest. In our example, if we click Click Rate a second time, the highest Click Rate appears in the first row and the lowest Click Rate in the last row, as shown in Figure 11-8. The arrow next to Click Rate is now pointing down to indicate the descending order.

After you view your report, you can click one of these buttons on the top right of your report screen to take a further action:

✔ **Permalink:** Create a link to this particular report screen so you can come back to that screen.

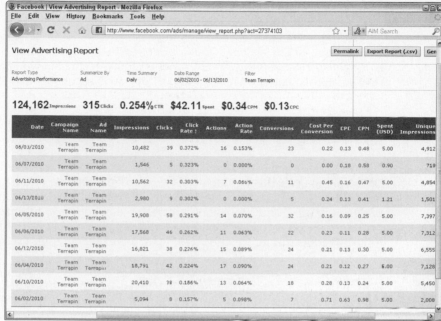

 ✔ **Export Report:** Download the report you're viewing in CSV format. When you click that button, you then choose whether to open this CSV file on your computer (in a program like Excel) or save the CSV file to your computer. (See Figure 11-9.)

Figure 11-9: Download or export your report after viewing it online.

✔ **Generate Another Report:** Return to the Reports main screen, with all the same customization options selected as before. If you click Reports from the left side of the screen to go back to the Reports main screen, you see all the system default options instead of the options you just selected. To generate another report similar to the one you just viewed, using this Generate Another Report button is recommended.

Creating a Responder Demographics report

Facebook gives you extensive targeting options so you can present your ad to very specific demographics. However, depending on which targeting options you choose, you might want to review which demographics are seeing your ad — and, most importantly, the demographic information of people who click or take action on your ad. Facebook provides an excellent report to show this information: the Responder Demographics report.

The Responder Demographics report shows you basic performance information on your ad or campaign based on a particular demographic, and then shows you that same information for specific ranges or subsets of that demographic. This helps you determine which demographics are appropriate for your ad, and which subsets of that demographic are the most and least responsive to your ad so that you can refine your targeting even further.

To generate a Responder Demographics report, follow these steps:

1. **Go to the Reports screen within Ads Manager.**

2. **Select Responder Demographics from the Report Type field.**

3. **Choose your customization options, such as Summarize By, Filter By, Format, and Date Range.**

   Time Summary is available only as Monthly for this report.

4. **Click the blue Generate Report button.**

   If you select the Webpage format option, your Responder Demographic report appears like that shown in Figure 11-10.

In this report, the report name and customization options appear at the top of the report, along with the Permalink, Export Report, and Generate Another Report buttons. Along the left side of the report table are the date (month name), campaign and ad name, and the following fields:

✔ **Demographic:** The name of the specific demographic by which the report has grouped data. As of this writing, Facebook defines three different demographic sets:

   • *gender_age:* The gender of the Facebook user in Bucket 1 and the age (as part of an age range) of the Facebook user in Bucket 2. More on Buckets in a bit.

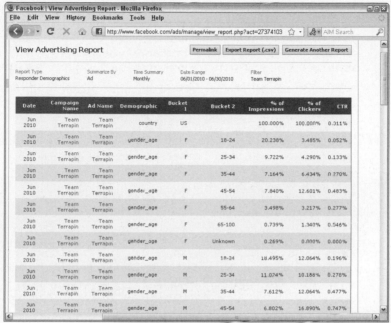

Figure 11-10: See which demographics are seeing and clicking your ad.

• *region:* The country where the Facebook user lives (as of this writing, this option works only if the country is the United States or Canada) in Bucket 1, and the state or province where the user lives in Bucket 2.

• *country:* The country where the Facebook user lives in Bucket 1 and nothing for Bucket 2. This option exists only if you're running the Facebook Ad in multiple countries besides the United States or Canada.

✔ **Bucket 1 and 2:** Specific information based on the value in the Demographic field. For example, if the Demographic value is gender_age, Bucket 1 will be F (for Female), M (for Male), or the entire word Unknown if the user never defined gender in his profile. Bucket 2 will list one of the following age ranges:

  • 13–17

  • 18–24

  • 25–34

  • 35–44

  • 45–54

  • 55–64

  • 65–100

  • unknown (if the user has never defined an age for the account)

If the targeting filter for your ad excluded everyone from a certain age range, you won't see a line item in your report for age ranges outside your targeting filter. For example, if you set up your report to show your ad only to people older than 18, you won't see the 13–17 age range in your report. (We discuss setting your targeting filters in Chapter 3.)

✔ **% of Impressions:** The percentage of unique people in the specified demographic range who were shown the ad, as compared with the total number of impressions for the ad.

✔ **% of Clickers:** The percentage of unique people in the specified demographic range who clicked the ad, as compared with the total number of clicks for the ad.

✔ **CTR:** The unique CTR for each specified demographic range by showing the number of unique clicks divided by the number of unique impressions.

Similar to the Advertising Performance report, you can click any column header to sort the data in ascending order by that field. If you click the same column header again, you can sort the data in descending order, or highest to lowest. For example, if we click the CTR field twice, we can see the specific demographic ranges that have the highest CTR for our given ad, as shown in Figure 11-11.

Figure 11-11:
Sort your data to see what demographics perform best.

Date	Campaign Name	Ad Name	Demographic	Bucket 1	Bucket 2	% of Impressions	% of Clickers	CTR ↑
Jun 2010	Team Terrapin	Team Terrapin	gender_age	M	55-64	3.681%	13.673%	1.117%
Jun 2010	Team Terrapin	Team Terrapin	region	us	Kansas	0.520%	2.059%	1.087%
Jun 2010	Team Terrapin	Team Terrapin	gender_age	M	65-100	1.100%	3.753%	1.026%
Jun 2010	Team Terrapin	Team Terrapin	gender_age	M	45-54	6.802%	16.890%	0.747%
Jun 2010	Team Terrapin	Team Terrapin	region	us	Arizona	0.996%	2.059%	0.567%
Jun 2010	Team Terrapin	Team Terrapin	gender_age	F	65-100	0.739%	1.340%	0.546%
Jun 2010	Team Terrapin	Team Terrapin	region	us	Maine	1.340%	2.647%	0.542%
Jun 2010	Team Terrapin	Team Terrapin	region	us	Hawaii	0.914%	1.765%	0.530%
Jun 2010	Team Terrapin	Team Terrapin	region	us	Georgia	2.462%	4.706%	0.525%
Jun 2010	Team Terrapin	Team Terrapin	region	us	Alabama	0.977%	1.765%	0.496%
Jun 2010	Team Terrapin	Team Terrapin	gender_age	F	45-54	7.840%	12.601%	0.483%
Jun 2010	Team Terrapin	Team Terrapin	gender_age	M	35-44	7.612%	12.064%	0.477%
Jun 2010	Team Terrapin	Team Terrapin	region	us	Oregon	1.545%	2.647%	0.470%
Jun 2010	Team Terrapin	Team Terrapin	region	us	South Carolina	1.391%	2.353%	0.464%
Jun 2010	Team Terrapin	Team Terrapin	region	us	Florida	7.971%	13.235%	0.456%

Creating a Responder Profiles report

The Responder Demographics report tells you a lot about what types of users are looking at and clicking your ads. However, those users' Facebook Profiles tell you even more. Facebook has a report called Responder Profiles to reveal information about users' likes and interests without compromising users' privacy rights.

The Responder Profiles report shows you the most common interests among Facebook users who looked at your ads in the past 14 days. Facebook groups this information and shows you the top recurring interests in categories such as Books, TV Shows, and Music. This information allows you to target filters to pick up new users who share the same interests. You might discover that your ideal target base likes a particular thing more than you expected.

To generate a Responder Profiles report, follow these steps:

1. **Go to the Reports screen within Ads Manager.**

2. **Select Responder Profiles from the Report Type field.**

3. **Choose your customization options, such as Summarize By, Filter By, and Format.**

   Date Range is available only as Last 14 Days for this report. Therefore, Time Summary is an irrelevant field.

4. **Click the blue Generate Report button.**

   If you select the Webpage format option, your Responder Profiles report appears like that shown in Figure 11-12.

This report pulls information only from the past 14 days.

In this report, the report name and customization options appear at the top, along with the Permalink, Export Report, and Generate Another Report buttons. Along the left side of the report table are the campaign and ad name as well as the following fields:

- **Interest:** A value found in multiple users' Facebook Profiles. Specifically, this value is pulled from the Interests field, within the Likes and Interests section of a users' profile. Examples of the Interest field from Figure 11-11 include reading, hiking, music, mountain climbing, and traveling.

- **Book, Music, or TV Show:** A book title, music type, or television show found in multiple users' Facebook Profiles. Specifically, these values are from the Books, Music, or TV Show fields, within the Likes and Interests section of a user's profile. Examples of the TV Show field from Figure 11-11 include *House*, *Family Guy*, and *The Office*.

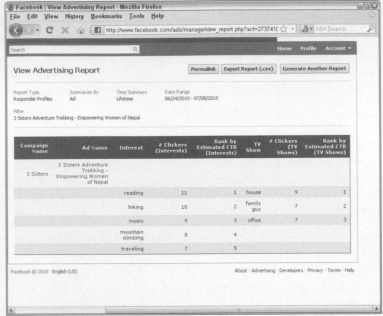

Figure 11-12:
Discover
which
demograph-
ics are
seeing and
clicking
your ad.

✔ **# Clickers (*field*):** The number of unique users who clicked the ad name mentioned in this line of the report, and who have the *field* specified in parentheses listed as an interest, book, music, or TV show in their Facebook Profile.

✔ **Rank by Estimated CTR (*field*):** The rank that Facebook assigns to the *field* in parentheses, in terms of the order of the most common interests, books, music types, or TV shows that your unique users (who clicked your ad) share with each other.

Unlike some of the reports mentioned earlier in this chapter, you can't re-sort the data presented to you in this report. That is why ranks are assigned based on the number of clickers who have that similar interest in their profile. You can still click the Export Report button to create a CSV file to download to your computer, or click the Generate Another Report button to start another report.

Gaining Insights from Facebook Insights

Besides your Facebook Ads reports, another rich set of data can help you target the right people for your ads, especially if you're using those ads to drive users to your Facebook presence. Know what it is? It's your current Facebook presence! If you've built your own Facebook Page or created a

Facebook Event, Facebook has been tracking the users who Like your Page or RSVP to your Event, and you can see reports and data of your current user base by using Facebook Insights.

Facebook Insights is a free function available for any Facebook Page administrator. *Note:* Only the person who is associated as the administrator can have access to Facebook Insights, as of the writing of this book.

To access Facebook Insights, do the following:

1. **From your Facebook home page, click the Ads and Pages link from the left navigation bar.**

2. **From the your Ads and Pages section, click the Pages link (below the list of your ad campaigns and above the Reports link) from the left navigation bar.**

   When you see the Pages screen, it should show the Pages You Admin list, as shown in Figure 11-13.

3. **Click the View Insights link for a Page that you administer to open the Insights dashboard for that page.**

Figure 11-13: Access Facebook Insights for any Page you administer.

View Insights links

When you get to your Facebook Insights dashboard for your Page, you will see a dashboard, broken up into two sections (see Figure 11-14):

- ✔ Users Who Interact With (*name of Page*)
- ✔ All People Who Like (*name of Page*)

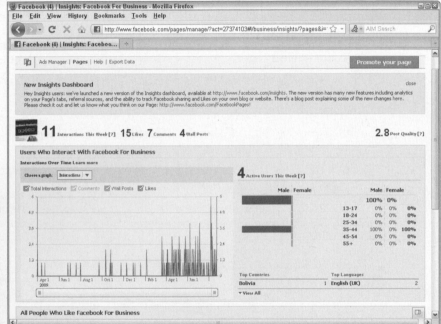

Figure 11-14:
See a concise dashboard of your Page Users and interactions.

These sections comprise interactive graphs and charts that give you a better idea about the users of your Page as well as the types of interactions they're having with you on the Facebook business Page.

Tracking interactions

The top dashboard on the Insights page focuses on the types of interactions you and your Users are having. Facebook describes these events as *interactive* because these events are really part of a two-way conversation between you and your Users: Every time you post something to your Page (a Wall post, a new photo, or some other form of new content), your post generates a user reaction in the form of Likes, comments, and Wall posts. The more that a user reaction is generated by your posts, the higher a Post Quality Score that Facebook assigns to your Page.

You can make your own inferences from this measured user activity as well. After all, if your users are contributing to your Facebook Page by writing, clicking, and commenting, that should indicate that your users find your Page valuable (or entertaining) — and therefore will be inclined to stay on your Page and hopefully draw positive conclusions about your business, your brand, and (if applicable) your products for sale. In other words, the more active your users are on your Facebook Page, the more "sticky" your Facebook Page is to your users, if you like to think of it in marketing terms. (*Sticky* is a marketing term meaning how long someone is "stuck" on your Web site instead of aimlessly surfing around. The more sticky your Web page, the better, since the average customer will spend more time with you and hopefully buy more, click more ads, and so on.) If they're using your Page, hopefully that means they have less time to spend on your competitor's Page or that they will be more likely to consider your company's product in the future.

Of course, the actual content of their interactions is important as well. After all, if your users are virtually picketing your site, writing post after post about how terrible you are, you will post very high interactive scores on your Insights dashboard — but that doesn't mean you're running a great business.

Total interactions

When you go to the Interactions part of the Insights page, you automatically see a graph from the past few weeks of your Page interactions with users. As we mention earlier, Facebook looks at different kinds of user response as an interaction with you and your Page, such as

- ✓ **Comments:** User leaves a comment under one of your posts.
- ✓ **Likes:** User becomes a Fan of your Page by clicking Like.
- ✓ **Wall Posts:** User writes something on your Page Wall.
- ✓ **Total Interactions:** This tallies Number of Comments + Likes + Wall Posts.

When you look at the Interactions graph (see the top of Figure 11-15), you see the four different options graphed out for the past week. To isolate any factor, simply clear its check box, and the graph will update itself with only the factors left marked, as shown in the bottom of Figure 11-15.

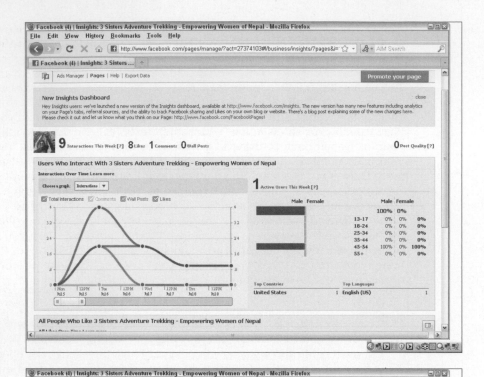

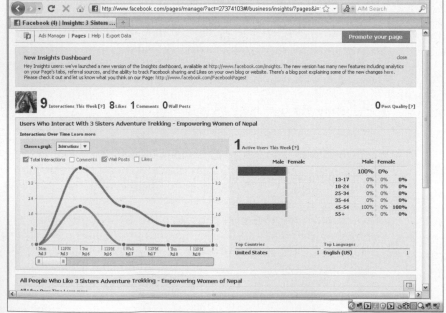

Figure 11-15:
Graph your
Page's total
interactions
for the past
week (top)
or just some
of your
interactions
(bottom).

You can click the drop-down arrow next to Interactions in the Choose a Graph section to see other graphs, which map out everything from interactions per Wall post to the number of mentions of your Page on Users' pages. When you get into the details part of your Insights page (which we discuss in a bit), you can graph these statistics as well.

As Facebook transitions to a new Insights interface, you will probably see a chart that shows just Likes and Comments, as shown in Figure 11-16. If you're monitoring your daily activity via Insights, you'll notice a Daily Post Views number and Daily Post Feedback percentage. Understand that these numbers change on a daily basis, and the percentage for feedback is based only on the feedback received *today* (not feedback received the previous day). You will need to monitor this on an ongoing basis to see any trends in how active your Posts are to your users.

See Details link

Figure 11-16:
Facebook
Insights for
Interactions
shows
Likes and
Comments.

When you're ready to see more detailed information about your interactions, simply click the See Details link, as indicated in Figure 11-16. In the next few sections, we talk about the graphs you can generate from this view.

Likes, Comments, and Unsubscribes

The first graph under the Interactions Insights report (see Figure 11-17) tracks three different measurements of your Users actions on your Page:

✔ The number of Likes received by a particular article or content piece of your Page

✔ The number of Comments under one of your (or one of your Friends') posts

✔ The number of Unsubscribes from your Page

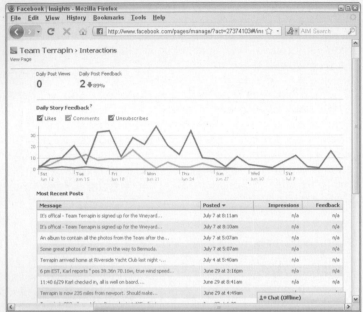

Figure 11-17:
See your
user inter-
action
numbers
over time.

By having these three statistics on one graph, you can visualize the positive or negative effect of your posts. By that, we mean that you can see where the approval is positive enough that users click the Like button, very positive enough that users are taking the time to Comment on the post, or the negative effect of causing users to lose such interest that they decide to unsubscribe from your page. Use this graph to see the trend of which action is more dominant as well as which actions are consistent or abnormal over a time period.

You can always not review any of the three elements by clearing its check box.

Wall posts

The second graph (see Figure 11-18) is basically a table that tracks the types of recent Wall posts that you (or another authorized admin of the page) made to the Page. If your users responded or interacted with those posts, you will see the number of interactions and feedback to each particular post in the table.

Here, your goal is to monitor your individual posts to see which ones are gaining more interaction and feedback. By seeing them together in a table, you can quickly see which posts are standing out from the pack and which posts are being overlooked by your audience.

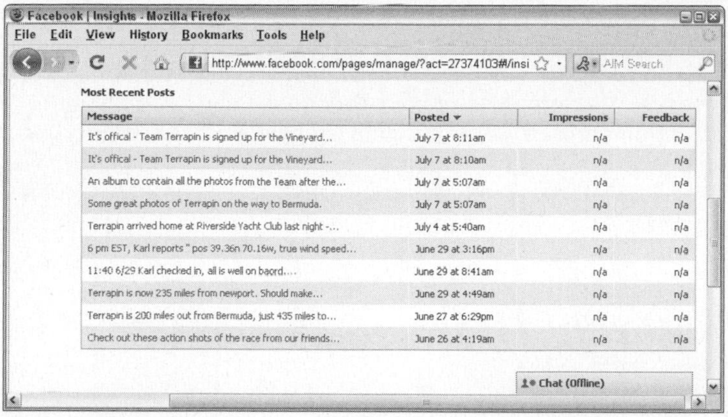

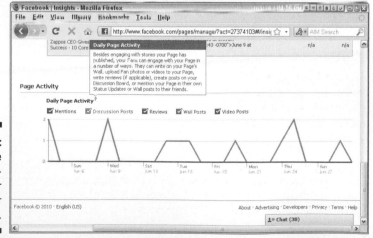

Figure 11-18:
See how
users are
interacting
with your
Wall posts.

Page interactions

Your users can do more than just Like your Page or Like your Wall posts.
Facebook provides a third and final graph in the Interactions report section
(see Figure 11-19), where you can see the measured number of Users who

- Mention your Page in their status update or Wall posts with their
  Friends
- Create posts on your Discussion Board
- Write reviews on your Page (if you have Reviews enabled)
- Write on your Wall
- Upload videos or User photos to your Page

Figure 11-19:
See how the
public per-
ceives your
Page over
time.

Here, you can study what parts of your Facebook Page, beyond the Wall, are being looked at and used by your audience. You can see the effect that a specific feature, such as a video post, has on your statistics over time, and get a sense of which parts of your Facebook Page need a shot in the arm to get attention and activity. Your goal isn't to generate activity for the sake of a colorful graph, but to have an active and interesting Page that supports your business goals through whatever functions your company has deemed necessary or your users require to stay engaged.

Measuring User engagement

In addition to tracking User interactions with your Page, you should look at the number and quality of Users of your Page. Facebook takes a look at your User base, the demographic information that Facebook can collect and present from everyone's own Facebook Profile, and the rise (and fall) of your User base on a weekly and total basis.

Total Users

No measurement would be complete without considering the total number of Users your Page has at the moment. The Facebook Insights page for User count starts with a graph of your total user count and active user count over the past three months (see Figure 11-20) along with a summary of the Monthly Active Users and most recent Daily New Likes count.

Figure 11-20: See your user count over time.

If you roll your mouse over either the Total Likes line or the Daily Active Users line, you can see the daily count of those figures. (See Figure 11-21.)

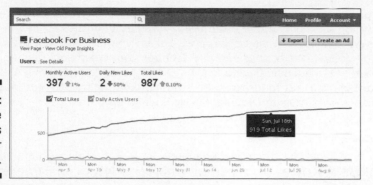

Figure 11-21:
Get precise
daily figures
on User
count.

New Users

When you click the See Details link for the User Insights page, you see several graphs of data: first, a close-up chart of the amount of daily active users on your Page for the past month; and second, a graph of new Users to your Page alongside the number of Users who have removed themselves from your user base on Facebook. (See Figure 11-22.)

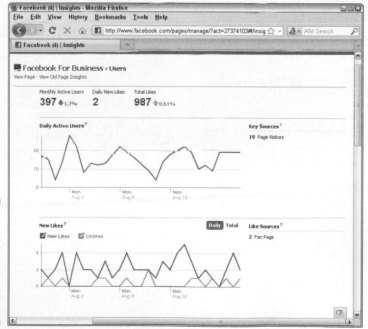

Figure 11-22:
See how
many new
Users you
gained in
the past
month.

One of the useful measurements you can detect from these two graphs is whether your daily count of active users is being influenced by the amount of new Users you've gained. In other words, is your Daily Active User count going up because of your new users, or are your new users taking the place of current Users who decide to leave, which creates a flat Daily Active User count? These are trends to watch out for, so definitely take advantage of Facebook Insights on a regular basis.

Country

Because Facebook is a global phenomenon — definitely not limited to just the United States — it's important to have a good idea of where your audience exists on a global scale. Facebook shows you the countries represented in your User base (for your Facebook Page) in the Users and Interaction reports, for both the past week and your overall User count.

After clicking the link entitled "View Old Page Insights," when looking at either the Users Who Interact With *<your business Page name>* or the All Users Of *<your business Page name>* header, you will see the View All link below the Top Countries listing. Click that link to see a drop-down list of all the countries that match the list type you're researching, as shown in Figure 11-23.

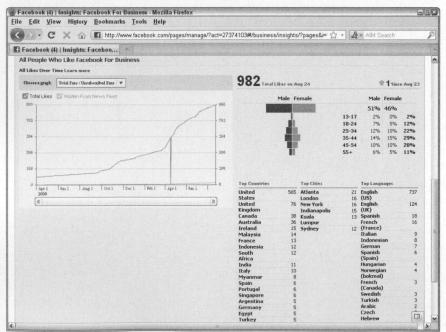

Figure 11-23: List the countries of your Page's Fans.

Breaking out demographics

After you study the sheer number of Users on your Page, the next question usually is about the types of Users you have: that is, their *demographic information.* Facebook organizes demographic information by gender, age group range, and then location, as you can see in the Demographics report in Figure 11-24. When you understand the most popular demographic ranges for your current user base, you will get a better idea of what to target with future ad campaigns if you truly need to maximize your budget and go after only the most likely candidates.

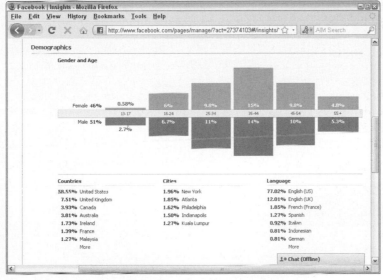

Figure 11-24: See the breakdown in demographic information for your Fan base.

If you see a More link under one of the location tables, like in Figure 11-24, just click it to expand the list to see all valid entries.

Exporting data

If you want to incorporate your ad performance data into a tracking system outside of Facebook's Ad reporting system, you can export the data from your Facebook Ad account to your computer, where you can view and manipulate the data; or import it into whatever tracking, analytics, or customer relationship management software you have.

When generating any report, simply change the Format option from Webpage (.html) to either Excel (.csv) or Multilanguage Excel (.csv), depending on how many languages you are implementing in your campaigns. (We discuss this in the section Generating Reports at the front of this chapter. You can see these options in Figure 11-4.) When you change that option and then click the Generate Report button, a pop-up window appears, asking whether you want to open or save your CSV report. When you save it to your system and then use Microsoft Excel to open this report, you should see something like Figure 11-25.

Figure 11-25: Download your ad reporting data onto your computer.

Date	Campaign Name	Campaign ID	Ad Name	Ad ID	Impressions	Clicks	Click Rate	Actions	Action Rate	Conversions	Cost Per Conversion
6/2/2010	Team Terrapin	6.00245E+12	Team Terrapin	6.00245E+12	5094	8	0.16%	5	0.10%	7	0.71
6/3/2010	Team Terrapin	6.00245E+12	Team Terrapin	6.00245E+12	10482	39	0.37%	16	0.15%	23	0.22
6/4/2010	Team Terrapin	6.00245E+12	Team Terrapin	6.00245E+12	18791	42	0.22%	17	0.09%	24	0.21
6/5/2010	Team Terrapin	6.00245E+12	Team Terrapin	6.00245E+12	19908	58	0.29%	14	0.07%	32	0.16
6/6/2010	Team Terrapin	6.00245E+12	Team Terrapin	6.00245E+12	17568	46	0.26%	11	0.06%	22	0.23
6/7/2010	Team Terrapin	6.00245E+12	Team Terrapin	6.00245E+12	1546	5	0.32%	0	0.00%	0	0
6/10/2010	Team Terrapin	6.00245E+12	Team Terrapin	6.00245E+12	20410	38	0.19%	13	0.06%	18	0.28
6/11/2010	Team Terrapin	6.00245E+12	Team Terrapin	6.00245E+12	10562	32	0.30%	7	0.07%	11	0.45
6/12/2010	Team Terrapin	6.00245E+12	Team Terrapin	6.00245E+12	16821	38	0.23%	15	0.09%	24	0.21
6/13/2010	Team Terrapin	6.00245E+12	Team Terrapin	6.00245E+12	2980	9	0.30%	0	0.00%	5	0.24

You'll notice that any days with 0 results are not exported into this new file. You should also notice that each column has a header as to what field it represents.

Piecing Together a Dashboard

Getting overloaded with data, statistics, and numbers is very easy when you look at all these various reports, day after day. As the saying goes, sometimes less is more. In this case, to manage an ongoing Facebook Ad campaign, the need for a very focused, precise, but informative set of reports or statistics is very real. Like for many other types of projects, having a dashboard, or clean set of high level numbers or statistics, can help you see the big picture to keep your campaigns on track.

Identifying what's important

The most important part of building your dashboard is deciding on the right elements and defining them correctly. If you stare at a bunch of numbers that have zero effect (or the wrong effect) on your ad budget and profitability, you're just wasting your time — and in some cases, your company's money. Conversely, if you become too focused on a tiny part of your campaign or chase the wrong goal for your brand, a dashboard can be more of a hindrance than a help.

Important stats to have for your dashboard include

- ✔ Cost per conversion (or cost per sale, cost per lead, and so on)
- ✔ Direction of average CPC (Going up? Down? Any reason?)
- ✔ Percentage of budget already spent
- ✔ Engagement stats (like those discussed earlier this chapter)

After you come up with the statistics for your dashboard, your next step is to figure out how to assemble or automate your dashboard so these statistics are always available to you for evaluation. Some companies put certain personnel in charge of pulling and presenting this data so it's always available online, or they use their information systems to create a tool to query the correct databases, calculate the necessary ratios, and present them on one screen, sometimes with graphical representations to make them easy to read.

If you don't have the dedicated personnel or resources to create an automated tool, perhaps you simply pick a fixed duration — say, once per week. Then you assemble the necessary data and share that data with management and any decision-makers to come up with short-term and long-term decisions. In the next section, we discuss several third-party solutions that can help you in this endeavor.

Exploring third-party tools

If you want a third party to help you coordinate all your Facebook Ad campaigns and show you detailed or specific reports on your progress, you can consider using a number of firms:

- ✔ **Alchemy** (www.alchemysocial.com): This firm, located in the UK, has handled campaigns for such companies as Nike, Nissan, Match.com, and HSBC. Alchemy offers a robust software solution that not only integrates with your choice of top analytic partners but also full-featured graphs (see Figure 11-26), bid management, and auto-optimization of your ads to get the lowest CPC and the highest results for your ads.

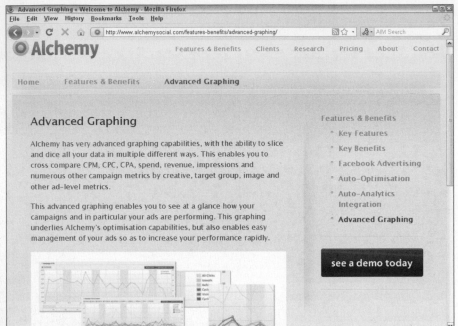

Figure 11-26:
Alchemy offers detailed reports and graphs.

✔ **BLiNQ Media** (www.blinqmedia.com): Billing itself as the "Social Engagement Advertising" company, BLiNQ Media provides companies with technology services and guidance to help those companies connect with customers on social media networks like Facebook. BLiNQ Media, which has worked with companies like AT&T, Delta Airlines, Sony Ericsson, and ING, can provide a centralized interface with intuitive dashboards, real-time analytics (see Figure 11-27), and help with devising social engagement strategies as well as computation of a company's "Cost per Social Action" when using Facebook Ads.

✔ **Clickable** (www.clickable.com): You can get started in seconds with Clickable's Pay per Click Management software. Offering an intuitive dashboard (see Figure 11-28), automated bid management, easy bulk-editing of multiple Facebook Ads, and extensive reporting and tracking options, Clickable can keep you informed and give you the information to make smart decisions regarding your Facebook advertising budget and spending. You can either choose the self-managed Clickable Pro software tool, or work with Clickable by using its Assist managed service. You might be able take advantage of a 15-day trial of Clickable their software from one of its Facebook Ads! (See Figure 11-29.)

Figure 11-27: BLiNQ Media offers a full-featured solution with real-time analytics.

Figure 11-28: Clickable offers an intuitive, readable dashboard.

Figure 11-29:
Clickable
reaches
out to new
users on
Facebook as
well!

You can find other third-party tools that interface directly with Facebook's system by checking the Facebook developer's Web site for their API tools vendor directory at `http://wiki.developers.facebook.com/index.php/Ads_API_Tools_Vendors`.

Chapter 12

Extending the Facebook Experience

In This Chapter

▶ Getting to know Facebook plug-ins

▶ Understanding the benefits of Facebook plug-ins

▶ Adding a Facebook plug-in to your own Web site

▶ Explaining the various Facebook plug-ins

*E*very year, Facebook holds a conference with its application developer community called F8. At the 2010 conference, Facebook CEO Mark Zuckerberg summed up many of Facebook's goals for their Web site in one sentence: "We are building a Web where the default is social." That conference was where Facebook launched its *Open Graph initiative,* which is a program designed for developers to add "hooks" or connections between Facebook, other popular Web site destinations, and regular Web sites that want to offer more content to their users.

In other words, the Open Graph initiative makes it easier for Web site developers to see social network connections between people, as well as those people's online interests. For example, special interest Web sites like Yelp use the Facebook Like button to capture information about users' favorite restaurants (based on Yelp reviews, for instance) and can use that information when trying to present new reviews. A movie Web site like Netflix or redbox can help record users' favorite movies based on their preferences and can use that information to recommend similar movies.

For online businesses, this means you can extend the Facebook experience to your own Web site so that hundreds of millions of users on your site can interact with your business using familiar Facebook elements. Facebook has created a system called Social Plugins, which we discuss in this chapter.

Introducing Social Plugins

When you hear the term *plug-in,* you might think of holding a power cord in your hand while looking for a power socket. However, Facebook's Social Plugins are purely software — code, that is. In essence, a Facebook social plug-in is a Facebook software feature that can be integrated or embedded into your own Web site. Typically, the easiest plug-ins only require one line of HTML code and can be added within seconds.

Here's the best part about Facebook's social plug-ins: All the heavy lifting and personalization is handled by Facebook, with no software or setup required on your part (aside from inserting the HTML code onto the correct Web page). Facebook hosts the plug-in on its site, which means that your plug-in will appear to be personalized because it will interface with your potential customer's Facebook account — while that customer is on *your* Web site, not Facebook!

The most important Facebook social plug-in is the ever-present Like button (or link). Place one line of HTML code on a page within your site, and your users will see the Facebook Like button. If users like what they see on your Web site, they can click that Like button, which posts a message on their Facebook profile that contains a preview of your Web site content for their friends to see. More importantly, when someone else views your Web pages, they automatically see which of their Friends have already Liked your content. In other words, the Friends of a new user are helping to sell your business automatically!

From the beginning, the response to this system was fast and overwhelming. Facebook launched this system with only 75 partners, but in one week, more than 50,000 Web sites had implemented at least one Facebook plug-in into their Web site. (Do the math — that's more than 300 Web sites per *hour!*) Today, Web sites large and small have Facebook plug-ins, from Yelp (see Figure 12-1) to local businesses like Meltdown Comics (see Figure 12-2), a Los Angeles-based comic book and memorabilia store.

Facebook personalization

Figure 12-1:
Yelp uses
Facebook
plug-ins to
customize a
user's expe-
rience.

Figure 12-2:
Local busi-
nesses
can use
Facebook
to connect
to their cus-
tomers.

Benefiting from Facebook Plug-ins

The first question most businesses have after hearing about Facebook plug-ins is: "Why do I need to put this on my Web site?" There are many answers to this question, and most of them have to do with a business's customers or users. These plug-ins provide a number of benefits to any size Web site, including the following:

- **Familiarity:** Facebook users know their Like buttons well. When you introduce Facebook-branded functions to your Web site, such as the Like button, you add a sense of familiarity for the hundreds of millions of Facebook users who are now on your site instead of Facebook.

- **Modularity:** Instead of building one specific "landing page" for your Facebook plug-ins, you can introduce different functions onto different pages on your Web site without an expensive programmer on staff. Most Facebook plug-ins require very little code or configuration on your end, and take up a small, set amount of width and height on your Web site, making them very plug-and-play–friendly and allowing you to drop in functions when appropriate in a very modular, or piece-by-piece, fashion.

- **Portability:** Regardless of how your users access your Web site or business content — mobile platforms, e-mail, Web sites, blogs, or by using any Internet-connected device — your Facebook plug-ins will go with your content, giving your users the same connected experience.

Fostering community

Most Internet users have a daily or weekly routine of Web sites they regularly visit that make up their active community. By integrating Facebook into your site with plug-ins, you make it easier for your users to include your Web site into that regular mix because your Web site becomes an extension of the Facebook experience instead of just another Web site to occasionally consider.

Most importantly, Facebook Social Plugins help put your Web site and your Web content in context with a user's Internet experience. For example, adding a Like plug-in to your Web site means that users may potentially discover that some of their Facebook Friends have Liked other articles on your site. This recommendation increases the chance of that user reading more content on your site. Then that user may click Like and share your content with his friends on Facebook, extending your content (and brand) even farther.

You have now extended the time that a user stays on your Web site (a term called *stickiness* in the Web community), and you have engaged this user on your own site, not Facebook. As users share and connect more of their interests, your Web site can become part of the overall user community.

Building engagement

As we discuss in other chapters, creating Facebook applications increases engagement with your customers and is a great way to keep your brand in front of customers and their friends. Facebook plug-ins allow you to continue that interaction to build more engagement and interaction.

One example is the Character Arcade, which is powered by the USA Network and has brought their games to Facebook. (See Figure 12-3.) This branded Web site allows people to play games against each other using different characters, some of which reinforce the programming seen on the USA Network. Although some plug-ins, such as the Like button, let Fans indicate their favorite games (see Figure 12-4), you can also challenge your Facebook Friends to a game. When you pick a Facebook Friend, the Character Arcade system determines whether that Friend is currently a user of Character Arcade and then sends that Friend a personalized invitation using Facebook and the person's status.

Figure 12-3: USA Network integrates Facebook into its Character Arcade.

Figure 12-4:
Games
in the
Character
Arcade
allow you to
Like and to
invite your
Friends to
play games.

Invite a friend   Like button

Adding Social Plugins to Your Web Site

When you're ready to add a Facebook plug-in to your Web site, be sure that you have access to the source files for your Web pages. Most Facebook plug-ins require you to add a line of HTML code to your source files.

For example, if you wanted to add a Like button to your Web page, you would follow these steps:

1. **Open up the HTML file for your Web site page, using whatever editor you normally use to make changes to your file (for example, Adobe Dreamweaver, Microsoft Word, or a UNIX editor like vi).**

2. **Go to the spot in the HTML file where you want the Like button to appear.**

3. **Input these lines of code into the HTML file. (replacing *http://* *example.com* with the name of your Web site):**

```
<iframe src= http://www.facebook.com/widgets/like.php?
href=http://example.com scrolling="no" frameborder="0"
style="border:none; width:450px; height:80px">
</iframe>
```

4. **Save the HTML file. If necessary, upload the new HTML file to your Web site.**

5. **Using a Web browser, go to your Web page (refresh your browser if necessary) and make sure that the Like button appears in the correct location.**

That's it! In most cases, installing a different plug-in only requires that you use a different line (or lines) of code in Step 3 of the preceding step list. Refer to the Facebook developers page for each plug-in for the specific code you will need.

Choosing Social Plugins for Your Business

You can go directly to the Facebook developers page for plug-ins (see Figure 12-5) to see the list of available plug-ins, details on how each plug-in works, and the specific code needed to add each plug-in to your Web site:

```
http://developers.facebook.com/plugins
```

Figure 12-5: See all the available plug-ins for your Web site.

The following sections review some of the more popular plug-ins.

Like button

The Like button — definitely the most popular plug-in available — can be used on multiple pages within your Web site. The purpose of this plug-in is simple: Putting a Like button on your Web site allows Facebook users who go to your Web page to click the button and add a content stream to their News Feed. If a Facebook user goes to your Web site and a Friend of theirs has already Liked your content, that Friend name will be indicated next to the Like button as already being a Fan of your content.

You can use a form on the Facebook developers plug-in page (see Figure 12-6) to build the code you need for your Web page. Simply complete the fields requested and then click the blue Get Code button to get the specific code you need to cut and paste into your HTML page. This way, you can customize how your Like button appears on your Web site.

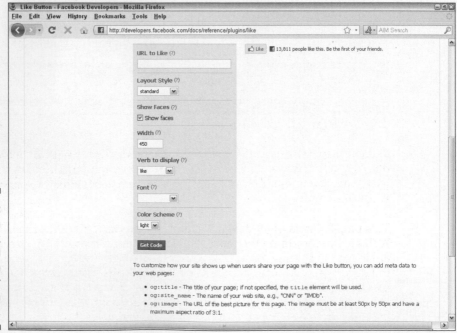

Figure 12-6: Use the Facebook Social Plugin form to build your Like button code.

So, as an example, we built a sample Like button (and used the other verb option, Recommend, instead of Like) to include on a comic book Web site, NewComix.com. We selected different options and then clicked the Get Code button to get the sample code, which can be seen in Figure 12-7. We can simply copy either the HTML code or the XFBML (eXtensible Facebook Markup Language) code into our Web page to complete the process.

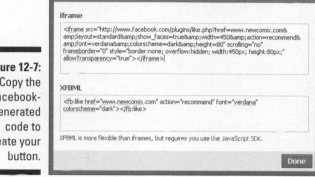

Figure 12-7: Copy the Facebook-generated code to create your button.

You can go directly to the developers plug-in page for the Like button:

```
http://developers.facebook.com/docs/reference/plugins/like
```

Recommendations

Recommendations allow you to display a personalized Recommendations box that lists specific content on your Web site recommended for a given user. This can be done by including the Recommendations plug-in on your Web site.

This plug-in looks at all the social interactions that reference the URL of your Web site to determine the most popular content for your Web site. If users are logged in to their Facebook account when they view your Web site with the Recommendations box, and they have Friends who viewed and Liked specific content, they will see the names of those Friends and the content where they clicked Like as highlighted and shown up front with preferential treatment, as part of their personalized Recommendations box.

You can use a form on the Facebook developers plug-in page (see Figure 12-8) to build the code you would need for your Web page. Simply complete the fields requested and click the blue Get Code button to get the specific code you need to cut and paste into your HTML page. This way, you can customize how your Recommendations box appears on your Web site.

Figure 12-8:
Use the Facebook plug-in form to build your Recommendations box code.

You can go directly to the developers plug-in page for the Recommendations plug-in:

```
http://developers.facebook.com/docs/reference/plugins/recommendations
```

Login (with Faces)

Because (after all) the Web site we're talking about is called *Face*book, and not *Name*book, or *Profile*book, or *Check*book (we think that last one is taken), it's only natural to discuss an option that includes actual faces. Facebook offers the Login with Faces plug-in. Nope, it's not a clever *Mission Impossible* security system with facial recognition, but actually exactly what it sounds like: a Facebook login box with faces (in this case, users' Facebook Profile pictures) of current users of your Web site.

You can generate the line of HTML by going to the developers plug-in page (see Figure 12-9) and setting up these three parameters:

✔ **Show Faces:** If you want your Login button to be accompanied by the profile pictures of Facebook users who have signed up for your Web site, keep this check box enabled. Otherwise, clear this check box.

✔ **Width:** This value determines how wide your Login with Faces box will display on your Web site (in pixels) Depending on where you plan to position this plug-in, the width can be very important.

✔ **Max Rows:** This parameter tells Facebook how many rows of profile pictures to display along with the Login button. If there aren't enough pictures to fill the number of rows you specified, Facebook will resize the box accordingly and show the max number of profile pictures that have joined your Web site.

Figure 12-9:
You can set up a Login with Faces box to appear on your Web site.

You can go directly to the developers plug-in page for the Login with Faces plug-in:

```
http://developers.facebook.com/docs/reference/plugins/login
```

Comments

One of the great advances with Web sites like Facebook is the ability for a two-way conversation, where customers, Fans, and casual observers alike can comment and interact with businesses and brands they see or enjoy. It's that interactive nature that makes sites like Facebook so addictive, so why not bring some of that two-way talking to your Web site? Facebook has a Comments plug-in that you can put on your Web site, allowing anyone to leave a comment about your Web content (see Figure 12-10), whether it's your business home page, an article, or other online page. Those comments can then be shared on the user's Facebook wall and show up in their Facebook Friends' streams.

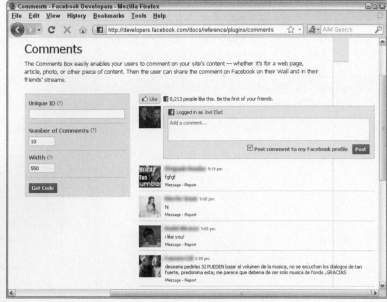

Figure 12-10:
Let your
Web site
visitors
leave com-
ments with
this plug-in!

You can generate the line of HTML by going to the developers plug-in page and setting up these three parameters:

- ✔ **Unique ID:** The unique ID number associated with the Comments plug-in. Typically, you can leave this field blank, and the value will be generated by the Web page when the box is being drawn.

- ✔ **Number of Comments:** This value determines the number of previous comments visible in your box. The default value is currently 10, but depending on your size limitations and where you want to place this box, you might want to lower the number of previous running comments.

- ✔ **Width:** This value determines how wide your Comments box will display on your Web site (in pixels) Depending on where you are going to position this plug-in, the width can be very important.

You can go directly to the developers plug-in page for the Comments plug-in:

    http://developers.facebook.com/docs/reference/plugins/comments

Activity Feed

In this "always-on" culture, sometimes people decide where to go by looking at where others have been. Showing recent activity on your Web site is not only a way to look hip and fresh to your users, but it encourages more interaction and exploration of your Web site by showing potential users what their Facebook Friends have been up to on your site (see Figure 12-11).

Figure 12-11: Show off your Web site's recent activity with the Activity Feed.

The Activity Feed box shows the recent activities of a user's Facebook Friends who are logged in to your Web site, and if necessary, contains recommendations on the most popular Web site content you have, according to Facebook users.

You can generate the line of HTML by going to the developers plug-in page and setting up the various parameters like the domain name of your Web site, the height and width of the Activity Feed box, the color scheme, font, and border color.

You can go directly to the developers plug-in page for the Activity Feed:

```
http://developers.facebook.com/docs/reference/plugins/activity
```

Like box

Sure, you can add the Like button to your Web site and count on your Web site to provide compelling content that'll make people click their way toward your business. But why not merge your Web site and your Facebook Page and gain Fans in general? Facebook allows you to put an entire Like box on your Web site to show people a dynamic, up-to-date snapshot of your Facebook Page, like how the Rio All-Suite Hotel & Casino does with its Web site. (See Figure 12-12.)

Figure 12-12:
Show off your Facebook Page content on your Web site.

Your Facebook Like box contains the following:

- An up-to-date count of your Facebook Page Fans, along with profile pictures of fans
- If the user is logged in to their account, which Friends already Like this page
- Recent posts from the business Page

You can generate the line of HTML by going to the developers plug-in page and setting up the various parameters, such as the Facebook Page unique Page ID, the width of the Like box, the stream of recent posts, and so on.

You can go directly to the developers plug-in page for the Like box plug-in:

```
http://developers.facebook.com/docs/reference/plugins/like-box
```

Friendpile

Say you want to show off the profile pictures of Facebook users who have logged in to your Web site, but you're not necessarily concerned with having your Web site visitors log in to their Facebook account (or your Web site) to see more. If that's the case, you might be interested in the Friendpile plug-in. Previously called the Facepile plug-in, this simple box shows profile pictures of current site members, and that's it.

You can generate the line of HTML by going to the developers plug-in page (see Figure 12-13) and setting up these two parameters:

✔ **Width:** How wide your Friendpile box will display on your Web site (in pixels). Depending on where you are going to position this plug-in, the width can be very important.

✔ **Num Rows:** How many rows of profile pictures to display in the box. If there are not enough pictures to fill the number of rows you specified, Facebook will resize the box accordingly and show the max number of profile pictures that have joined your Web site.

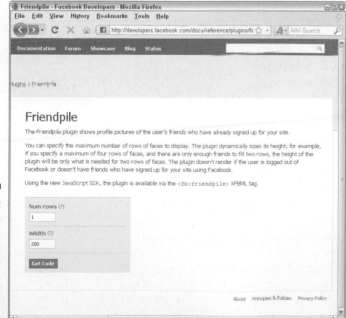

Figure 12-13: You can set up a Friendpile box to appear on your Web site.

You can go directly to the developers plug-in page for the Friendpile plug-in:

```
http://developers.facebook.com/docs/reference/plugins/friendpile
```

Live Stream

If you have a lot of steady activity on your Web site, like a webcast, live streaming event, or an online multiplayer game, you might want to show the constant activity on your site (or Facebook application, for example) by having a Live Stream box on your Web page. The Live Stream plug-in allows users to share their activities and their comments with each other in real time. This type of plug-in is best suited for an active online event or an application with a lot of steady users.

You can generate the line of HTML by going to the developers plug-in page (see Figure 12-14) and setting up these four parameters:

✔ **App ID:** If you are tying your Live Stream plug-in to a Facebook application, you can provide that application's unique ID number here so the Live Stream plug-in can properly interface with that application.

Figure 12-14: Show real-time interactions with the Live Stream plug-in.

✔ **Width:** This value determines how wide your Live Stream box will display on your Web site (in pixels). Depending on where you are going to position this plug-in, the width can be very important.

✔ **Height:** This value determines how tall your Live Stream box will display on your Web site (in pixels). Depending on where you are going to position this plug-in, the height can be very important.

✔ **XID:** This value is a number that you can assign to this Live Stream box to make it unique. This field is a required value if you want to place more than one Live Stream box for a given Web site and you want to differentiate them so that they can follow different events or applications.

You can go directly to the developers plug-in page for the Live Stream plug-in:

```
http://developers.facebook.com/docs/reference/plugins/live-stream
```

Part V
The Part of Tens

The 5th Wave   By Rich Tennant

"That's the problem—on Facebook, everyone knows you're a dog."

In this part . . .

As you develop your Facebook ad campaigns, you will do a lot of writing, testing, and rewriting. Some of these tasks will be easier than others, and some tasks that might seem easy will be harder than expected. We thought it was time to cover some information that makes things easier, not harder.

As we come to the end of *Facebook Advertising For Dummies*, we leave you with the Part of Tens, where you'll find chapters that list ten (or so) helpful items. They're advice, tips, and references that just fit best in a ten-item list format.

Chapter 13

Ten Facebook Page Promotion Techniques (Besides Ads)

In This Chapter

▶ Promote your Page offsite

▶ Put compelling or unique content on your Facebook Page

▶ Have a clear focus on your Page's purpose

▶ Make your content easy to share

▶ Get your users to collaborate

▶ Provide something exclusive to your Facebook Page

▶ Build a Facebook app

▶ Create and interact with Facebook Groups

▶ Post a Facebook Marketplace listing

▶ Market yourself, not just your Page

As you maintain a presence on Facebook and use ad campaigns to promote your business on and off Facebook, keep in mind other techniques you can use to promote your Facebook Page. Some of these techniques are common sense, and others are unique to Facebook. The point, though, is that you should be as active and open as possible because you never know where your next customer will see you, or what feature will turn out to be the "killer app" that drives traffic to your Facebook Page. In this chapter, we highlight ten concepts that we think are beneficial to implement as you build and promote your Facebook presence.

Promote Your Page Offsite

It might seem like the whole world is online and using sites like Facebook, with its hundreds of millions of users, but don't forget about all your other encounters that might or might not happen online and happen outside Facebook. You should promote your Facebook Page in as many mediums as possible, including adding a Find Us on Facebook button or graphic on elements such as

- ✔ Your e-mail marketing efforts (see Figure 13-1)
- ✔ Your Web site
- ✔ Physical signs in your store
- ✔ Store receipts or online order invoices
- ✔ Your company (or personal) e-mail signature

Figure 13-1: Announce your Facebook presence via e-mail to your customers.

And here are other benefits of promoting your Facebook Page in other mediums: Not only is announcing your Facebook Page a news item worth sharing with your audience (that is, it's a great reason to contact your user base, and while you're at it, to mention other related news, like limited-time-only product offers) but it's also a way to show your audience that you are approachable via a new communications avenue. Even if users don't look at your Facebook Page, they associate your business with one that stays ahead of the curve or strives to be relevant and accessible.

Put Compelling or Unique Content on Your Page

You have to be on Facebook with a business Page to be part of the conversation. After you build your Facebook Page, though, ask yourself whether anything unique, interesting, compelling, or "gotta have" is available on your Facebook Page. Is there something that will compel people to give up some of their free time to go on your Facebook Page?

One example is the Magic Bullet compact blender made by Homeland Housewares. Homeland didn't just build a token Facebook presence, but instead included an entire tab of how-to videos using the Magic Bullet (see the left image in Figure 13-2) and an entire interactive recipes section of foods and drinks you can make by using the Magic Bullet (see the right image in Figure 13-2) on top of the Wall, discussion threads, and photos for that Page. The owners of the Magic Bullet blender provided hours of free content without asking for any money up front.

Figure 13-2:
Include how-to videos on your site (left) or add a library of unique recipes that involve your product (right).

Have a Clear Focus on Your Page's Purpose

Businesses commonly build a Facebook Page because someone "at the top" said that they needed one. However, just having a Page is no longer good enough in today's market. Instead, your Page should serve at least one clear purpose, something that will be obvious to any new Fan or customer who arrives on your Page.

Look again at the Magic Bullet Facebook Page and note that everything about that Page is essentially geared to one thing — selling Magic Bullets. The wealth of video and information is designed to show the usefulness and benefits of the Magic Bullet. The interaction between potential customers and company representatives is meant to allay any fears and reduce any objections to the sale. The friendly and nonthreatening nature of the conversations that Magic Bullet starts with its Fans (see Figure 13-3) gets current users to talk about their devices in a positive and happy way, which essentially become testimonials for anyone browsing or considering buying a device.

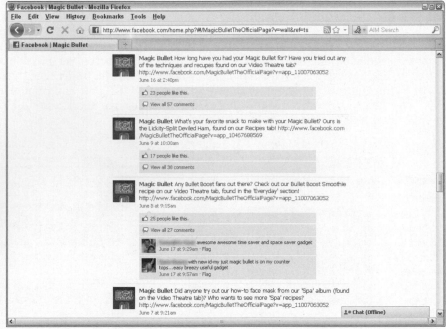

Figure 13-3:
Make sure your Facebook Page has a clear purpose.

Make Your Content Easy to Share

After your Fans are on your Facebook Page, make sure they can spread the word about what they find to their Friends and the world in general. Facebook is a success because it allows people to connect with each other and share their favorite content, whether it's a photo, hyperlink to a Web site, or funny video. Let your Fans become your "viral army," spreading the good word 24/7 so you can focus on making your followers happy and informed.

This means putting buttons or links so people can share information with their Facebook Friends; post a Twitter message to their followers; or alert other social media sites like Digg, Del.icio.us, or StumbleUpon. You can make sure your Web site content has an RSS feed so that Fans can subscribe and automatically receive updates of your newest content.

You can also share products with other people. For example, Best Buy created a program that allows you to pick out something from its catalog, post it to your Facebook Wall, and solicit advice from your Friends on whether to buy it (see Figure 13-4). Not only is this extending the Best Buy experience to your Facebook Page and all your Friends' Pages, but it also gets people to recommend products they like (which is one of the top motivators for buying something) that you can then buy . . . from Best Buy!

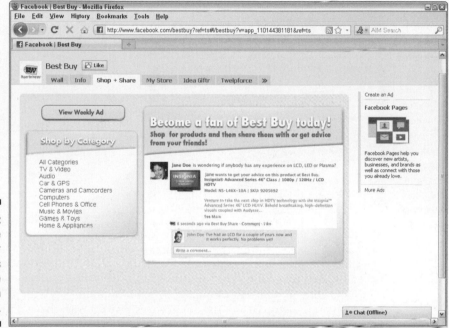

Figure 13-4:
Encourage
your
customers
to share
content with
Friends.

Get Your Users to Collaborate

It works for *American Idol,* so why not your business? Because Facebook allows you to have a two-way conversation with your potential customers, why not use that medium to the fullest, and have your members vote or collaborate on something to get them involved and invested in your brand? Companies big and small offer different ways to get the opinions and ideas of their customers. Not only does your customer feel more of a connection with your business, but this also usually increases the amount of times they visit your Facebook Page and think about your business.

Every year, Target donates 5% of its profits to a nonprofit organization. Instead of having the executives pick the charity, though, Target decided to leave the choice to its customers. So, Target created a poll on its Facebook Page, asking people to vote for their favorite charity from a list of prescreened, worthy organizations. Based on the votes received, Target awarded the top vote-getting organizations with a part of this profit (see Figure 13-5).

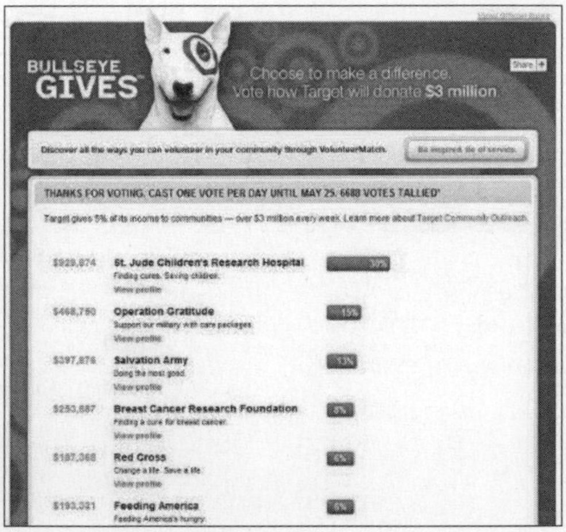

Figure 13-5: Target allows its community to pick worthy nonprofits to receive donations.

You can also have your customers pick the winner of an upcoming contest (see Chapter 15 for an example of ad campaigns that support Facebook Page contests) by posting the top entries on your Facebook Page and having your Fans vote on their favorite ones. When Mountain Dew wanted to add a new flavor, it offered users the chance to come up with three different flavors, which were bottled and distributed. Fans were able to go back to the Mountain Dew Facebook site and vote on their favorite one, and the winner will become a regular flavor of Mountain Dew to be distributed with the other regular flavors.

Provide Something Exclusive to Your Facebook Page

One way to make your Facebook Page so compelling is to make sure you put something on your Facebook Page not available anywhere else. That means putting some sort of exclusive content or an exclusive offer that causes people to check out or Like your Facebook Page to benefit from this exclusive. This can be an introductory exclusive or some form of ongoing exclusive.

An early adopter of Facebook, Victoria's Secret has an extensive Facebook Page where Fans are part of a PINK Nation. Victoria's Secret provides an exclusive offer if you sign up for its Facebook Page (see Figure 13-6) and also tied in a number of events and other content to its Facebook Page. (See Figure 13-7.)

Figure 13-6: Offer something exclusive through your Facebook Page.

Figure 13-7: Tie in events and other content to keep your Page active.

Build a Facebook App

According to recently published statistics about Facebook, about one-half of its hundreds of millions of users access the site at least once per day. This heavy usage is attributable to the number of things someone can do on Facebook. Besides communicating with their Friends, Facebook users love to play games and use applications. Therefore, just like brands that sponsor TV shows, radio programs, or outdoor events, you can get your brand in front of people by creating your own application — typically, branded with your name — so people can use or play with your app, and see your brand every time they do so.

Some companies integrate their products with the application. Zappos.com, a leading online shoe retailer, wrote its own Facebook app (see Figure 13-8), which a Facebook user can install on their Page. The app user can share with their Facebook Friends different products from the Zappos catalog, especially recently purchased items. This keeps the Zappos brand, and product catalog, very close to users' level of awareness.

Figure 13-8:
Write an application that integrates your products into your users' lives.

Other applications are geared more for fun and games. For example, Red Bull recrafted a game called Red Bull Roshambull, based on the old Rock-Paper-Scissors game. (See Figure 13-9.) This game allows you to challenge your Facebook Friends to a game, while the application keeps track of all your games and allows you and them to enter and compete in tournaments. Because you're inviting people to play against you, you're extending Red Bull's reach to other people, and those people might invite their Friends, and so on.

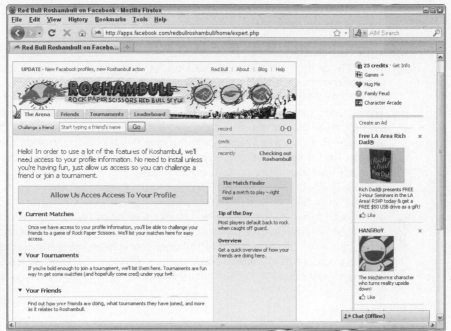

Figure 13-9:
Add a
game app
that allows
Friends to
compete.

Of course, writing your own Facebook application takes time and money, so you have to decide whether it's a worthwhile investment. You can do a search for Facebook application developers, or search the official Facebook developers Web site at `http://developer.facebook.com/docs`.

You can also find more information about how to build a Facebook application by checking out *Building Facebook Applications For Dummies* by Richard Wagner.

Create and Interact with Facebook Groups

Before Facebook business Pages became very popular, Facebook users would organize themselves around a common topic or theme that interested them by creating and joining a Facebook Group. A Facebook Group allows people to be members of the Group without requiring every member to "Friend" every other member; and anybody in the Group can share photos, news items, and have discussions around their common topic.

One way that you as a business can extend your brand is to form a Facebook Group around an issue or topic that pertains to your business. We're not saying that you should form a Group about your business because that is what your business Page is for. Rather, you can promote yourself by being an active participant, or even the founder, of a related Group that matters to your customers.

The easiest way to start is to simply join a Facebook Group or two, and start participating by joining in discussions and sharing opinions, information, and photos. If you see the value in participating and being the ambassador of your brand in these Groups, but there's not a Group that addresses a concern your business or your customers would be interested in, feel free to start one.

If you start a Group with the sole intention of pushing your products, you will probably be in a Group by yourself. Facebook users are interested in socializing with each other, not in getting even more marketing messages. Use your time in a Facebook Group to share advice, tips and tricks, and support so people can observe that your brand is interested in more than pure sales.

Post a Facebook Marketplace Listing

Another section of Facebook that could provide you with some opportunity is the Facebook Marketplace. This section is designed with pure commerce in mind: Any Facebook user can list merchandise for sale to sell to other Facebook users. The process works similar to other community Web sites like Craigslist, where you can see merchandise for sale in a variety of categories, as shown in Figure 13-10.

Depending on your market, you can simply list items from your business on the Marketplace, or you can perhaps clean out some old office furniture or unused prototypes on the Facebook Marketplace. As you list items for sale, you can share this information with your Friends or your Fans, so they can spread the news to their Fans as well.

If you're a services business, you can list your service as a Marketplace item. You can see a list of categories available (see Figure 13-11) with many options for advertising a local services business on Facebook via the Marketplace. These listings can have photos and comments, and can link back to your profile.

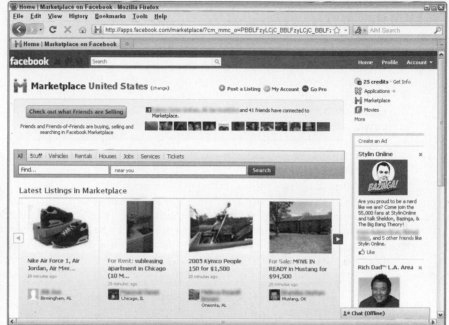

Figure 13-10: See what's available for sale, or sell yourself, in the Facebook Marketplace.

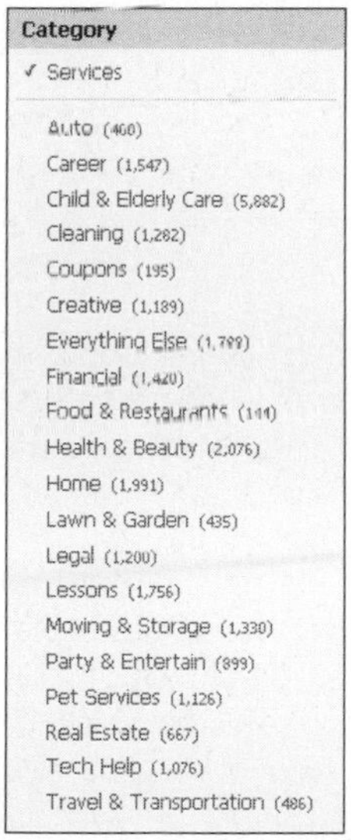

Figure 13-11: Many categories are available for local service business listings on Facebook Marketplace.

Category

✓ Services

Auto (460)
Career (1,547)
Child & Elderly Care (5,882)
Cleaning (1,282)
Coupons (195)
Creative (1,189)
Everything Else (1,799)
Financial (1,420)
Food & Restaurants (144)
Health & Beauty (2,076)
Home (1,991)
Lawn & Garden (435)
Legal (1,200)
Lessons (1,756)
Moving & Storage (1,330)
Party & Entertain (899)
Pet Services (1,126)
Real Estate (667)
Tech Help (1,076)
Travel & Transportation (486)

Market Yourself, Not Just Your Page

Getting attention on Facebook for your business or brand is never limited to just your company Facebook Page. You can be the ambassador of your brand, so remember that you can promote yourself (no, not as in giving yourself a raise and a new title) on Facebook, and make connections with other people through your Friends, discussions, Facebook Groups, Pages, applications, and the Marketplace.

As you build connections, provide commentary, and lend your expertise to others on Facebook, you're implicitly extending your business or brand as well. Of course, this method does have its consequences, especially if you decide to share behavior that's, well, unbecoming of your business or brand. Remember, Web sites might change, but after it's on the Internet, it lives forever in the cache of a search engine, so try to limit your embarrassing moments, and promote your community building activities instead.

Chapter 14

Ten (or So) Facebook Ads Beginner Mistakes

In This Chapter

▶ Not using a picture or graphic in your ad

▶ Not refreshing the ad often

▶ Not split-testing the ad at least once

▶ Not targeting your audience

▶ Targeting your audience too tightly

▶ Testing your ads for too short or long a time period

▶ Focusing on CPC or Page membership and not profit per click or engagement

▶ Writing a simple/boring headline

▶ Not including a strong call to action

▶ Not connecting with your audience on a relationship basis

▶ Not following Facebook Advertising Guidelines

After speaking with a number of people and companies that have advertised on Facebook, as well as running numerous campaigns ourselves, we thought it beneficial to talk about the mistakes people make: what you should *not* do when building a Facebook Ad campaign. Sometimes, it really is easier to give advice on what *to do* by illustrating what *not to do* first.

Not Using a Picture or Graphic in Your Ad

When you build ad campaigns in other systems like Google AdWords, you focus on elements such as the headline, offer, call to action, and destination URL because those are important elements. However, when building a Facebook Ad, one of the most critical components of your ad is the image that goes along with the advertisement. Although, for Facebook this is an optional step, it's very important in terms of people who advertise on Facebook.

Look at the example in Figure 14-1. In this group of nine ads, which is the ad that's easiest to ignore? Probably the one that doesn't have a graphic. And this advertiser had several options, say showing a person standing next to a computer or hunched over a laptop, or using clip art of a laptop or a stock photo of a computer, or showing someone frustrated with his computer.

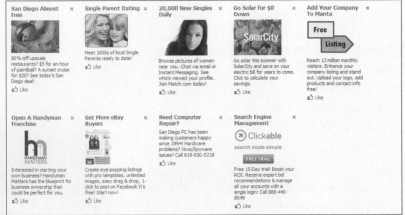

Figure 14-1:
Which
ad is the
least likely
noticed?

If you can't find a picture, clip art, or even the logo to your Web site, consider using a graphic of several big words of text. (See Figure 14-2.) Of course, the simplest solution is just to show a picture of somebody smiling (see Figure 14-3). Facebook users and advertisers say that ads with people in them — especially smiling people — typically capture more attention than ads without people in the photos. As clichéd as it sounds, this site is called *Face*book for a reason. We're trained to look for our Friends' faces in their profile pictures, and we respond more to photos on a site like Facebook because so many people use the site to show and exchange photos with each other.

Figure 14-2:
Sometimes
words can
become
your
graphic.

Figure 14-3: Smiling people can definitely catch your eye when looking at ads.

If you're not an expert at locating photos or graphics to use in your ads, don't worry. Stock photography sites like iStockphoto (www.istockphoto.com) are available. Check out Chapter 16 for more information.

Not Refreshing the Ad Often

In the early stages of your ad campaign, as you test different concepts and try different combinations to find the best result, your ads will change often, especially for different people. After you stabilize on an ad or two, though, don't rely on that ad for too long. Your users will likely see the same set of ads again and again, and if they notice that your ad doesn't change or update itself, they will more easily ignore your ad in general throughout the life of your campaign.

Run the top two or three ads from your test efforts in a rotation, or come up with a way to keep your ads fresh.

Rosetta Stone, for example, runs a special every month (see Figure 14-4), so not only does the ad seem more appealing and specific, but Rosetta Stone can also run a different ad every month that's not so different and has good response rates.

Figure 14-4: Change out your ads, at least slightly, on a regular basis.

Not Split-Testing Your Ad at Least Once

It can be very easy to design and launch your ad without testing and revision that turns out to be profitable. You might think, "I don't need to test this, I've got my winner, and I will run with this ad until it becomes unprofitable." However, wouldn't you like to know whether one simple change could make a large, noticeable difference?

Advertisers have seen a dramatic difference when they swap out even one element of their Facebook Ad. Using a more interesting picture, changing a message to include a strong call to action, or even changing one word in a message can make a lot of difference. The point of split-testing is to compare two nearly identical ads with exactly one difference, to see which ad performs better in terms of a higher click-through rate — and, if you're measuring it, a higher conversion or action rate.

Nick O'Neill, the founder and editor of All Facebook (www.allfacebook.com) commented in one of his articles that "an advertiser told me once that women tend to react more often to advertisements that have the color pink in them." Although O'Neill doubted whether this applied for all women, he assumed it could have been true for a significant portion of them. Something like this can be tested with an ad split test.

Of course, you can split-test more than one concept with two ads: for example, trying three different graphics while keeping the ad identical (see Figure 14-5) to see what type of graphic garners the biggest response.

Figure 14-5: Try different concepts to look for a difference in response.

 If you run a split test and the results are almost the same, keep the ad you like, toss out the other, and test a different concept to see whether that new concept makes a change.

Not Targeting Your Audience

Even if you think your ad, product, or company applies to everybody, you can still optimize your ad campaign by making sure only the most interested or the most targeted people see your ad. If you were advertising with an out-door billboard or a TV commercial, you'd have to pay to show your ad to a lot of people who are *not* interested just to get your ad in front of an audience who *is* interested. Facebook offers so many targeting controls and options, though, that you can prevent your ad from being shown to those who do not want to see it, so you pay only for those people who are most likely or your exact target audience.

This is especially true for local service companies. For example, if you're a plumber in Boston, why would you want to show your ad to someone in San Diego? Use the location feature to target only those people within a certain radius. You can always experiment with a larger radius, but ignoring that factor altogether can cost you big money. We discuss setting the location filter in Chapter 3.

Because you have the ability to target by demographic or likes/interests, why wouldn't you want to put your ad in front of people who are eager and most likely to consider responding? Look at your business records to see which types of customers are the most likely to buy, and perhaps target the cus-tomer demographics that match your highest spending customers. Then add those targeting factors, and see what happens to your advertising statistics, and of course, your resulting sales or actions from the ad.

If you're unsure what demographics to target, run your ad for an entire range. Then, from Facebook Reports, run a Responder Demographics report to see which demographic ranges have the highest response rates. Consider updating your ad with those demographic ranges to see whether focusing your audience causes an even bigger reaction. See Chapter 11 for more information about this report.

Targeting Your Audience Too Tightly

Of course, if not using any targeting is a mistake, so is using too much targeting. The allure of targeting factors can cause people to keep narrowing down and narrowing down until they reach their "perfect" demographic. The problem is that if your audience is too narrow, you might not see the volume you need to justify the ad campaign. Keep in mind that your estimated audience needs to be big enough so that a response rate of even 0.1% will generate enough clicks and profit to be worthwhile.

As an example, co-author Paul Dunay ran a campaign to promote the 3 Sisters Trekking group (which helps train job-seeking women in Nepal to become guides for travelers). When he put together the appropriate targeting filters, he chose to target women over 18 in the United States who are interested in mountaineering, trekking, women's rights, or mountain climbing, because he felt this target audience would be most interested in contributing, sup-porting or learning about this cause. After applying all the targets, Facebook estimated the reach of this ad was only 17,820 people (see Figure 14-6). And after running this campaign, he found that he was averaging about 20 clicks per day, of which less than one-half converted to Fans of the Page. Although the targeting was reaching the ideal candidate, the results were not enough to meet the short-term goals, leaving him to consider expanding his targeting filters to reach a wider audience.

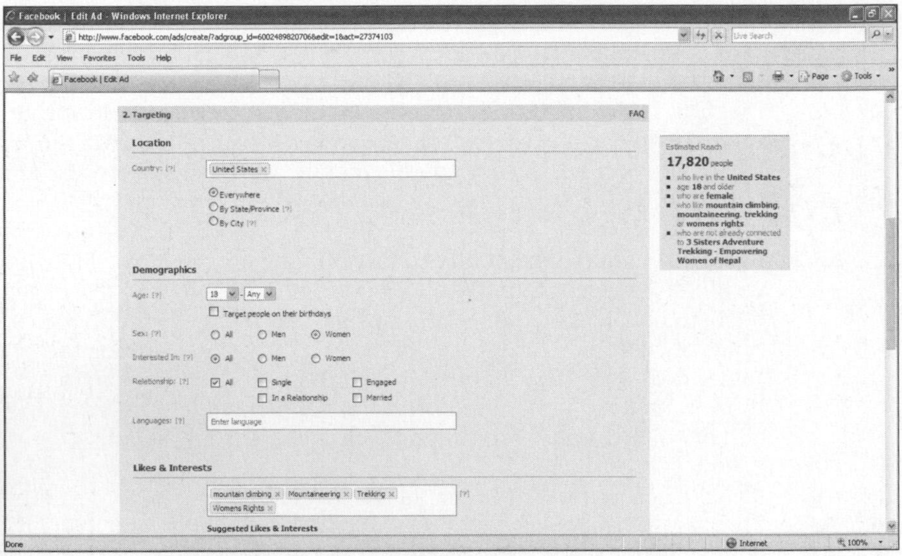

Figure 14-6:
Make sure
your esti-
mated reach
is enough
for a viable
campaign.

Testing Your Ads for Too Short or Long of a Time

Throughout the book, we talk about the importance of testing your Facebook Ads, but how long should you test those ads? Some advertisers make changes after getting only a few clicks, and some advertisers never seem to get out of testing mode. The key is to find a comfortable range of bids that take up a small but measurable part of your overall budget.

One benchmark could be your overall ad budget. Some advertisers set aside 5% to 15% of their total ad budget for testing purposes. Put another way, after they spend 5% of their total ad budget on their test campaigns, they start looking at their test results to see whether they can make a valid conclusion. And then, after 10% of their budget is spent, they wind down any remaining tests and start making bigger decisions for their main campaigns.

Other advertisers like to see a number of clicks per test ad before they make their call. Some advertisers, for example, wait to get 100 clicks on an ad before making any decision. Others amassed 50 to 75 clicks for each of their test ads before comparing click-through rates (CTRs). After the ratios start to stabilize, whether it's 50 or 100 clicks, the advertiser can start to make a truly educated decision.

Conversely, some companies find themselves spending 25% to 50% or more of their entire ad budget just on the testing while they split-test ad after ad in search of the perfect result. Avoid testing for too long — or over your spending limit — and simply go with the best results you found up to that point.

Focusing on CPC or Membership, Not Profit per Click or Engagement

One easy trap lots of people fall into is obsessing about the cost per click (CPC) or CTR numbers from their Facebook Ad campaigns without determining whether those new clickers actually buy anything or stick around the business' Facebook Page. You could have phenomenal CTRs, but if everybody you "recruit" through Facebook completely ignores your business, you're spending money for little more than brand awareness.

The key here is to either be able to track each new lead all the way to completion, so you know exactly what each lead is ordering and so you know the profit for that customer. Once you know the profit per customer, you know how much to spend in order to get that customer. (You also know if you overspent your ad budget to acquire that customer), Another way to track this is to be familiar enough with your average sales from that Web channel so that you know your average profit per order, lifetime value of a customer, and your average conversion rate from when someone arrives at your Web site to when they purchase an item or two. Let's say that you know that 10% of your new Web site visitors become paying customers, the average profit per order is $50, and the lifetime value of a new customer is $250. In the short term, each new visitor is worth $5 to you; and in the long term, each new visitor is worth $25. These are much better numbers to obsess about than cost per click.

After you know one of these sets of numbers, you have a better idea whether your Facebook Ad campaign is truly profitable. Say that you're getting 100 clicks per day for your Facebook Ad, and 2 of those clicks turn into orders. Also say that your average profit per order is $40. Those 100 clicks are earning you $80, so if you're paying more than $0.80 per click, you're losing money.

Look at another type of goal. Say you want to build your Facebook Page up to 1,000 Fans for a given ad budget. If you're not earning enough new Fans to meet your goal when your ad budget runs out, you're going down the wrong road, and you need to work on improving that conversion before running more ads.

Writing a Simple or Boring Headline

Pick up a newspaper or read the news online, and you'll see the power of a good headline. Ever since the days of newsboys shouting "Extra! Extra!" to passersby, people pay attention to a headline. It's the biggest text on the page and can be seen from a distance, so make it count. When it comes to Facebook Ads, there are a number of restrictions on the headline. You have only 25 characters, you can't use certain punctuation marks (like an exclamation point), and your headline has to be relevant and pertain to your ad. For example, you can't scream about sex and free products if you're advertising an online university.

However, you can try to write a headline that stands out from the pack without breaking any of these rules. Although you can't use exclamation points, you can use a question mark, so get people's attention by asking a question (see Figure 14-7). "Why should you consider X?" Entice people with questions like, "Want to join the FBI?"

Figure 14-7: Get attention by asking a question.

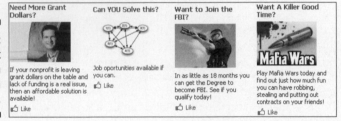

You can also try to write a headline that offers specific benefits: for example, *4 Flat Stomaching Foods, 7 Ways to Get Trimmer, Get Solar for $0 Down*. If you can boast of an award or status, use your headline to announce it: *The #1 Game on Facebook*. Finally, add keywords to your headline to draw attention; for example, why say *Home Rentals* when you can say *Home Vacation Rentals* or *Private Home Rentals*?

Not Including a Strong Call to Action

As we mention elsewhere, Facebook advertising is different than other forms of online advertising because when folks are on Facebook, they're not purposely searching for something specific, not necessarily in a buying mode, or not even in the mood to look for something. Typically, they're catching up with their Friends, enjoying some Facebook applications, or just goofing off. The ads are served along the right side of the page, hoping to catch the user's eye.

Therefore, it's even more important that your ad include a call to action to encourage every visitor to click the link and find out more. Remember that your ad is basically asking someone to stop what she is doing, click the link, and find out more about your products or services as mentioned in the ad. So, you have to present a compelling reason, even if the call to action is as simple as Liking your Facebook Page.

Here are some examples:

- ✔ Saying you're giving something away for free is great. Being *specific* about what you're giving away for free — and, if possible, describing why that free thing will help someone — is even better.

- ✔ Compare two MBA programs whose ads just happened to show up side by side (see Figure 14-8). The ad on the left has a generic statement about what the school offers. The ad on the right is not only specific about some of the benefits (21-month program, local alumni network) but also encourages people to accept an application for the upcoming semester. Timed deadlines can be an excellent motivator.

Figure 14-8:
Be specific to encourage that call to action.

Not Connecting with Your Audience on a Relationship Basis

Just because you're writing an advertisement doesn't mean that it has to read like an advertisement. You're free to write about the why or the history of your brand or whatever it takes to connect with your audience. Remember that you're reaching out to users in a friendly, nonthreatening active environment that's more conducive to relationship marketing than pure sales or rapid conversion. Advertising on Facebook is more of a long-term relationship instead of a fast-paced, product-sales cycle that other online advertising platforms can encourage.

One way to connect to your audience is to use a particular cause, charity, or non-sales approach so you can form more of a social connection between you and the people who make up your potential customer set. Companies partner with nonprofits and causes all the time, and companies advertising on Facebook should be no different.

Another way to connect with your audience is to use your ad message as a way to speak directly to your potential customers about why you are in business. Compare these two photography services advertising on Facebook. The first ad (see Figure 14-9) is a decent, clear ad that gives the name of the business as the headline and the types of services offered, with a fun picture. The second ad, however, has a nice picture but also talks about *why* the photographer loves the job. If you were reading both ads while looking for a photographer, which ad would you click first?

Figure 14-9:
Would you consider reading an ad like this (left) or an ad that speaks to the why of their service (right)?

Not Following Facebook Advertising Guidelines

The last big mistake that most beginners commit when building their Facebook Ads has to do with not following the Facebook Advertising Guidelines. As Facebook launched and grew its ad system, Facebook put into place a strict set of guidelines to control the types of ads it would display. Partially to protect users from placing the wrong kinds of ads, and partially to protect the Facebook brand against ads that would turn off their user base, Facebook management put together its Advertising Guidelines, which are different than other online advertising systems (such as Google AdWords).

Here's how these guidelines work: When you create your ad to be run on Facebook, you submit your ad to Facebook for approval. Facebook checks your ad copy, image, destination URL, and landing page against its Advertising Guidelines and decides whether to approve or disapprove your ad. Only after Facebook approves your ad will your ad show up in search results and earn clicks. If your ad gets rejected, you receive a message about the guideline(s) that you violated. Then, if you want, you can fix those issues and resubmit your ad for approval. This process can occur multiple times until Facebook feels you are in full compliance with its Advertising Guidelines.

You can go straight to Facebook's Advertising Guidelines (`www.facebook.com/ad_guidelines.php`) to see the most recent policies in effect, which, essentially, can be grouped into three categories:

- **Editorial and Format Guidelines:** These guidelines focus your attention on issues such as types of grammar used, the number of languages you choose, and additional ad text issues.

- **Content Guidelines:** These guidelines focus on the types of things you can advertise on Facebook, and more importantly, the types of ads and content that are *not* allowed as Facebook Ads.

- **Ad Destination Guidelines:** These guidelines focus on the necessary elements you need to have in place for Facebook to consider it an acceptable landing page. When your ad takes people off Facebook and onto your private site, Facebook wants to make sure your landing page is almost identical to the ad to prevent any misconception or feeling of fraud.

In case you were curious, here are some of the most common things Facebook will flag if it declines your Facebook Ad:

- Incorrect use of capital letters: Facebook is very picky about the ad copy. You can't use all-capital letters. You also can't use title case (Text Like This) in the ad body, and so on.
- Incorrect grammar and spelling, and using slang
- Inaccurate ad text
- Deceptive claims
- Inappropriate images
- Misguided targeting
- Improper sentence structure
- Use of language deemed inappropriate
- Incorrect usage of punctuation
- Symbols exchanged for words

Chapter 15

Ten Nontraditional Facebook Ad Campaigns

In This Chapter

▶ Paging a party of one

▶ Showing off contest entries' creativity

▶ I want to work for *you*!

▶ Can you solve the riddle?

▶ Bring the community to the mountain

▶ Wanted: A few young minds

▶ Are you a Tough Mudder?

▶ Build a better book group

▶ No purchase is too large

▶ Be your own brand

*W*hen you look at the various advertisers using Facebook, you see a lot of traditional campaigns, as companies try to promote their products for sale, or offer services ranging from dating sites to social media tools. Some businesses are trying to grow their Facebook Page Fan count, whereas others are simply promoting hot Facebook applications, new movies or TV shows, or fun online games.

Still, a growing number of campaigns don't fit the regular mold of a traditional online advertisement. People and companies are coming up with new and interesting ways, concepts, and strategies to achieve their goals. We thought it could be interesting and educational to take a look at ten such campaigns. Who knows? Some of these ideas could become part of your next campaign.

Paging a Party of One

Facebook's targeting filters allow you to reach out to your desired target demographic with a great degree of control. Given the immense pool of hundreds of millions of Facebook users, though, what if your specific target demographic were exactly one person? Say you're trying to reach a specific decision maker at a certain company. Facebook Ads can indeed deliver you a targeted audience of one.

Tim Kassouf, the director of marketing for the G.1440 company, was testing the capabilities of Facebook Ads and their targeting filters, and decided to see how much of a micro-niche he could create. After targeting an ad that went specifically to his girlfriend (now fiancée), he decided to attempt to contact someone from his B2B prospect list. As it turns out, co-author Paul Dunay was who he chose, so he created an ad targeted just for Paul (see Figure 15-1) to click.

Figure 15-1: Use a Facebook Ad to reach a party of one.

Paul, This ad is for you!   ✕

Paul, I'm glad I got your attention! I have an interesting Marketing idea that I wanted to run by you.

👍 Like

Tim decided to reach out by using five pieces of information from Dunay's public profile:

- ✔ Lives in the United States
- ✔ Male
- ✔ Relationship status is Married
- ✔ Workplace is Avaya
- ✔ Likes the Grateful Dead

When Tim used these five targeting filters, he got an estimated reach of "fewer than 20 people" from Facebook. (See Figure 15-2.) He assumed that if this ad didn't show up for Paul directly, it would show up for someone at Avaya who works with Paul, and that person would forward the ad or alert Paul to its presence.

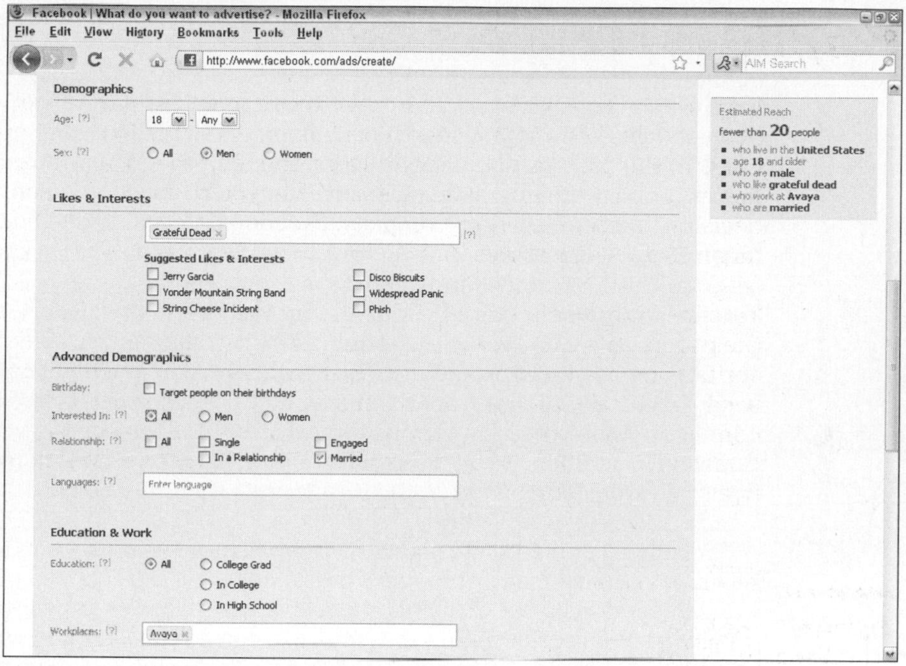

Figure 15-2:
Use
Facebook
targeting
procedures
to target
your party of
one.

Because the ad was so perfectly targeted, it did show up in Paul's ad space when he was using Facebook. Interestingly enough, even though the ad included Paul's profile picture, he initially skipped over it. Tim then tried another image of Paul at home. Paul immediately recognized the image and clicked the ad. He was taken to a personalized landing page on the G.1440 site, which explained why Tim wanted to contact him and the offer that Tim's company had for him. From here, Paul was able to contact Tim to talk about the offer.

The cost for this bold experiment was a whopping $1.94. Tim placed a $10 per-click price on this ad campaign, and within a few days (the time it took for Paul to notice the ad while he was using Facebook), the campaign was successful because this ad captured Paul's attention and got him to contact Tim, which was Tim's goal with this campaign in the first place.

Showing Off Contest Entries' Creativity

If you've ever entered a Facebook contest, you've given out some personal information, perhaps answered some questions, guessed a particular amount, or performed some other small task to put yourself in the running to win. Given the interactive nature of Facebook and the two-way conversation that companies have with their customers, contests that encourage active participation from their customers are on the rise. In some cases, the audience even helps pick the winner.

For example, some contests ask people to come up with a new advertising slogan, message, or even a jingle. But imagine a contest in which participants upload the jingle so that other Facebook users decide which one is the best. Oreo created a new treat called the Cakester, and decided to hold a jingle contest (see Figure 15-3) where people could create a jingle and upload the video to the Oreo Facebook Page. The winner got the chance for national exposure for the jingle as well as compensation.

A number of companies are using Facebook Photo Albums to ask users to enter contests by contributing photos of their product or service. Hyatt Resorts, for example, has a Best of All Worlds contest (see Figure 15-4) where guests not only vote for their favorite resort but also can upload a picture of their favorite vacation activity. (Don't worry if you don't have a picture because you can choose from Hyatt's own Photo Album of Resort activities.) If the resort you voted for was the top resort picked, you could win a resort getaway. In addition, if you uploaded a photo, you had a chance to win extra Hyatt reward points.

Other companies hold similar contests in which users submit a picture of themselves with the company's product. For example, you can submit a picture of yourself performing one of the Dairy Queen Blizzard Photo Challenges with the Blizzard cup somewhere in the picture to enter for a chance to win a year's supply of DQ Blizzard treats in Dairy Queen's Capture the Cup sweepstakes.

Figure 15-3:
Hold a jingle
contest.

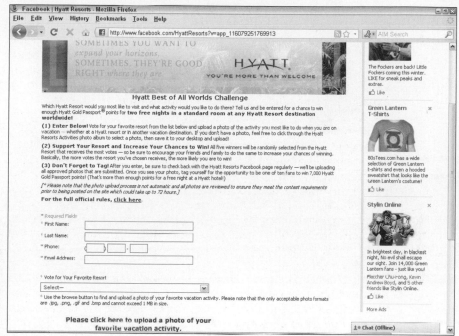

Figure 15-4:
Upload
photos for a
giveaway.

1 Want to Work for You!

You can do a lot of things online to help find a job. You might post your resume on a job search site or peruse your newspaper's online classifieds section. You might get certified in a particular skill, or use your friend and contact network on a Web site like LinkedIn to check for opportunities, and that search could extend to personal social networking sites like Facebook. But what if you were proactive and used a site like Facebook to go after the specific job you really wanted?

Damon Lewis wanted to be the new Social Media coordinator for his favorite hockey team, the Detroit Red Wings. To that end, he not only built his own Facebook Page to promote this goal (which he named *Hire Me, Red Wings!* — see Figure 15-5), but he also ran a Facebook Ad campaign to alert others to his goal.

Lewis's Facebook Page and campaign used some familiar elements (his picture for the ad was Dave Coulier from the TV show *Full House* in a Red Wings jersey), and he filled his Wall with posts from new Fans, relevant stories, and tips for gaining an audience for a need like this. His goal is to grow his Fan base and gain attention until his intended employer, the Red Wings, sees his page and considers his offer. After all, what better way to prove that you could serve as a good social media coordinator than to practice the skills necessary for your job? As of this writing, Lewis is rebranding his page to take advantage of the attention and audience he has earned to be considered for other social media opportunities.

Figure 15-5:
Damon
Lewis
has one
request —
Hire me,
Red Wings!

Can You Solve the Riddle?

In the movie *Good Will Hunting*, a math professor at Harvard posts a complex assignment on the blackboard in hopes of finding his next prodigy. Little did he expect the janitor (played by Matt Damon) to be the one to solve the problem. Dating back hundreds of years, the practice of posting a riddle or impossible problem to solve has been a recruitment tool for the right person to step forward and provide a solution. That concept has come to Facebook, in the name of job recruitment.

Similarly, RapLeaf posted a Facebook ad (see Figure 15-6) with the simple title "Can YOU solve this?" and a picture of a diagram. (Since only the word YOU is capitalized, and not the entire title, this was not considered a violation of Facebook's Advertising Guidelines regarding capitalization.) When you click the ad, you go to the RapLeaf Web site where the problem and a non-elegant solution are presented for your perusal. At the RapLeaf Web site, you can find out about the company and what positions are available, especially for people who can solve that problem.

Figure 15-6:
Solve the
puzzle and
win a
prize . . . er,
a job!

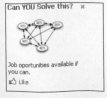

Bring the Community to the Mountain

Many Facebook users don't just bring their likes and interests to the Web site; they also bring their favorite nonprofit organizations, organizing Facebook Pages, charity events, and creating applications to further the goals of their designated charities and nonprofits. To help get the word out and expand the memberships of (and donations to) these great causes, Facebook users are turning to ad campaigns to educate, inform, and rally. Even we authors have been moved to help.

Co-author Paul Dunay went to a speech where he heard about the 3 Sisters Adventure Trekking group of Nepal. Three sisters, who worked very hard to become trekking guides to have a job in their country, started this organization to help women train to become trekking guides so they can have a job and make money for their family. Very few women had become trekking guides, so this organization has its work cut out for it. Their story was one of inspiration and hope, and Dunay was moved into action.

He created a Facebook Ad campaign to drive traffic to the 3 Sisters Facebook page (see Figure 15-7), using CPC methods and targeting older women who were interested in mountain climbing, trekking, or women's rights. His goal was to increase the membership of this organization here in the United States so they could work on clothing and fundraising drives to help the organization do more in Nepal and give more of those women a chance at a future.

Figure 15-7: Facebook Ads can point to stories of inspiration and hope.

Wanted: A Few Young Minds

Many companies use their Facebook Pages to conduct informal market research about how their customers feel about subjects beyond the company's products and brands. But what happens when you really need to conduct a thorough and accurate research study and need quick access to a specific target group? Why, come to Facebook . . . and find them with Facebook Ads!

WiseChoice provides an online "personalized path to college" for high school students and their parents. By getting to know prospective students through personality assessments, they try to fit students with the leading universities in the United States. Furthermore, they offer information on paying for college, applying for college, and everything else a college-bound kid plus the kid's parents need to know. To provide the best information, they needed to reach current college juniors and seniors at different universities throughout the United States. Because they had to do it quickly (a new season of applicants was preparing college applications and needed current and relevant guidance from WiseChoice) and efficiently, they turned to Facebook and took out ad campaigns that targeted college-age students at specific schools with ads that look like Figure 15-8.

After students started replying, WiseChoice gathered information through research study interviews with these college students to offer the right advice to their high school clients. Respondents to the WiseChoice ad campaigns had a better success rate of following through with the research study interview (compared to WiseChoice's previous methods of outreach to this audience) and giving quality information.

Figure 15-8:
Target very
specific
audiences
in a timely
way.

College Juniors,
Seniors

Need money? Tell us about
your school for a chance to
win $10,000. Fun and easy
survey. Pure research, no
selling.

Are You a Tough Mudder?

A number of groups and organizations encourage you to push yourself to be a better person, whether through physical, mental, or spiritual means. These groups can use Facebook as a social platform to encourage, motivate, and spread their causes to people every day. Some groups, however, take this "improvement" to a whole new level, and Tough Mudder is definitely one on those groups, putting together an event billed as "the *toughest* one-day event on the planet." Tough Mudder uses Facebook Ads (see Figure 15-9 below) to recruit people to check out their local events, like the one in California, to help train them for the bigger challenge.

After clicking the ad, they are taken to the Tough Mudder Facebook presence, shown in Figure 15-10. Not only can the organization provide information about the events they produce and how you can get involved, but teams can post comments, post videos, and swap stories; and the organization can relay all their media mentions on Facebook, and use the interactions from their Facebook Page in their other advertisements. They have course maps uploaded as documents you can view, and photos from the event organizers and participants from their events.

Figure 15-9:
Invite
people to
your event.

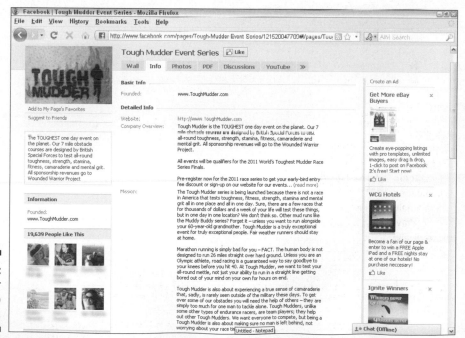

Figure 15-10:
Use your
ad to link to
your site.

Build a Better Book Group with Facebook

Some books explode onto the market and grab a large market share, often because someone famous like Oprah recommended it, or because it's a part of an established franchise like the *Harry Potter* books. Other books start small and build a grassroots campaign to increase visibility and buzz, one new Fan at a time. Although many authors have turned to Facebook to built special Pages to promote their books, few of them have turned to Facebook Ads to augment that presence — until now.

In some cases, the Page and ads in question are all about the book, like *Fragile: The Human Condition*, written by Howard G. Buffett and featuring a foreword by the singer Shakira. This book has been running ads to get people interested in the subject matter (see Figure 15-11), and when you click the ad, you're taken to *Fragile*'s Facebook Page, where readers can find out more about some of the cultures that Buffett discusses in the book.

In other cases, the Fan Page focuses more on the author, like Brian J. Cleary, who used a quote from one of his books that pertained to Facebook (see Figure 15-12) to get people interested in his business Page (see Figure 15-13) where people could find out about all of Brian's books and his definitions of certain words.

Figure 15-11:
Promote a book and the story behind it.

Figure 15-12:
Cleary's ad is getting people to think about their Facebook Friends.

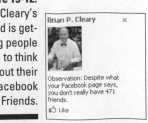

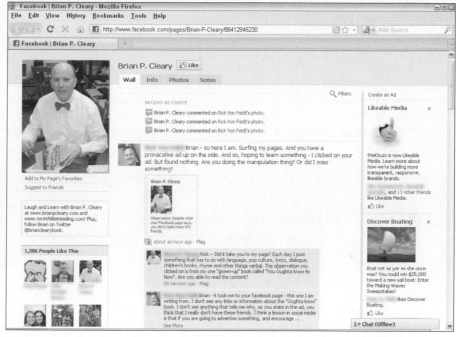

Figure 15-13:
At Cleary's
site, visitors
can find
out more
about all
of Cleary's
books.

No Purchase Is Too Large

Some people wonder about the price threshold when customers shop online, meaning how much a customer will spend on something without being able to actually see the item first. Typically, rural-area people spend more because their distance from bricks-and-mortar stores makes them more inclined to catalog and phone shopping. As people become more comfortable with online research and shopping, bigger purchases happen online. But what about the biggest purchase of all? Would you use Facebook to buy a house? Someone decided to find out.

Erik Lerner, an AIA Real Estate Broker, used Facebook Ads to advertise a $2.6 million steel house in Los Angeles. (See Figure 15-14.) You can see that Lerner is advertising the solar power capability of the house in his listing, in hopes of promoting the home listing to those people looking for an eco-friendly home.

When you click the link, you are taken to an online listing for the house, hosted by RealEstateArchitect.com, which not only has an impressive slideshow (see Figure 15-15) but goes into the design features, architecture, neighborhood information, and links to press articles about the house. Although we acknowledge that any eventual buyer will take at least one walkthrough of the property, this ad helps illustrate the fact that Facebook is being used as a lead generator for all sorts of items that some people might have not considered.

Figure 15-14:
Facebook
Ads now
promote
large-ticket
items, such
as houses.

Figure 15-15:
Use an ad
to lead a
user to more
information.

Be Your Own Brand

When you sign up for a Facebook Page, there are three Page-creation options: Business, Brand, or Celebrity/Public Figure/Artist. In terms of audience count, some of the top Facebook Pages are for public figures like President Barack Obama, music sensation Lady Gaga, and actor Vin Diesel. So, while some figures like comedian Dean Napolitano (see Figure 15-16) or producer Christopher Coppola (Nicolas Cage's brother) are using Facebook Pages, and using Facebook Ads to advertise those pages, there is a growing number of businesses where the top person is quite literally the face of the business, and they use Facebook Ads to promote themselves and their brand in one ad.

Dr. Karen Becker is a "proactive and integrative wellness" veterinarian, and she decided to run a Facebook Ad campaign to garner more than 10,000 followers. As of this writing, she is approaching 12,000 followers, and the numbers continue to go up. She plans to use her Facebook Page (see Figure 15-17) to "connect like-minded pet owners to discuss holistic solutions for pet health problems" as well as share tips and interact with the community herself.

Figure 15-16: Entertainers use Facebook to connect to their audiences.

Figure 15-17: Use Facebook Ads to grow your community.

There are a growing number of other examples, like Annie Jennings, who runs her own public relations firm, aptly called Annie Jennings PR. She's using Facebook Ads (see Figure 15-18) to increase her following in hopes of building her client base. As more and more businesses understand the power of Facebook, they're using this social network community to build up themselves and their businesses together. After all, if a smiling face helps attract attention to an ad more than most images, why shouldn't that smiling face be you, the owner?

Figure 15-18: Business owners use Facebook Ads to promote their businesses.

Annie Jennings PR - × USA Public...

Get booked on TV shows & big Radio. Famous pay for play biz model. No booking, no fee. Reach 10 MILLION REAL listeners with Radio!

likes Annie Jennings PR - USA Public Relations.

Like

Chapter 16

Ten Resources for Facebook Advertisers

In This Chapter

▶ All Facebook is all about Facebook

▶ Go Inside Facebook

▶ Turn about face with AboutFaceDigital

▶ Hear the Buzz (Marketing for Technology)

▶ It's the Age of Advertising

▶ Live in the now with Social Media Today

▶ Take stock of iStockphoto

▶ Get the source with Facebook's own blog

▶ Collaborate with the developers on their document site

▶ Read about Facebook Ads' own Facebook Page

As you use Facebook to build and run advertisements, and maintain your own Facebook presence for your business or brand as part of your advertising structure, you can also take advantage of a wealth of information and resources to help you in your endeavors. In this chapter, we showcase ten online resources that we think are beneficial to keep track of as you pursue Facebook advertising. Good luck!

All Facebook Is All about Facebook

As Facebook continues to expand and change, it's important to stay informed of how Facebook relates to their users and what social media professionals are doing to best use the Facebook site and platform. Therefore, you want to stay current on any issues that could affect you as an advertiser and Facebook Page owner. As you read about different announcements and see how different people are using Facebook, you'll probably get ideas for ways to use Facebook more effectively for your situation, with or without advertising.

In 2007, Nick O'Neill started a blog called All Facebook (www.allfacebook.com), dedicated to covering the Facebook platform. Blog posts talk about everything Facebook-related, from any news articles about the growing social networking site, to announcements regarding new functionality or changes to the site, to discussion and prediction about the future of Facebook. O'Neill, along with guest bloggers, provides multiple articles on a daily basis that discuss everything from usage statistics to security issues and everything in between.

Today, All Facebook (part of a larger network called Web Media Brands) dubs itself "the unofficial Facebook resource" and contains a wealth of information about Facebook, including

✔ **Articles:** The most valuable part of All Facebook is the articles, or blog posts, written about the various functions within Facebook and how to best take advantage of them. One example is a recent article advising people how to use Facebook Advertising effectively. (See Figure 16-1.)

✔ **Page Statistics:** See which pages on Facebook have the most Fans, the highest growth rate, and the highest rate of drop-off subscribers.

✔ **App Statistics:** See which Facebook applications are being downloaded and used by the most Facebook members, along with the top Facebook developers, and the fastest-growing and shrinking Facebook application user bases.

✔ **Events:** All sorts of conferences, live events, and any parties or events targeted for the professional worker involved with media in any form.

Figure 16-1:
All Facebook has useful articles for the Facebook advertiser.

Get Inside Facebook with Inside Facebook

Another great resource that keeps track of Facebook news and announcements is Inside Facebook (www.insidefacebook.com). This site, part of the Inside Network of sites, was started by Justin Smith in 2006 to not only benefit developers and entrepreneurs looking to understand Facebook better, but also marketing and advertising professionals, industry analysts, and the financial community by providing news, insights, and analyses backed by their own research. Inside Facebook also has a special focus on social gaming applications, both on Facebook and on other social networking sites such as MySpace, Bebo, hi5, and other related Web sites.

One of the reasons why Inside Facebook is such a good resource for news is that it publishes its own market research reports about Facebook; the Facebook platform in particular; and social media concerns that affect developers, marketers, and ad agency personnel. You can join its proprietary network — Inside Facebook Gold — that gives you access to specially prepared research papers. Some examples of recent Inside Facebook proprietary research reports (see Figure 16-2) include

- **Facebook Global Monitor:** This report presents the latest traffic stats on 96 countries and 6 regions around the world, and also includes historical data and future growth projections. This report is designed to give marketers, application developers, and business analysts the data to spend trends and opportunities within Facebook.

- **Facebook Marketing Bible:** This report is designed as a guide for the wide variety of marketers out there regarding the marketing possibilities within Facebook for companies and brands of any size.

- **Tracking Virtual Goods on Facebook:** This report provides exclusive original research, data, and analysis on virtual goods, social gaming, and monetization on social platforms.

- **Spending and Usage Patterns on Facebook:** This report provides an extensive look at how Facebook users are spending their money in regard to social gaming and what social gaming applications are being used and how often.

Research from Inside Facebook is widely quoted in numerous publications and media sources such as CNN; *The New York Times;* Reuters; *BusinessWeek; Forbes;* and all types of magazines, Web sites, and information sources. Anyone can subscribe to Inside Facebook Gold on a monthly basis, and there are some pricing breaks for businesses who want a multimember access plan.

Like All Facebook, Inside Facebook also maintains pages regarding statistics about Facebook usage (PageData) and Facebook Application usage (AppData. com; see Figure 16-3) so you can find out quickly which developers, applications, and pages are capturing (and losing) people's attention.

Figure 16-2: Get leading industry research through Inside Facebook.

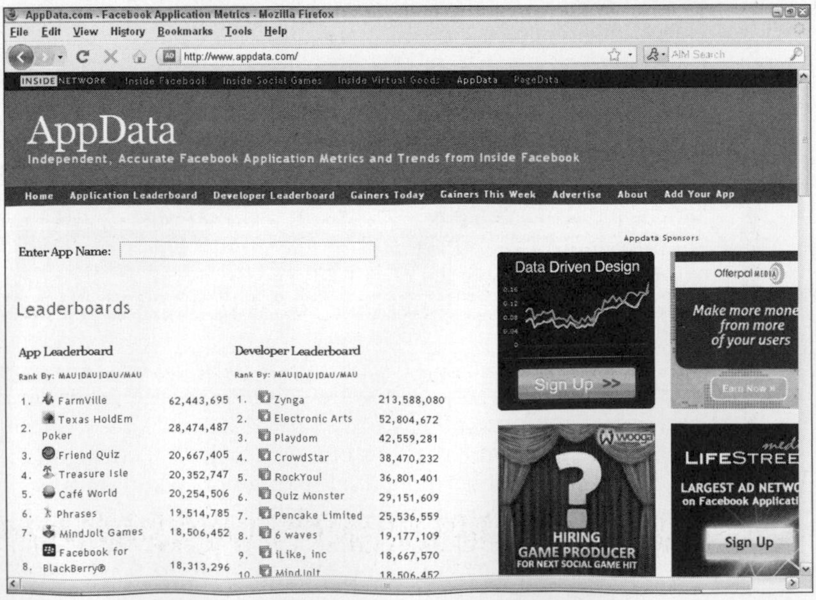

Figure 16-3: Inside Facebook tracks Facebook app statistics.

Do an About Face with AboutFaceDigital

When companies large or small need help navigating the Facebook and social media space to figure out their overall strategy and specific tactics, they typically enlist the help of an expert, or an agency of experts, to help them in their quest. AboutFaceDigital (www.aboutfacedigital.com) is one of those agencies, focused on all the necessary services related to a successful Facebook presence. From creative design to custom application development to media buying and optimization, AboutFaceDigital services provide that strategic support backed by a team well versed in the traditional and new marketing arenas. They offer techniques and solutions grounded in the traditional marketing world, but optimized and tweaked to take advantage of this new world of social media.

The AboutFaceDigital blog has now become a mixture of advice and information as the company analyzes the issues that face their clients and helps give a window to others struggling with a similar situation. Their mix of team members and guest bloggers touch on strategy and theory (see Figure 16-4), and balance that discussion with just-released functionality or announcements from Facebook and how that can impact any company, not just their clients. (Full disclosure: Co-author Richard Krueger is one of the team members of AboutFaceDigital.)

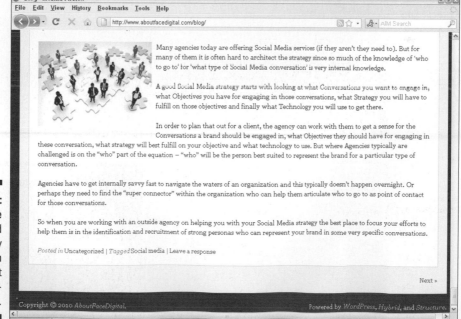

Figure 16-4: Get some sound strategy advice from the folks at AboutFace-Digital.

Hear the Buzz — Marketing for Technology

Buzz Marketing for Technology (www.buzzmarketingfortechnology. com) began in March of 2006 defining new trends in the market that were creating "buzz" for companies, such as the advent of social media and the rise of Facebook marketing. As the blog developed, owner Paul Dunay (yes, the same Paul Dunay who is a co-author of this book) began to expand it to include a more focused discussion on how the new buzz approaches and tools can work best for business-to-business (B2B) technology firms. Obviously, there was a lot of great discussion already going on about buzz marketing, but a great deal of it was more focused and appropriate for consumer marketing than for B2B technology firms. This blog was meant to fill that market need and focus on just business-to-business.

Now that new techniques like social media and Facebook marketing have matured, Buzz Marketing for Technology has again recast itself into a great resource for any B2B marketer looking to find out more about cutting-edge techniques that span from Facebook advertising, location-based advertising, and social customer support, among other things; as well as the ways these subjects intersect with social media.

As the discussion continues, Buzz Marketing incorporates ongoing features like relevant interviews with important players in the marketplace (see Figure 16-5) and analyses of larger business issues that affect this space. (Full disclosure: Co-author Paul Dunay is the author of Buzz Marketing for Technology.)

Figure 16-5:
Get info from the experts by reading Buzz Marketing for Technology.

It's the Age of Advertising: Ad Age, That Is

No one knows the concerns of advertisers better than a group of advertisers, right? The advertisers who run Advertising Age (Ad Age, for short) offer "news and intelligence" to the advertising industry as well as to the marketing and media industries that rely on advertising. They use their print magazine, Web site, and special insight papers to communicate with their readers in hopes of offering strategies for brand building and advice on how companies should present their messages in such a complex business world.

At the Ad Age home page (http://adage.com; see Figure 16-6) you can see the different categories of news, features, columns, blogs, and podcasts offered through the Web site. You can use the search box in the top-right corner to search archives and current content for Facebook-related content, or peruse the special reports along the right side of the screen.

Figure 16-6: Ad Age offers a variety of useful articles, columns, and reports.

As you dig into online Advertising Age content, pay special attention to some particularly useful sections:

- ✔ **DigitalNext** (`http://adage.com/digitalnext`) is the Ad Age consolidation of news and original opinion pieces regarding the emerging new media opportunities, like online marketing, as well as how this new technology will impact all kinds of marketing professionals.

- ✔ **MediaWorks** (`http://adage.com/mediaworks`) is a collection of Ad Age articles that focus on the new media opportunities and the marketing capabilities within those arenas.

- ✔ **Branded Content** (`http://brandedcontent.adage.com/`) is a special section of Ad Age that focuses on topics like customer relationship management and mobile marketing.

Stay Up to Date with Social Media Today

Because a total strategy for social media advertising and marketing involves different skill sets, it's important to have as many perspectives as possible. Started in 2007, Social Media Today (`www.socialmediatoday.com`; see Figure 16-7) is an ongoing collection of perspectives, insights, and articles from bloggers, media professionals, project managers, and journalists who look at the issues, especially as they apply to business to business and public policy issues, and talk and relate to each other.

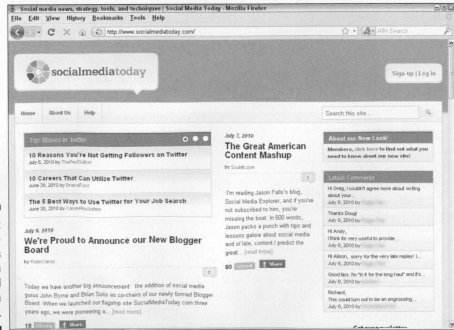

Figure 16-7: The conversation is always on at Social Media Today.

At the Social Media Today Web site are stories, comments, features, and feedback about social media concerns happening today, tomorrow, and every day. Not only can you connect with them through its newsletter, Twitter feed, Facebook fan page, or RSS feed, but you can also become a blogger and contribute your own views as well after your submission is reviewed by the fine folks at Social Media Today. (See Figure 16-8.)

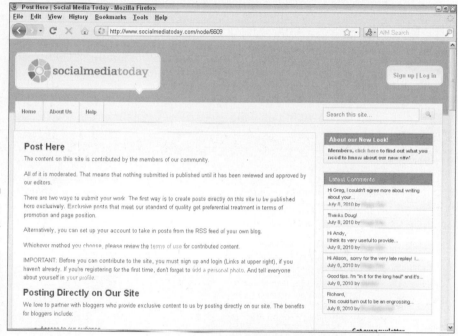

Figure 16-8: Submit your own material to be considered for Social Media Today.

Get the Picture with iStockphoto

One of the advantages of a Facebook advertisement compared with other types of online advertising is that you can include an image with your ad, say your product or company logo. You don't want to run your ad without any image whatsoever (see Chapter 14), and if you don't have a photo ready to go, hiring a graphic designer to come up with a standard image could blow your budget out of the water.

Thankfully, you have options. Take a look a variety of ads (see Figure 16-9), and you'll notice that a lot of them use generic photos — people smiling, surfing, doing whatever — or just an appropriate graphic. Online, you can easily find similar generic or stock photos to use for your ads. We recommend iStockphoto (www.istockphoto.com), which bills itself as "the Internet's original member-generated image and design community."

At the iStockphoto home page, you can type in a query like "Smiling woman" to bring up a set of search results (see Figure 16-10) you can choose to purchase. With iStockphoto, you purchase a set of credits, which you can then use to buy photos for use in your ads, Web site, or any other forum, without having to pay royalties for the right to use that image. The number of credits you need for the image depends on the size of the image you want. (See Figure 16-11.) In the case of Facebook ads, because your picture shouldn't be more than 110 x 80 pixels, the XSmall (extra small) size is sufficient.

If you're going to use a lot of photos or illustrations, iStockphoto offers several subscription plans that give you a refilled daily balance of credits you can use for 3, 6, or 12 months. You can find out more about subscriptions at `www.istockphoto.com/royalty-free-subscriptions.php`.

As of this writing, you can also download more from iStockphoto than just photos, depending on your needs. Also available from the site are

- Illustrations
- Flash files
- Audio files
- Video files

For the high-volume account user, iStockphoto offers Corporate Accounts that provides not only credits for buying images, but also extra tools and features to help the company fulfill any image needs.

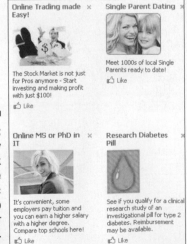

Figure 16-9: Many Facebook ads use generic photos to convey their message.

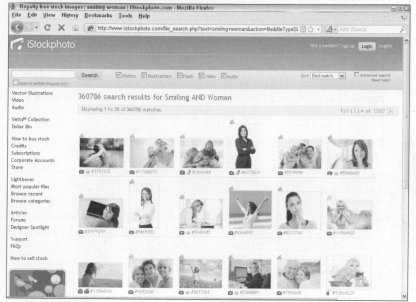

Figure 16-10: Search a stock photo house for the picture you need.

Figure 16-11: At iStockphoto, the cost of an image is based on its size.

Get the Scoop Directly from Facebook

If you want to truly know what's going on with Facebook, why not go to the source? Facebook runs its own extensive blog (`http://blog.facebook.com`), posting topics that affect parts of the site or the whole infrastructure. (See Figure 16-12.) Facebook uses blog posts to expand upon topics that interest a lot of their readers, or announce new features to the site with the explanation and background of that change to help people understand why something changed. Keeping up to date on Facebook inner workings not only affects you as an advertiser and your brand, but anything that affects Facebook users also affects how you interact with users to make them your customers.

One of the benefits of the Facebook blog is the Comments section. Facebook, and the entire community, can see what the user base thinks of a particular post by judging the number of Likes and the number of comments any particular discussion receives, as shown in the Most Popular stories section of Figure 16-12. This interactive nature allows the original blog poster to expand upon ideas touched upon in the post, depending on the questions posted after the initial question.

Figure 16-12:
Facebook's blog keeps their users informed on updates and features.

Access the Libraries Created by the Facebook Developer Team

When you have a question or technical concern for how to get something done on Facebook, a great resource is the documentation stored and maintained by the Facebook developer team at `http://developers.facebook.com/docs`. (See Figure 16-13.) These documents are free, and some of them are geared toward computer programming experts. Rest assured, though, the guys and gals who wrote the code that makes Facebook run so well will have the answer for your technical question.

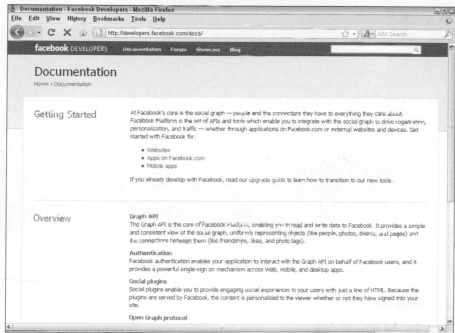

Figure 16-13: Facebook developers provide libraries of technical information on their Web site.

Libraries of information are organized and stored by subject:

- (Facebook) Web site
- Facebook Applications
- (Facebook) Mobile Apps
- Graph API Overview
- Authentication Overview
- Social Plugins Overview

- ✔ Open Graph Protocol Overview & API calls
- ✔ Facebook Application Programming Interface (API)
- ✔ Facebook JavaScript (FBJS)
- ✔ Facebook Markup Language (FBML)
- ✔ Facebook Query Language (FQL)
- ✔ Facebook Software Development Kits (SDKs) for these platforms
  - JavaScript
  - PHP
  - Python
  - iPhone
  - Android

Like Facebook Ads? Why Not Like the Facebook Ads Page?

As we mention in the early part of the book, Facebook has an Advertising Sales team available to help customers (mostly large customers with a preset limit per month) with their Facebook Ad needs. The benefit for you, the reader, is that Facebook Ads uses the Facebook platform themselves to share information, thoughts, and advice with Facebook Ad customers. They do this through several mechanisms:

- ✔ **Facebook Ads newsletter:** When you start taking out ads on Facebook, you will be automatically entered into Facebook's system to get newsletters about Facebook Ads. (See Figure 16-14.) These newsletters provide the most recent announcements along with interesting case studies of actual Facebook advertisers and links to the relevant Web pages within the Facebook Ads system.

- ✔ **Facebook Ads Page (www.facebook.com/FacebookAds):** The Facebook Ads team has put together its own business Page on Facebook (see Figure 16-15), which you can Like to receive status updates. Their Wall posts are announcements, tips, or articles with information that matters to any Facebook advertiser using their system.

Figure 16-14:
Get the latest news and information from the Facebook Ads team.

Figure 16-15:
Stay connected to the Facebook Ads team using Facebook.

The Ads team also makes a lot of other documents available through the different tabs on their Facebook Page, such as

- **Reference Guides:** Download everything from guides on how to optimize your ad to industry-specific guides, such as how to reach the retail or health industries most effectively.

- **Case Studies:** You can read about specific examples of companies using Facebook Ads to achieve their goals, along with examples of their ads and the results of their ad campaigns.

- **Notes (Updates):** This page contains only the Wall posts that are announcements of updates to the Facebook Ads system.

- **Discussions:** Read questions or postings that people have made. You will see some responses from the Facebook Ads team, which makes this discussion area a nice repository for questions and answers. (See Figure 16-16.)

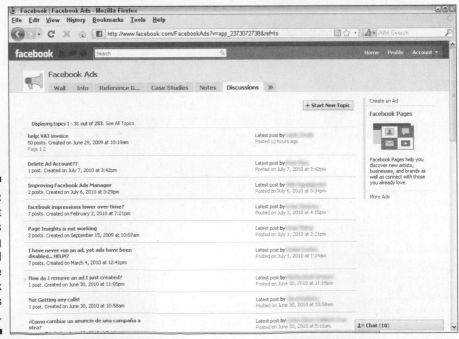

Figure 16-16: See what topics are being discussed in the Facebook Ads community.

Index

• *Symbols* •

Clickers field, 214

• *A* •

AboutFaceDigital (advertising services company), 293
account, Ads
  other Facebook accounts, 12
  settings, 195–197
  sctup process, 27
  user list, 196
Account Charged notification, 186
ACT! (CRM system), 171
Action data
  described, 77
  reports, 157, 207
action photo, 90
Action Rate data, 207
Active campaign, 188
Activity Feed plug-in, 243
Ad Approved notification, 185
ad copy
  ad campaign adjustments, 79
  brand building, 53
  character limit, 10, 34
  defined, 13
  described, 34–35
  Facebook Guidelines, 273
  first ad, 28
  in images, 90
  local campaign, 48
  marketing writers, 96
  test campaign, 100
Ad Created notification, 185
Ad Destination Guidelines, 273
Ad Disapproved notification, 185

Ad Preview, 32
ad pricing
  bidding systems, 15–16, 65–67
  budget reports, 77
  campaign adjustments, 78–79, 143–146
  campaign optimization, 143–146
  described, 15
  tips for bidding, 70–71
  traditional media, 64
Ad Requires Editing notification, 186
Ad Space arca, 12
Add a User button, 196
Add to My Page link, 130
address
  of business, 38
  verification program, 168–169
Administrator function, 84, 132
Ads and Pages link, 72, 215
Ads Board feature, 35, 97
ads, creating
  Ads Manager feature, 185, 194
  alternative advertising options, 108–111, 252–262
  application development, 110–111
  campaign adjustments, 78–79, 97, 148–149
  copyright, 14
  Facebook library, 301–302
  Facebook sales team, 102–105
  first ad, 27–33
  marketing objectives, 52–62
  multiple ads, 90–94
  notification, 185
  online-offline ad integration, 98
  process of, 12–13
  schedule for ads, 93–94
  scope of campaign, 47–52
  test campaigns, 99–101
  unique aspects of Facebook, 14

Ads Manager feature. *See also* monitoring
    ad campaigns
  access to, 138
  account settings, 195–197
  Advertising Performance report, 205
  budget reports, 72–78
  campaign notifications, 184–187
  deleted campaigns, 80
  described, 72, 181–182
  Facebook Reports, 200
  graphs, 189–191
  home page features, 182–184
  Lifetime statistics feature, 187–189
  multiple campaigns, 192–193
  report types, 138
  Responder Demographics report, 210
  Responder Profiles report, 213
  weekly data, 193–194
Ads page, 27, 48
Ads Report
  budget reports, 72–79
  described, 72
  paused campaign, 80
Adtester CX (software), 175
Advertiser Information form, 102
advertising
  elements of, 33–38
  goal of, 20
  networks, 69
  principles of, 9
  types of, 81–86
Advertising Age (Web site), 295–296
Advertising Performance report
  ad analysis, 138–140
  defined, 201
  described, 75–76, 205
  elements of, 206–210
  example of, 206
  generation of, 205–206
age, user, 30, 44, 144
Alchemy (advertising services company),
    227–228
All Facebook (Web site), 266, 290

AllPosters.com (Web site), 18
analyzing ads. *See also* Insights feature;
    monitoring ad campaigns
  alternative Facebook options, 108–111
  audience perceptions, 146–148
  budget reports, 71–79
  campaign optimization, 143–149
  conversion tracking, 175–178
  dashboards, 227–230
  demographic reports, 140–143
  Facebook sales team, 102–105
  importance of, 95
  international campaigns, 154, 224
  landing pages, 119
  Lifetime Statistics feature, 187–189
  methods for, 99–101
  online-offline ad integration, 98
  performance objectives, 105–107
  performance reports, 138–140
animated image, 36
announcement, 114–116
application
  development of, 110–111, 258–259
  directory, 110
Application ad
  described, 84
  example of, 108–109
  popularity of, 108
approved ad, 32, 185, 273
Aps Directory, 129–130
aspect ratio, 36
auction, 68–69
audience, targeting. *See* targeting users
audio clip, 155

• *B* •

badge, 98
banner advertising, 1, 64
Becker, Karen (veterinarian), 287
Best Buy (retailer), 39, 40, 128–129, 255
bid-based model, 68–69
bidcactus (Web site), 177

bidding system. *See also specific systems*
  brand building, 54
  budget reports, 77
  campaign optimization, 143–146
  common mistakes, 269
  defined, 15
  described, 15–16, 70
  performance reports, 138–140
  recommended bids, 70–71
  tips for bidding, 70–71
  types of, 65–67
  value of, 67–69
BikerOrNot.com (social hangout), 53, 55
billing information
  financial resources, 96–97
  first ad campaign, 32
  notifications, 186
Bing (search engine), 66
birthday, user, 30
blast, e-mail, 114–116
blind bidding, 68–69
BLiNQ Media (advertising services
      company), 228–229
blog
  about Facebook, 266, 289–290, 300
  cross-promotion tips, 112–114
  marketing tips, 294
Blue Sky Factory (e-mail provider), 46
body text
  ad campaign adjustments, 79
  brand building, 53
  character limit, 10, 34
  defined, 13
  described, 34–35
  Facebook Guidelines, 273
  first ad, 28
  in images, 90
  local campaign, 48
  marketing writers, 96
  test campaign, 100
Book field, 213–214
book group, 284–285
bookmark, 128

Box Title field, 133
brand
  Application ads, 108–109
  application development, 110
  campaign strategies, 53–55
  consistency among pages, 39
  customer service, 173
  feedback from customers, 61
  referrals, 88
  self-promotion, 262
  sense of community, 57
  tips for building, 53
Branded Content (Web site), 296
Branded Gift ad, 84, 86
BrandLift survey, 88
Bucket field, 211–212
budget
  Ads Manager features, 182, 188, 192
  changes in, 78–79, 143–146, 186
  creation, 15
  described, 14
  financial resources, 96–97
  first ad campaign, 31
  Lifetime Statistics feature, 188
  need for, 63
  notifications, 186
  paused campaign, 79
  performance report, 207
  reports, 72–79
  sponsored ads, 102
  test campaigns, 100
  tracking methods, 71–78
Budget/Day field, 188, 192
Buffett, Howard G. (*Fragile: The Human
      Condition*), 284
*Building Facebook Applications For
      Dummies* (Wagner), 259
business category, 24, 25
business Page. *See* Page, business
business-to-business technology firm, 294
Buzz Marketing for Technology (blog), 294
By City radio button, 48
By State/Province radio button, 50

• C •

calendar, 204–205
call to action
  audience perceptions, 147
  benefits of Facebook Ads, 18–19
  brand building, 54
  common mistakes, 270–271
  defined, 18
  described, 34
  example of, 35
  lead conversions, 122, 160–161, 177
  sales generation, 55–56
campaign notification, 184
Campaigns link, 80
capitalization, 273
Case Studies tab, 304
celebrity, 286
Character Arcade (games), 235–236
charity donation, 281
chat session, 169
Chex Mix cereal, 162–163
Choose a Graph section, 219
circulation date, 98
Cities Within check box, 48
City field, 48
Cleary, Brian P. (author), 284–285
click rate
  Ads Manager, 183, 188–189
  Advertising Performance report, 139–140
  campaign optimization, 143–145
  common mistakes, 268–269
  conversion tracking, 176
  Lifetime Statistics feature, 188
  Responder Demographics reports,
    141–143, 212
  Responder Profile reports, 214
Clickable (software company)
  ad copy, 96–97
  described, 228
  lead conversion, 164
  trial products, 106
closed bidding system, 15
Coca-Cola (beverage company), 165, 166

college graduate, 30, 44
column, table, 208
Comic Bug (retailer), 39–40
comma-separated values file, 74, 204
comment
  described, 217
  Insights feature, 219–220
  link to, 156
  plug-ins, 241–242
communication
  CRM systems, 171
  from Facebook, 184
  lead conversion, 165, 172–173
  lead follow-up, 167–173
community building
  audience perception, 147
  feedback from customers, 61
  landing page selection, 120, 122
  plug-ins, 234–235
  tips for, 57–60
company
  contact information, 38
  credit cards, 96
  e-mail address, 169
  logo, 37, 39, 264
comparison shopping, 68–69
computer, 4
Connections filter, 30
contact information
  companies, 38
  users, 168
Content Guidelines, 273
contest
  brand building, 110
  compelling content, 256
  cross-promotion, 115
  landing pages, 120
  lead conversions, 162
  nontraditional advertising, 277–279
contract negotiation, 68
conversion
  defined, 107, 160
  described, 122
  performance objectives, 107

performance reports, 207
process of, 159–167, 172–173
rates, 122
relationship marketing, 165–167
tracking tips, 175–178
types of, 162–164
copyright, 14, 36
CoreMetrics (tracking tool), 47
Cost of Conversion data, 207
cost per click (CPC) method
    Ads Manager feature, 188, 193
    bid ranges, 70–71, 143–146
    brand building, 54
    campaign optimization, 143–146
    cost determination, 67–69
    customized landing pages, 119
    described, 15, 65–66
    Lifetime Statistics feature, 188
    performance reports, 140
cost per customer, 174–175
cost per thousand impressions (CPM)
    Ads Manager feature, 188, 193
    benefits of, 65
    bid ranges, 70–71, 143–146
    brand building, 54
    campaign optimization, 143–146
    common mistakes, 269
    cost tracking, 65
    defined, 67
    described, 15–16, 65
    Lifetime Statistics feature, 188
    performance reports, 139–140
    value of Fans, 135
Country field, 50–51
coupon, 32, 186
CPC. *See* cost per click method
CPC Bids header, 193
CPM. *See* cost per thousand impressions
Create a Facebook Account screen, 26
Create a Page screen, 24–25
Create a Similar Ad button, 194
Create button, 128
Create Official Page button, 26
Create Your Ad button, 48

creating ads
    Ads Manager feature, 185, 194
    alternative advertising options, 108–111, 252–262
    application development, 110–111
    campaign adjustments, 78–79, 97, 148–149
    copyright, 14
    Facebook library, 301–302
    Facebook sales team, 102–105
    first ad, 27–33
    marketing objectives, 52–62
    multiple ads, 90–94
    notification, 185
    online-offline ad integration, 98
    process of, 12–13
    schedule for ads, 93–94
    scope of campaign, 47–52
    test campaigns, 99–101
    unique aspects of Facebook, 14
credit card
    financial resources, 96
    first ad campaign, 32
    payment notification, 186
credit, game, 108–109
currency, 31, 108–109
custom tab, 127–134
customer
    acquisition cost, 160
    database, 46, 164
    inquiries from, 105
    service, 165, 173
customer information
    bid ranges, 143–144
    bidding systems, 67–68
    budget reports, 72–79
    collection methods, 134–136
    conversion tracking, 176–177
    customer relationship management systems, 170
    demographic reports, 77–78, 140–143, 210–212
    external landing page, 125
    Facebook features, 16
    Facebook sales team, 102

customer information *(continued)*
first ad, creating, 30
Insights feature, 150–157, 225
landing page selection, 37, 120
lead verification, 168
targeted attributes, 16–17, 44–47
test campaign, 100–101
types of, 16–17
customer relationship management (CRM)
system
described, 169–170
examples of, 171–172

● *D* ●

Daily Active Users graph, 152, 224
Daily Active Users line, 222–223
Daily Budget Change notification, 186
Daily Fan Views graph, 157
Daily New Likes count, 222
Daily Page Activity, 157
Daily Post Feedback percentage, 219
Daily Post Views number, 219
daily report, 73
Daily Spend feature, 182
Daily Stats for the Week Of header, 194
Daily Story Feedback réport, 157
Dairy Queen (restaurant), 278
dashboard
benefits of, 226
creation, 227–230
defined, 199
Insights feature, 215–216
management of, 199
data, customer
bid ranges, 143–144
bidding systems, 67–68
budget reports, 72–79
collection methods, 134–136
conversion tracking, 176–177
customer relationship management
systems, 170
demographic reports, 77–78, 140–143,
210–212

external landing page, 125
Facebook features, 16
Facebook sales team, 102
first ad, creating, 30
Insights feature, 150–157, 225
landing page selection, 37, 120
lead verification, 168
targeted attributes, 16–17, 44–47
test campaign, 100–101
types of, 16–17
database, customer, 46, 164
data-mining software, 74
Date Range field, 74, 204
date, viewing, 68, 93
Default Landing Tab for Everyone Else
list, 134
deleting campaigns, 79–80, 194
Demographic field, 210–211
designing ads
Ads Manager feature, 185, 194
alternative advertising options, 108–111,
252–262
application development, 110–111
campaign adjustments, 78–79, 97, 148–149
copyright, 14
Facebook library, 301–302
Facebook sales team, 102–105
first ad, 27–33
marketing objectives, 52–62
multiple ads, 90–94
notification, 185
online-offline ad integration, 98
process of, 12–13
schedule for ads, 93–94
scope of campaign, 47–52
test campaigns, 99–101
unique aspects of Facebook, 14
Destination URL field
first ad, 27, 28
multiple ad campaigns, 37–38, 92–93
Poll ads, 84
URL selection, 37–38
Detroit Red Wings (hockey team), 279–280
DigitalNext (Web site), 296

direct marketing
  benefits of Facebook, 20
  defined, 20
  described, 20
  Facebook's unique features, 21
  landing pages, 122
discussions page
  customer feedback, 61–62
  Facebook sales team, 304
  Insights feature, 221
  tracking tools, 157, 221
downloading
  ad data, 184
  products, 177
Dunay, Paul (author), 276–277, 281
Dynamics CRM (Microsoft), 171

• *E* •

Edit Ad Creative button, 194
Edit Page link, 132
Edit X rows button, 192
editing ads
  ad development, 94
  Ads Manager feature, 192, 194
  payment notification, 186
Editorial and Format Guidelines, 273
education level, 30, 44
eLance.com (freelance site), 110
election, political, 110, 111
e-mail
  alternative Facebook advertising
      options, 252
  confirmation of account setup, 26–27
  cross-promotion, 114–116
  initial contact with leads, 169
  lead verification, 168–169
  notifications, 184–187
  scams, 27
  targeted campaigns, 46
emoticon, 33
employee involvement, 58, 61
engagement ad
  common mistakes, 269
  described, 81

Insights feature, 222–224
  plug-ins, 235–236
  referrals, 88
Event, Facebook
  compelling Page content, 257
  described, 39, 82
  example of, 85
  Live Stream plug-in, 246–247
  locked titles, 33
  performance objectives, 105
  referrals, 86–88
  tracking tips, 150–157
eVoice (transcription service), 161
Excel (Microsoft software), 74–75, 184, 204
exclusive product, 256–257
expense, advertising
  common mistakes, 269
  Lifetime Statistics feature, 188
  return on investment, 174–175
expired coupon, 186
Export Format option, 203
exporting
  reports, 80, 184, 209, 226
  user information, 225–226
external landing page
  ad types, 82, 84
  benefits of, 125–127
  cross-promotion, 112–116
  described, 124
  development of, 127
  first ad, 27
  Like box plug-in, 244
  local ad campaign, 48
  multiple ad campaigns, 37–38, 92–93
  review by Facebook staff, 125–126
  selection, 37–38
External Referrers list, 155

• *F* •

Facebook
  Ad Guidelines, 14, 272–273
  founding of, 1
  functions of, 10
  number of users, 1, 10

Facebook *(continued)*
  popularity of, 9–10
  sales team, 102–105, 302–304
Facebook Ads for Pages and Events
    feature, 18
Facebook advertising
  described, 1, 10–12
  elements of, 10–11
  goal of, 20
  home page, 12–13
  origin of, 1
  strengths of, 1
  types of, 81–86
*Facebook Application Development For
    Dummies* (Stay), 5, 129
Facebook Global Monitor report, 291
Facebook Marketing Bible report, 291
Facebook Markup Language (FBML)
  benefits of, 128
  custom tab creation, 127–134
  defined, 5, 127–128
  versus HTML, 128
Fan ad, 82
Fan, Facebook
  Action data, 77
  community building, 57–58
  conversions, 162
  feedback from, 61–62
  internal landing page, 123
  Like box plug-in, 244
  photos from, 39
  recommendations from, 86–88
  tracking tools, 150–157
  value of, 135, 174
Fan Page. *See also* Page, business
  defined, 23
  described, 11
  maximum fans allowed, 24
  origin of, 1
  transition to business Page, 24
FBML. *See* Facebook Markup Language
FedEx (shipping company), 110
feedback, customer. *See also specific types*
  audience perceptions, 146–148
  described, 61–62

graphs, 219
  lead conversion, 165
F8 conference, 231
filter. *See also specific filters*
  audience perceptions, 146–147
  nontraditional ads, 276
  report settings, 202
Filter By criteria, 73, 202
financial resource, 96
Find Us on Facebook button, 252
fixed cost, 174
Flash image, 36
flat-rate model, 68
following up leads, 167–175
form
  described, 134–136
  lead conversion, 163, 166–167
format, report, 74, 203–204
Fragile: The Human Condition (Buffett), 284
fraud
  CPM system, 67
  e-mail confirmations, 27
  Facebook Guidelines, 274
free item
  lead conversion, 162
  sales, generating, 105–106
freelance developer, 110
frequently asked questions, 61
fresh ad, 146, 265
Friend, Facebook
  Activity Feed plug-in, 243
  Comment plug-in, 241–242
  interactive games, 235
  internal landing page, 123
  Like button plug-in, 238
  recommendations from, 86–88, 239
  sample copy, 34
Friendpile plug-in, 245–246
Friends of Connections field, 86–87

• *G* •

game application
  development of, 258–259
  nontraditional ads, 108–109

GameLoft (video game company), 58, 60
gender, user, 30, 44, 210
General Mills (food company), 162–163
Generate Another Report option, 210
Generate Report button, 74, 205
geo-targeting, 68
Get Code button, 113, 238
gift, 84–85
giveaway, 105
golfstakes.com (retailer), 126–127
Google (search engine)
  AdWords, 107
  Analytics, 37, 47, 128
  bidding systems, 66–67
GoStats (tracking tool), 37
grammar
  body text, 34
  Facebook Guidelines, 273
  titles, 33
graph
  Ads Manager, 183, 189–191
  Insights feature, 150–157, 216–226
  user interactions, 217–222
graphic. *See* image
Group, Facebook
  alternative advertising methods, 34, 84,
    259–260
  described, 259

• H •

Header option, 113
headline. *See* title, ad
hobby, 45, 149
how-to information, 173, 253
HTML code
  versus FBML, 128
  Like box widget, 113–114
  plug-ins, 232, 236, 238–239
  report format, 74–75, 204
Hyatt Resorts, 278, 279

• I •

I Have a Coupon to Redeem link, 32
icons, explained, 5

identifier code, 176
iframe window, 113–114
image. *See also* photo
  brand building, 53
  common mistakes, 263–265
  financial resources, 96
  first ad, creating, 28
  importance of, 89
  local campaign, 48
  online-offline campaign integration, 98
  previews, 32
  profile picture, 28
  selection, 36–37, 89–91
  size limit, 10, 28, 36
  test campaigns, 100
impression
  Advertising Performance report, 138–139
  bidding systems, 15, 65, 67
  defined, 188
  Lifetime Statistics feature, 188
  Responder Demographic reports, 212
Industry setting, 195
information, user. *See* user information
in-game ad, 108–109
Inside Facebook (Web site), 291–292
Insights feature. *See also* analyzing ads
  audience perceptions, 147
  dashboard, 215–216
  data export, 225–226
  demographic information, 225
  described, 19, 150, 214–215
  engagement ads, 222–224
  interactions among users, 156–157,
    216–222
  media consumption, 155
  overall Fan base, 150–152
  Page views, 154–155
  user demographics, 153–154
Instant Message, 169
Integrated Solutions: Contact Us form,
    102–104
Interactions Detail report, 156–157
Interactions graph, 150
interactive advertising
  community building, 58
  feedback from customers, 61–62

interactive advertising *(continued)*
Like links, 11
plug-ins, 235
tracking tools, 156, 216–222
types of interactions, 217
Interactive Advertising Bureau Revenue
Report (PriceWaterhouseCoopers), 16
interests, of users, 45, 149, 213
internal landing page
benefits of, 122–124
creation, 127–134
described, 122
example of, 123
forms, 134–136
international ad campaign
analysis of, 154, 224
number of international Fans, 1
scope of campaign, 50–52
Internet
access to, 4
most popular sites, 9–10
service providers, 177
technology growth, 16
introductory offer, 98
inventory, 79–80
InvolveSocial (application development
company), 110–111
Island Life (game), 108–109
iStockphoto (Web site), 297–299

• J •

Jennings, Annie (public relations
expert), 288
Jigsaw (address verification service), 169
job search, 279–280
job type, 30
jump page, 125–126

• K •

Kassouf, Tim (marketing director), 276–277
Key Sources list, 152

keyword
audience perceptions, 146–147
bidding systems, 66
first ad, creating, 29
refined campaigns, 149
sales generation, 55–56
targeted campaigns, 45
test campaign, 100
text in photos, 90
tips for use, 30
titles, 33
Web site usage logs, 47
Keywords target field, 29

• L •

landing page. *See also* Page, business
ad analysis, 119
body text, 34
creation, 127–134
cross-promotion, 112–116
customization, 119
defined, 119
described, 39
Facebook Guidelines, 273
forms, 134–136
Insights feature, 155
multiple ads, 37–38, 92–93
ordering process, 178
selection, 37–38, 119–127
types of, 39–40
usage log, 47
Language filter, 31, 44, 51
language, report, 204
language-specific campaign, 51
Last Updated field, 188
Launch a Package (application), 110
lead capture page. *See* landing page
lead conversion
communication tips, 172–173
described, 122, 159–167
lead generation
follow-up, 167–175
performance objectives, 105–106
tracking tools, 169–172

LeClaire, Jennifer (*Web Analytics For Dummies*), 176
Lerner, Erik (real estate broker), 285
letter, 169
Lewis, Damon (Facebook advertiser), 279–280
library, Facebook, 301–302
Lifetime Statistics feature, 187–189
lifetime value, 174
Like Box plug-in, 112–114
Like button
  Action data, 77
  brand building, 54
  business versus Fan Page, 24
  conversion tracking, 176–177
  described, 11, 217, 232
  familiarity of, 234
  Insights feature, 150–153, 156, 219–220
  internal landing page, 123
  lead verification, 168
  referrals, 87
  stories, 156
  targeted campaigns, 45
  tips for adding, 232, 236–237, 239
  Video ads, 84
Live Stream plug-in, 246–247
local ad campaign, 47–48
local business, 29, 68
Location filter
  demographic reports, 142
  described, 44–45
  first ad, creating, 29
  local campaign, 48
  test campaign, 101
locked title, 33
Login button, 240–241
Login with Faces plug-in, 240–241
logo, company, 37, 39, 264
Lowden, Sue (Senate candidate), 110–111
loyal customer, 173

• *M* •

magazine ad, 98
Magic Bullet (kitchen appliance), 166–167, 253–254

mailing list, 162
Mango Harvest (game), 110
market research, 282
marketing
  alternative Facebook advertising, 252–262
  application development, 110
  cross-promotion, 112–116
  objectives, 52–62
  online-offline integration, 97–99
  performance objectives, 105–107
  resources, 96–97
  self-promotion, 262
  test campaigns, 99–101
  types of, 19–20
  writers, 96
Marketplace, Facebook, 260–261
Marriott (hotel chain), 124
Max Bid field, 70
Max Rows option, 241
measuring results. *See* analyzing ads
media consumption, 155
MediaWorks (Web site), 296
Meltdown Comics (retailer), 232–233
membership conversion
  common mistakes, 269
  described, 162, 164
Merrill (outdoor community), 120
message, advertising
  ad campaign adjustments, 79
  brand building, 53
  character limit, 10, 34
  defined, 13
  described, 34–35
  Facebook Guidelines, 273
  first ad, 28
  in images, 90
  local campaign, 48
  marketing writers, 96
  test campaign, 100
Microsoft (technology company)
  customer relationship management system, 171
  data-mining software, 74–75
  downloaded ad data, 184
  investment in Facebook, 1
  report format, 204

mission statement, 38

mistakes, common, 263–273

monitoring ad campaigns. *See also* Ads
    Manager feature; analyzing ads
 ad testing, 99–101, 147–149
  alternative Facebook options, 108–111
  audience perceptions, 146–148
  budget reports, 71–79
  campaign optimization, 143–149
  Facebook sales team, 102–105
  Insights feature, 150–157
  lead conversions, 160, 175–178
  ongoing maintenance, 97
  online-offline ad integration, 97–99
  performance objectives, 105–107
  resources for, 96–97
  test campaigns, 99–101

monthly membership, 164

monthly report, 73, 204, 210

More Ads link, 35

More link, 225

Mountain Dew (soda), 256

movie studio, 84

Multilanguage Excel option, 204

Music field, 213–214

MyPartyShirt.com (retailer), 161–162

• N •

naming
 business Pages, 26
 campaigns, 31, 183

national campaign, 50–52

Navigation bar, 182–183

negotiating advertising rates, 68

new user, 223–224

News Feed
 Comments plug-in, 242
 internal landing page, 123
 Like button plug-in, 238
 referrals, 87

newsletter
 account settings, 197
 Facebook sales team, 302
 lead conversions, 160, 162, 165

newspaper ad, 98

Nike (retailer), 82, 85, 92

No Filter option, 202

note taking, 170–171

Notes (Updates) tab, 304

Notification feature, 182, 184–187, 196

Clickers field, 214

NuSpark Marketing (marketing company),
  53, 55

• O •

offer wall, 108

Official Page header, 24

Omniture SiteCatalyst (tracking tool), 47

Oncontact (CRM system), 171

O'Neill, Nick (blogger), 266, 290

online advertising
 alternative Facebook options, 108–111,
  252–262
 elements of, 14
 growth of, 9, 16
 integration with offline ads, 97–99
 nontraditional examples of, 275–288
 payment models, 64
 principles of, 9
 purpose of, 18, 20
 types of, 81–86

online impression
 Advertising Performance report, 138–139
 bidding systems, 15, 65, 67
 defined, 188
 Lifetime Statistics feature, 188
 Responder Demographic reports, 212

Online Yard Sign (application), 110–111

Open Graph initiative, 231

operating system, 4

optimizing your campaign, 143–149

opt-in form, 135–136

ordering process
 conversion tracking, 178
 forms, 166–167

Oreo (cookie brand), 278–279

organic ad, 88

Outlook (Microsoft), 171

• P •

Page, business. *See also* Fan Page; landing page
  community building, 58
  consistency with business site, 39
  content of page, 253–257
  cross-promotion, 112–116
  customer feedback, 61
  described, 10–11, 23
  first ad campaign, 30
  function of, 19, 24
  maintenance, 97
  maximum fans allowed, 24
  multiple ad campaigns, 92–93
  name of, 26
  preparation for ads, 38
  purpose of, 253–254
  referrals, 86–88
  stickiness, 217, 235
  tracking tools, 150–157
  transition from Fan Page, 24
  unique Page ID, 112–113
  updates, 38–39, 59, 97, 146
Page Name box, 26
Page Views Activity graph, 154–155
Pages You Admin list, 215
paid membership, 164
Pala Play & Stay (spa giveaway), 162–163
pausing campaigns, 79–80, 183–184
pay per click (PPM). *See* cost per click method
paying customer, 164
payment model. *See also specific models*
  notifications, 186
  performance reports, 138–140
  selection, 64–69
PayPal account, 96
Pei Wei (restaurant), 110
people, photo of, 89, 264
performance, ad. *See* Advertising Performance report
Permalink option, 208
phone call, 169

photo. *See also* image
  albums, 39
  common mistakes, 263–265
  contests, 278
  selection of, 89–91
  sources for, 36, 39, 265, 297–299
  tracking tools, 157
Pick Up Stix (restaurant), 163–164
PINK Nation Page, 257
pixel, 10, 36
plug-in
  available plug-ins, 237
  benefits of, 234–236
  described, 232
  example of, 233
  most popular, 238–247
  selection, 237–247
  tips for adding, 236–237
political election, 110–111
Poll ad
  described, 84
  example of, 85
  sponsored ads, 103, 105
postcard, 169
PPM. *See* cost per click method
previewing ads, 32
PriceWaterhouseCoopers (Interactive Advertising Bureau Revenue Report), 16
pricing ads
  bidding systems, 15–16, 65–67
  budget reports, 77
  campaign adjustments, 78–79, 143–146
  campaign optimization, 143–146
  described, 15
  tips for bidding, 70–71
  traditional media, 64
product preview, 165
product review, 39
profile, Facebook
  campaign optimization, 146–147
  profile pictures, 28, 245
profit
  budget reports, 77
  return on investment, 174–175

progress report, 97
promotional code, 32, 92, 161
province, 50
public figure, 286
punctuation
  body text, 34
  Facebook Guidelines, 273
  titles, 33
puzzle, 280

• *Q* •

Queen of Auctions (mailing list), 114–115

• *R* •

Rank by Estimated CTR field, 214
RapLeaf (Web site), 280
rate card, 64, 68
real estate, 285–286
RealEstateArchitect.com (Web site), 285
recommendation, user, 86–88, 239–240
Red Bull Roshambull game, 258–259
Redbox (retailer), 115–116
Reference Guides tab, 304
reference landing page, 119–120
referral, 86–88
region field, 211
regional campaign, 48–50
Relationship Interests filter, 30
relationship marketing
  common mistakes, 271–272
  described, 20, 22
  goals of, 22
  landing page selection, 37
  lead conversions, 165–167
Relationship Status filter, 30, 146
relevant ad, 146
renaming campaigns, 183
repetitive words/phrases, 33
report
  audience perceptions, 146
  budget analysis, 72–79
  demographic data, 140–143

Facebook resources, 291
  Insights feature, 150–157
  performance analysis, 138–140
Report, Facebook. *See also specific reports*
  ad performance, 205–210
  customized settings, 201–205
  described, 200–201
  profile attributes, 213–214
  report generation options, 201–205
  types of, 201
  user demographics, 210–212
Reports link, 72–73
Reports screen, 138, 205
request for information, 105
resized image, 36, 98
Responder Demographics report
  ad refinement, 148–149
  audience perceptions, 146
  creation, 210
  defined, 201
  described, 77–78, 140–143
  elements of, 210–212
Responder Profiles report
  ad refinement, 149
  defined, 201
  described, 78, 213–214
Rest-of-Site page, 12
return on investment (ROI)
  formula for, 175
  sales generation, 56
  tracking tips, 173–175
  value of Fans, 135
revenue, 174
Review Ad page, 32
reviewing
  ads, 32, 183
  products, 39
Reynolds Wrap (retailer), 59–60
Rio All-Suite Hotel & Casino, 244
Rockstar Games (video game company), 53
ROI. *See* return on investment
Rosetta Stone (retailer), 265
RSVP (attendance count), 105

• S •

sales cycle, 173
sales, generating
  budget reports, 77
  Facebook sales team, 102–105, 302–304
  lead conversions, 159–167, 172–173
  multiple ad campaigns, 92
  performance objectives, 105
  referrals, 86
  tips for, 55–57
Salesforce.com (CRM system), 171–172
Salesforce.com For Dummies (Wong), 171
scheduling ads, 93–94
search engine
  conversion tracking, 176
  cost per click ad, 66, 69
  defined, 9
  external landing page, 125
  optimization, 125
  popularity of, 9
  results page, 69
  user information, 16
See Details link, 223
segment, 141–142
self-service solution, 184
Set a Different Bid link, 70
settings
  account, 187, 195–197
  report, 201–205
Sex filter, 30, 142
sharing content, 254–255
sharing videos, 84
Shop Now! (retailer), 92
shopping
  carts, 177–178
  engines, 68–69
Show Faces checkbox, 240
Sign Up Now button, 26
slang, 273
slider, 190
slogan, 39, 53
So Cal Comic Convention, 133–134

social ad
  defined, 11
  described, 81
  illustrated, 12
Social Media Today (Web site), 296–297
Social Plug-in
  available plug-ins, 237
  benefit of, 234–236
  described, 232
  example of, 233
  most popular, 238–247
  selection, 237–247
  tips for adding, 236–237
Sort feature, 183
sorting tables, 208
Sostre, Pedro (*Web Analytics For Dummies*), 176
spam, 108
special offer, 173
spelling, 33–34
Spending and Usage Patterns on Facebook report, 291
split ad campaign
  common mistakes, 266
  defined, 100
  refined campaigns, 149
sponsored link/ad
  budget, 102
  defined, 66
  described, 102
  example of, 66
  users' home pages, 103–105
squeeze page, 122
state campaign, 48
Static FBML application, 128–134
Status column, 184
Status field, 188, 192
status update, 221
Stay, Jesse (*Facebook Application Development For Dummies*), 5, 129
sticky Page, 217, 235
stock photo, 36, 265
store hours, 38
story, 156

Stream option, 113
streaming event, 246–247
Summarize By option, 72–73, 201
summary line, 206
survey, 178, 255–256
symbol, 33, 273

• T •

tab, custom
  creation, 127–134
  forms, 136
  tracking tools, 154–155
Table of Campaigns, 182
table, report, 207–208
Tabs View list, 155
tag, tracking, 175–177
Target (retailer), 256
targeting users
  ad campaign adjustments, 78, 148–149
  audience perceptions, 146–147
  bidding systems, 67–68, 70
  body text, 34
  brand building, 52–55
  budget reports, 77–79
  common mistakes, 266–268
  community building, 57–62
  customer attributes, 16–17, 44–47
  demographic reports, 140–143, 211–212
  described, 43
  direct marketing guidelines, 21
  filters, 29–31
  first ad, creating, 29–31
  Insights feature, 153–154
  referrals, 86–88
  sales generation, 55–57
  scope of ad campaign, 47–52
  test campaign, 100–101, 148–149
Team Terrapin (sailing team), 142–143
technical problem
  campaign adjustments, 79
  Facebook library, 301–302
  financial costs, 96
test pricing, 21

testing ads
  benefits of, 137–138
  bid ranges, 144
  campaign optimization, 144, 147–149
  common mistakes, 265–266, 268–269
  described, 147–148
  goal of, 138
  images, 90
  Insights feature, 152
  methods for, 99–101
  reports, 79, 138–143
  targeted audience, 100–101, 148–149
text message, 33
third-party application, 58
Threadless (retailer), 55–57
3 Sisters Adventure Trekking group
    (training company), 281
thumbs-up approval, 11
time limit, 100
Time Summary option, 73, 202–204, 210
Timeslinger (adventure series), 82–83
timestamp, 176
title, ad
  character limit, 10, 33
  common mistakes, 270
  defined, 33
  described, 33
  disapproved ad, 185
  Facebook Event, 33
  first ad, creating, 28
  local campaign, 48
title case, 273
title, tab, 133
Top Countries listing, 224
Total Likes line, 222
Tough Mudder (Web site), 282–283
tournament, 258
tracking
  codes, 98, 102
  conversions, 169–172, 175–178
  dashboards, 227–230
  engagement ads, 222–224
  Events, 150–157
  Insights feature, 150–157, 214–222

return on investment, 173–175
viewers, 37, 47, 125, 150–157
Tracking Virtual Goods on Facebook
    report, 291
trademark, 36
transaction landing page, 119–120, 122
trial product/service, 105–106, 163
TripAdvisor (Web site), 58–59, 85
TV Show field, 213–214
Twitter (Web site), 171, 254
two-step close system, 125–126

• U •

Unique Clicks data
  conversion tracking, 176
  described, 77, 207
unique ID
  conversion tracking, 176, 177
  plug-ins, 242, 246
Unique Impressions data, 76, 207
Unique Page Views, 154
university name, 30
unsubscribing, 156, 219–220
updating fans, 58
URL (Web address)
  described, 4
  Page ID, 112–113
  tracking tools, 37, 47
  usage logs, 47
USA Network (television network), 235
User base, 222–224
user information
  bid ranges, 143–144
  bidding systems, 67–68
  budget reports, 72–79
  collection methods, 134–136
  conversion tracking, 176–177
  customer relationship management
    systems, 170
  demographic reports, 77–78, 140–143,
    210–212
  external landing page, 125
  Facebook features, 16

Facebook sales team, 102
first ad, creating, 30
Insights feature, 150–157, 225
landing page selection, 37, 120
lead verification, 168
targeted attributes, 16–17, 44–47
test campaign, 100–101
types of, 16–17
Users graph, 150
Users Who Interact With link, 224

• V •

Vanguard Productions (publisher), 87
Ventegy (business development company),
    122–123
verifying leads, 168–169, 177
Victoria's Secret (retailer), 257
Video ad
  described, 84
  example of, 85, 173
  Insights feature, 221–222
  sources for videos, 298
  sponsored ads, 103, 105
  tracking views, 155
View All Ads link, 183
View Insights link, 150–151, 215
View Old Page Insights link, 224
Viking Grills (retailer), 120–121, 173
viral marketing, 135
virtual currency, 108–109
Vitrue (marketing company), 135

• W •

Wagner, Richard (*Building Facebook
    Applications For Dummies*), 259
Wall page
  Comment feature, 242
  landing page development, 133–134
  posts to, 217, 220–221
  tracking tools, 154
Web Analytics For Dummies (Sostre and
    LeClaire), 176

Web page, external
benefits of, 125–127
company logo, 37
consistency with business Page, 39
cross-promotion, 112–116
described, 124
development of, 127
first ad campaign, 27
landing page selection, 37–38
Like box plug-in, 244
review by Facebook staff, 125–126
URL address, 4
usage log, 47
webcast, 246–247
Webpage option, 204
WebTrends (tracking tool), 47
weekly data, 193–194
Wendy's (restaurant), 115
widget, 112–114
Wildchild (retailer), 92–93
WiseChoice (college-student matching
service), 282
Wong, Tom (*Salesforce.com For
Dummies*), 171
word choice, 34, 53, 56
workplace, 30, 195
writing expert, 96

writing style
ad campaign adjustments, 79
audience perception, 146–147
body text, 34–35
brand building, 53
business Page content, 253–254
common mistakes, 270–272
Facebook Guidelines, 273
sales generation, 55–56
titles, 33

XID value, 247
Xobni (CRM system), 171

• Y •

Yahoo! (search engine), 66
Yelp (Web site), 232–233

• Z •

Zappos.com (retailer), 258
Zuckerberg, Mark (Facebook founder),
1, 231
Zynga (game developer), 108–109